# COMMITTEE OF VIGILANCE
*Revolution in San Francisco, 1851*

*Books by*

GEORGE R. STEWART

*Bret Harte*

*Ordeal by Hunger*

*John Phoenix*

*East of the Giants*

*Doctor's Oral*

*Storm*

*Names on the Land*

*Man: An Autobiography*

*Fire*

*Earth Abides*

*The Year of the Oath* (in collaboration)

*Sheep Rock*

*U.S. 40*

*American Ways of Life*

*The Years of the City*

*N.A. 1*

*Pickett's Charge*

*The California Trail*

*Committee of Vigilance*

# COMMITTEE
# OF VIGILANCE

### REVOLUTION IN
### SAN FRANCISCO, 1851

*An account of The Hundred Days
when certain citizens undertook the
suppression of the criminal activities
of the Sydney ducks*

*by*

GEORGE R. STEWART

*illustrated*

★

**BOSTON**

**HOUGHTON MIFFLIN COMPANY**

The Riverside Press Cambridge

*Second Printing*   W

# CONTENTS

(The chapter titles are from
contemporary newspaper headlines.)

# ILLUSTRATIONS

These are, with one exception, taken from Frank Soulé, John H. Gihon, and James Nisbet, The Annals of San Francisco, 1855. Many of them, however, were originally published in 1851. Contemporary testimony indicates that the drawings are highly accurate. For the source of "Proposed Plan," etc., see the accompanying caption.

A map showing San Francisco in 1851 appears on page x.

# COMMITTEE OF VIGILANCE

*Revolution in San Francisco, 1851*

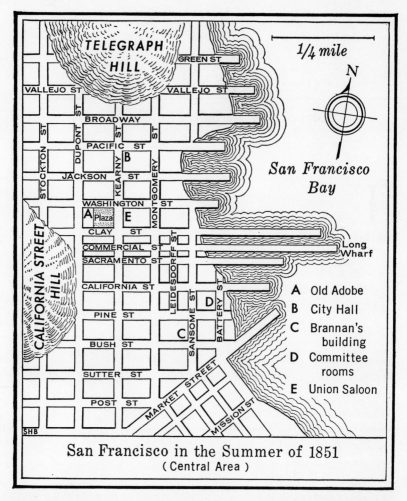

San Francisco in the Summer of 1851
( Central Area )

The map can be used for a general guide, but the city itself was changing so rapidly that the situation shifted from month to month. New wharves were being built, new streets being laid out, the waterfront being extended eastward by filling in. Except for Long Wharf, all of the wharves bore the names of the streets which they extended. California Street Hill is the present Nob Hill. Sydneytown lay to the south and east of Telegraph Hill. Names and locations of the streets have remained the same, except that Dupont Street has become Grant Avenue.

# CHAPTER 1

# DARING ASSAULT AND ROBBERY

*(February 19)*

T HE NEWSPAPER ACCOUNTS, the testimony in court, and the confessions, make possible the detailed reconstruction of the circumstances and the enactment of the crime. . . .

The place was San Francisco, at the dry-goods store of C. J. Jansen & Co., on the west side of Montgomery Street, one door from Washington. The year was 1851, when the city was just leaving the simple crudities of the frontier behind, and was entering, for good and for bad, into the full complexities of civilization. The time was shortly before eight o'clock on the evening of February 19. The thermometer, reported for that very hour, stood at 48 degrees. The moon had not yet risen, but the night was clear and star-lit. On such an evening a man might muffle himself in a cloak, or otherwise cover his face, merely for protection against the chill.

The custom was that many stores remained open into the evening, and a business street, such as Montgomery, was still well frequented. There were no street lamps, but the stars were bright, and broad beams of light from the windows of stores cut through the darkness. A man had no difficulty in getting about, and could easily make out other people at a distance, though without being able to recognize their faces.

At this time a group of eight men came along, though they formed a group only because of a shared motivation, since they moved by twos and threes, some on the east side of the street, some on the west. There was nothing distinctive about their appearance. But a passer-by, if he had heard them talking, would have recognized British accents. Moreover, if his ear was at all keen to note turns of speech, he would have thought: "Sydney ducks!"

He might, indeed, have thought "Sydney coves," or "Sydney birds." But whatever nickname came to his mind, he was not likely to linger in that vicinity. Men from Australia had a bad reputation. Many of them had been transported there as convicts from the British Isles. Since the discovery of gold some of these had made their way, legitimately or otherwise, to California. Soon discovering that mining was not as easy or as profitable as they had hoped, many of them lapsed into their former ways, and supported themselves by robbery. They lived mostly in "Sydneytown," north of the business-district and at the foot of Telegraph Hill, a slum of disreputable rooming-houses, dubious gambling-joints, and cheap groggeries.

On this evening, then, these "Colonials" — as they liked to call themselves — moved along Montgomery Street. They had designs upon Jansen's store. One of them, Sam Whittaker by name, had recently lived next door to Jansen, and had picked up some acquaintance with him. Whittaker had said that Colonials, when returning to Australia, needed English coin. Jansen, always ready to earn an honest penny, replied that he usually had a good stock of gold sovereigns and would be glad to exchange. Tips from another source had come to the leaders of the gang that the cash in the store might be as much as ten or even fifteen thousand dollars.

As they approached, the men had no definite plan, and had not even decided as to whether they should make the attempt at that time. But they soon realized that the situation could scarcely be more favorable. The store, like others in the vicinity, was open. It consisted of one room with a narrow frontage, but extending back fifty feet. This large room was dimly illuminated by a single candle, almost at the rear.

Thus encouraged, some of the men went up and looked in at the window. They did so with impunity, since they could pose as prospective customers. Among those who thus looked were a small man called "Old Jack" and a tall man called "English Jim." The latter was one of the leaders of the gang.

After sizing the situation up, Old Jack entered the store quietly. He hoped to do a sneak-thief job, and lift the money from some place in the front of the store without even arousing whoever was at the back, where the light was. The others continued to look through the window.

English Jim, however, had little confidence in his comrade or in the possibilities of sneak-thievery. The situation seemed likely to demand bolder methods. After watching for a few moments and seeing no sign of success, he muttered, "If I do not go in, there will be no money got."

He prepared to enter, and we may assume that he looked to his weapon or weapons. He may well have carried both a revolver and a knife, but he did not plan to use them. The one produces an embarrassing amount of noise; the other, what may be an equally embarrassing amount of blood. Moreover, both revolver and knife are likely to kill. English Jim may have had no particular aversion to killing in itself, but he knew that a community becomes unduly aroused at murder. Therefore, with him as among the Colonials generally, the slung-shot was a favored weapon.

The usual slung-shot was merely a chunk of lead held in a folded piece of cloth. Even a handkerchief would serve. The slung-shot had many virtues. It was cheap, and easily disassembled and thrown away. It was almost noiseless and bloodless. Properly wielded, it knocked a man out, but did not kill.

English Jim, however, did not like the ordinary slung-shot, and he had produced his own adaptation. This was a short and light stick, one end of which was inserted into a lump of lead, variously described as being the size of a hen's egg and the size of a man's fist. We must take the latter as epic exaggeration; such a lump would have been needlessly heavy. Lead of the size of a hen's egg would weigh about two pounds, and would suffice. . . .

While all this was happening, the proprietor of the store was unconscious of approaching trouble. Charles J. Jansen was of slight physical build, not pugnacious or bellicose, but of an amiable disposition, and having many friends among the other merchants. One of these was Theodore Payne, who had a store across the street and was one of the city's wealthy and prominent men. Jansen and Payne were planning to go out to dinner together, later in the evening.

We must conclude that Jansen was of an unsuspicious nature. To make friends with a Sydney duck, and confide about money matters! Also, his conduct on this particular evening seems singularly trusting.

It also presents an anomaly. Why did he invite trade by keeping his store open, anad yet keep his store so dark that it repelled rather than attracted? The reason may have been the simple one of economy. The year was '51, and the great boom of '49 and '50 was over. Though the community in general enjoyed prosperity, the merchants were suffering. Too optimistic importing had glutted the market, and storekeepers were being forced to dump their goods at heavy losses. The single candle may thus have resulted from mere penny-pinching. The same reason may account for the proprietor having let his clerks go, while he himself remained to pick up any late trade.

The merchant's day, in those times, was a long one, and now Jansen was relaxing, sprawled out. He became aware of someone moving about in the front of the store. Arousing himself, he made out a small man with a hat pulled low over his forehead. Jansen inquired the customer's need. The man said that he wanted some blankets. Being told that these were at the back of the store, near the candle, he then came in that direction. Jansen pointed to some dark blankets.

"No, white," said the customer, laconically.

At this moment Jansen was aware that another man had entered the store. Darkly silhouetted against the front windows he showed up as tall and muffled in a cloak. Turning toward the newcomer, Jansen again inquired. This man, too, wanted blankets, and so he came back to where the blankets were. The three were then standing in a row, with the storekeeper in the middle.

Suddenly Jansen heard the exclamation "Now!" and immediately he received a stunning blow on the head. He cried out, and slumped to the floor.

Apparently he did not altogether lose consciousness. He knew, at least in some vague way, that his store was being hastily ransacked. In a short time he realized that the robbers had left, and he judged it safe to move.

Keeping his wits about him, he recollected that he was closer to the back of the store than to the front. He therefore crawled to the back door, and called.

The whole affair had occupied only a few minutes. Many people were still in the streets, and some of these came to the injured man's assistance. Shortly his friend Payne arrived to help.

Jansen was got to bed. A hastily summoned physician reported a concussion — serious and painful, but not fatal. The patient lapsed into a coma.

A search showed that the robbers had carried off a shot-bag containing cash, and had also taken Jansen's watch. Payne made a find, picking up the discarded weapon, which the assailant had used with such enthusiasm as to break its handle. . . .

That same evening, at a drinking dive kept by the brother of one of the gang, the eight men divided the money into equal shares, which came out at $196 apiece. A small remainder was immediately expended upon drinks. The keeper of the dive was given Jansen's watch. Either this was of little value or its recipient thought it incriminating, and so he threw it into the bay. One notes that the eight shares totaled $1586.

The eight could sleep soundly that night. They had made a good haul, committed no murder, and got away cleanly.

# CHAPTER 2

# CRIME AMONG US

*(February 20–21)*

N EXT DAY English Jim and his comrades could not have felt so complaisant. Their little affair was creating what they may well have thought to be an unjustified amount of excitement.

In the weeks preceding, crime had been common enough in San Francisco. A murder and robbery on December 30 had even led the *Herald,* one of the important morning dailies, to editorial comment — the citizens could well band together for self-protection; lynch law, dreadful as it was, might even be necessary.

During January and the first weeks of February the *Herald* reported some twenty crimes; and doubtless there were others which the newspapers, crowded for space, did not report. Such events got a modest headline of ROBBERY, or THEFT, or DARING THEFT, and received about an inch of one column. Homicides were rare, and were likely to get such a headline as AFFRAY, indicating a high-spirited encounter between two belligerent individuals, in which the survivor could reasonably plead self-defense.

But the present affair coupled robbery with violence in a way which was out of the current pattern of crime. Jansen was a solid citizen, and other solid citizens immediately began to think, "I might have been the victim!" Besides, they were already worried about continuing and increasing crime.

The *Alta California,* another important morning daily, declared the case to be, though with obvious hyperbole, "one of the most bare-faced, and audacious robberies to which the annals of any country give a history." The *Herald* under the heading DARING ATTACK AND ROBBERY, gave the story four inches.

Both accounts ended with a little editorializing. The *Herald* declared, "Something must be done to strike terror into the hearts of these miscreants. There must be an example made." The *Alta* offered a prediction about Jansen's assailants: "If the law will not punish them, an indignant community will."

The *Courier* declared, "This is one of the boldest and at the same time one of the most brutal attempts that we have ever yet chronicled in this city." As for the assailants, the editor queried: "Is it worthwhile, if caught, to offer them a trial in our Courts? Is it not better to make examples of them, if found, by hanging them up at once?"

All three editors, in their moral enthusiasm, were neglecting the details that guilt should be properly established and that nothing would be gained and much lost by hanging the wrong men.

Moreover, the editors were overlooking the circumstances that almost no clues existed. The broken instrument of assault, in the times before the use of finger-prints, was almost valuless. Jansen, though still suffering from shock, had supplied a little information. He described the first man as small; the second, as tall, having a mustache, and wearing a hat with broad rim and round top. Since any criminal might change his hat, these vague descriptions allowed the arrest of almost the entire male population.

The editorials were an expression of lack of confidence in the police. . . . The force was organized under an elected official known as Marshal. Under him were about seventy-five officers. Since the permanent and floating population of the city scarcely reached thirty thousand, the size of the force appeared to be adequate. Nor was it lacking in certain good qualities. The officers were courageous, and they were generally alert and efficient in controlling incidents. A high-spirited visiting miner discharging his revolver in Portsmouth Square or a saloon brawl on the waterfront that threatened to become a riot — any such outbreak would find the police arriving on the run.

The real question about the force was to what extent its members were in alliance with professional criminals. A great many San Franciscans were beginning to believe that there was such an alliance. The editorial suggestions that the people should take affairs into their own hands implied either inefficiency or corruption.

The peculiar excitement about the Jansen affair thus put the already unpopular and suspected police into an uncomfortable corner. Their obvious way to get out was to arrest some suspects, and quickly. Jansen's two clerks were first questioned, but they established their innocence.

By the next morning the attack was a day and a half old, and had receded out of current news. There were no new developments. The police might well hope that everyone would forget about it.

But the case showed strange vitality. The *Alta* came out with a leading editorial, CRIME AMONG US, which was an attack upon the whole system of police and courts:

> How many murders have been committed in this city within a year! And who has been hung or punished for the crime? Nobody.

Most alarming of all was the last paragraph, in which the editor stated that he was receiving many letters from aroused citizens. Some made one suggestion and some another. Then the editorial concluded:

> Others threaten to resort to Lynch law as the only remedy, in case the powers that be do not do something for the public relief and protection.

With such a threat breathing down their necks, the police arrested a man within a few hours — "on suspicion." He was a Colonial named Windred (or Wildred or Weldred), his first name being William (or Robert). Quite possibly, he deserved arrest. At the time of his apprehension he was playing "strap," a popular bunco game. According to the police, he corresponded to "the short man."

On this same day an alert officer from Sacramento, happening to be in San Francisco, spotted a face that looked familiar. Was not this a man who had recently escaped from custody in Sacramento? The officer made the arrest, and turned his prisoner over to the local authorities for safe-keeping, identifying him as James Stuart, known as English Jim, a notorious Sydney duck, suspected of various crimes and specifically wanted in connection with two murders.

The San Francisco police grasped at the possibility that this man might furnish them a means of solving their embarrassing problem. Since his height seemed proper, could he not be "the tall man" of Jansen's description?

They questioned him, but learned nothing. He denied any connection with the Jansen case. He even denied being Stuart. The police, sure of their identification, were acquiescent. If he preferred to be called Thomas Berdue, that made no difference, as long as they had him in hand. These Sydney ducks had plenty of aliases! Likely enough, his name was neither Stuart nor Berdue, but something that had long since been discarded on the arduous England-Australia-California route.

They searched him, but found nothing to connect him with Jansen. The search proved Berdue, *alias* Stuart, to be well-heeled, suspiciously so. He had a gold watch and chain, two gold rings, a certificate of deposit on a bank for $1720, two bags of gold dust, and $338 in gold coin.

The identification of the man with a reputed murderer justified his detention until further information was available. As for his connection with the current case, there was an obvious move to make. He, along with Windred, could be taken to visit the injured man, who could perhaps identify them as his customers.

Jansen, though judged to be out of danger, was still in bad condition. His face was much swollen, and had turned black. He was still resting most of the time in stupor.

A number of men, including the two prisoners, crowded into the room where the injured man was lying. He was roused to consciousness. Asked about identification, he pointed to the taller prisoner, and said, "That was the man." He then said that the shorter prisoner "resembled" his other assailant. Under interrogation he repeated his identification several times, but was less certain of the short man than of the tall man.

Jansen thus proved to be an excellent witness for the police. A prosecuting attorney, however, might have his doubts as to whether a jury, under the promptings of a defending attorney, would accept this testimony of a man who might still be suffering from shock and who had seen his muffled assailants for barely a minute by the dim light of a single candle burning in a large room.

# CHAPTER 3

# A WAY TO STOP CRIME

*(February 22)*

T HE EDITORIAL suggestions for lynch law were not at all what was to be expected in San Francisco, even in 1851. That city had a long tradition of legal authority, thus displaying a difference from much of the United States, particularly in the West.

Graphically to indicate that difference we might prepare a map of the country, marking in blue those areas in which some establishment of legal and judicial authority was simultaneous with European settlement, and by marking in red those areas where settlement preceded such establishment. Eventually we would have a map mostly of blue, but with large areas of the West standing out in a color which might symbolically be called blood-red.

The colonial settlements — whether Spanish, French, Dutch, or English — functioned under established authority from the beginning. Some of the first wood cut from the forest might be used for the erection of a gallows. Law-and-order, in a general sort of way, kept up with the frontier in its slow advance during two centuries. Only after 1800 did the situation tend to reverse itself, as the frontier began to advance rapidly. At that time the national government — whether by mere negligence, or by reluctance to expend money, or by a new philosophy of individualism — allowed things to get out of hand, so that many areas were settled before legal authority was more than a shadow and a gesture.

The result was the Wild West. In a curious way Americans are proud of it, and there are, indeed, certain phases of it which are both heroic and even morally admirable. But most of it should be written off as a national disgrace, and in a hundred years more we may get around to doing so.

It was essentially a rule of violence and of the exploitation of natural resources and of weaker individuals and peoples. The genocide of the Indians (in some instances tribes were annihilated) was its worst feature. That the Wild West did not need to happen is shown by the example of Canada.

Historically, the gold rush of 1849 produced a large red area on our supposed map. Scores, even hundreds, of mining camps sprang up in places where there was not, and had never been, any sheriff, or judge, or constable, or justice of the peace.

The story of the miners' "Struggle for Order" has received classical treatment in Charles Howard Shinn's *Mining Camps,* written in the early eighties when memories were still alive. There is in this struggle much that is fine. We see a genius for self-government which we may proudly think to be typically American. The miners organized, passed regulations for the size of claims, enforced justice when need was. Since the communities were small and the culprits were generally caught red-handed, the chances are that fewer mistakes were made than in the ordinary courts of law. The common sentence was merely banishment from that particular camp. Flogging, a punishment then recognized by several states, was sometimes inflicted. Murder might be requited by hanging. Occasionally, emotions got out of control, and the result was a hasty and brutal lynching.

But the period without established authority was short. Even before California was admitted as a state on September 9, 1850, the officer of the law made his appearance in most places.

But San Francisco was not a mining camp, and its region would have to be colored blue. The Spaniards had founded the Presidio in 1776, and legal authority along with it. Spanish rule had given way to Mexican, and the village of Yerba Buena had sprung up, with its *alcalde*. American rule had followed Mexican, and Yerba Buena had become San Francisco, still maintaining its *alcalde,* and adding justices of the peace and other officers. Finally, on May 1, 1850, the citizens had adopted a city charter, elected the first mayor, and set up a full city government. At no time since the beginning had there been a lapse of constituted authority.

Only once, moreover, had there been an important instance of the flouting of the laws by criminal elements and of an emergency counter-action. . . . This affair of "The Hounds" occurred in the summer of 1849 when the city had grown so rapidly because of the gold rush that the legal authorities were unable to exert much control. A number of men banded together, ostensibly for self-protection. Calling themselves the Hounds, they soon began a life of open license. Under color of protecting the city they later called themselves Regulators, and initiated a campaign of violence and robbery against the numerous and generally inoffensive Latin Americans. On July 15, in broad daylight, they attacked the district known as Little Chile, beating many people, robbing, and destroying. The better citizens were outraged, and alarmed, and on the next day two of them waited upon the *alcalde,* urging action through the people. As the result, a meeting was held that afternoon, and 230 men were enrolled as special constables, and organized into armed companies. These companies immediately moved into action. During the rest of the afternoon some twenty of the most notable of the Hounds were put under arrest. Still later on that same day, special courts were organized, the *alcalde* acting as chief judge. On the next day the trials began. In the end nine men were found guilty on various counts, and sentences were imposed. Because of the disturbed conditions of the time these sentences were never enforced, but the gang disappeared.

The official participation of the *alcalde* prevents this incident from being classifiable as an example of "popular justice." Still, it was close to being such. In 1851 people were likely to mention the affair of the Hounds as having been one occasion when the good citizens had seen to their own law-enforcement.

Properly speaking, however, the city had no valid tradition of action that by-passed the legal authorities. If the San Franciscans, swayed by the inflammatory urgings of their newspaper editors, should move to set up some kind of citizens' court, they would be acting much more violently and much more questionably than the miners had done. In an early mining-camp there had been mere social chaos, and any attempt at organization for the ends of justice was necessarily a movement toward order. But in San Francisco such a movement would be one against crime, but also one against the established government — in essence, a revolution. The participants would have to accept the responsibility that revolutionists accept. And, in the case of an unsuccessful revolution, the consequences may be unpleasant.

The more responsible citizens realized the serious nature of any rising that would imitate the setting-up of a miners' court. Such a move would at first bring conflict only with the powers of city and county, though even these were far from negligible. But, beyond, loomed the power of the state and finally the might of the federal government. Besides, once the rule of force, should be invoked, where could anyone stop? "He who rides a tiger . . ."

On the other hand, many San Franciscans were not wholly responsible or clear-thinking citizens. The gold rush, by its very nature, had brought to California many men given to quick and rash actions, even though they might be essentially law-abiding. Moreover, in the winter months, the city was thronged with miners who could not work their claims during high water and came down to enjoy spending what they had gained in the previous months. Many of them, having participated in miners' courts, would have thought, and would not have been slow to say, that the San Franciscans were indolent and cowardly not to take a stronger stand against criminals. Finally, in any city at any time, there are many people who do very little thinking at all, and are ready, by the contagion of excitement, to rise with any mob. . . .

February 22, Washington's Birthday, was not an official holiday. It was a Saturday, but a six-day working week made a Saturday little different from the days that preceded it. There were no unusual numbers of people in the streets, but the floating population of the city was large and many such idle visitors were loitering about, the tinder and kindling of mob action.

The morning newspapers served as the chief sources of information. If a man read the *Herald,* he found that the editor had given space to a half-whimsical article on the prevalence of audacious rats. Another paragraph commented upon the reclamation of the bay: "Clay street has been filled up with earth down to Sansome." The editor even became nostalgic: "Formerly, the tide flowed up to Montgomery street — now it stops a square below, and soon many other places that know it now, shall know it no more!"

The reader could also learn of the arrests in the Jansen case, and of the identification of the prisoners — the identification being stated in such positive terms as to leave no doubt in the reader's mind that the proper men had been caught.

There was also an editorial, "A WAY TO STOP CRIME." After reiterating much that had been stated already about crime in the city, the editor advised, "Let us then organize a band of two or three hundred 'regulators,' composed of such men as have a stake in the town, and who are interested in the welfare of this community." The final sentence read, "If two or three of these robbers and burglars were caught and treated to 'Lynch law' their fellows would be more careful about future depredations."

The *Alta,* usually the most moderate of the newspapers, was moderate. But the reader of the *Courier* found a heading, THE ROBBERS, and a sentence advising that the assailants of Mr. Jansen should be hanged immediately, if identified.

Throughout the morning, in spite of these editorial incitements, the streets were quiet. The Washington Guards and the California Guards, the two local military organizations, prepared to parade in honor of Washington's Birthday.

About noon the police again took their two prisoners from the station-house, located in the City Hall, and visited Jansen. This time they brought with them a justice of the peace and several witnesses. Once more roused from stupor, Jansen was put under oath, and repeated what he had told the police already. He refused, however, to swear that these were his assailants, but he "believed that they were."

The party then set out to return to the City Hall. By this time the news had got around, and a crowd followed along, shouting "Hang 'em!" "Lynch 'em!" The mob, as it might now be called, made a rush to seize the taller prisoner, but the police beat back the attempt.

About two o'clock the examination of the prisoners commenced in the Recorder's Courtroom at the City Hall. Windred, "the short man" attempted to prove an alibi, but no one had much confidence in the reliability of his witnesses. As the examination progressed, people pressed into the courtroom until it was jammed. The crowd filled the corridors, and even outside the building hundreds of excited people were collecting, the crowd growing larger every minute, until some thousands had gathered. These men were much excited and highly indignant against the prisoners. They lacked, however, a plan and a leader.

Moreover, they faced an organized opposition. Mayor John W. Geary had served as colonel of the Second Pennsylvania in the war with Mexico; he had smelled some gunpowder, and knew how to meet force with force. In addition to seeing to it that the police were present for duty he mobilized a volunteer force some 250 strong, and threw it as a cordon around the City Hall.

These men were armed. Many of the citizens had derringers or revolvers, and even a workingman would have his knife. The danger of a bloody collision was thus acute. The crowd made several attempts to break through the cordon, but these pushes were thrown back without resort to arms.

The most critical point, however, was the courtroom itself,

THE CITY HALL, FEBRUARY 22D, 1851

Note the orator addressing the crowd from the top balcony, and the cordon of men drawn up to defend the building.

jammed with excited men. Just as the magistrate was adjourning until Monday, there was a sudden cry, "Now's the time!" and the crowd made a rush, overturning benches and breaking through the railings. The few police were at the point of being overpowered.

At this moment, as if by magic, the Washington Guards, uniformed and with bayonets fixed, rushed into the room, and confronted the mob. In unlimited confusion they even mounted upon the desk and the benches, thrusting with their bayonets, and managing to clear a space. On the other side the crowd, inside and outside, roared "Hang 'em!" "Lynch 'em!" "Bring 'em out!" Those in the courtroom violently cursed the military.

Gradually, however, the bayonets got control. The room was cleared, and the prisoners were taken to the station-house.

When the Guards came out, they met hisses and hoots as they passed into their near-by armory. The crowd even began to throw stones at the windows. The captain of the Guards then came out, and spoke to the crowd, saying that his men had merely done their duty, that on Monday, if it became necessary, they would march out to ensure the hanging of the two prisoners. Recognizing the justice of his position, the crowd cheered him loudly, and ceased its violence.

About this time an anonymous handbill was being circulated, addressed, CITIZENS OF SAN FRANCISCO. Somewhat more violently than the newspapers had already done, it incited the people to take affairs into their own hands. It declared that failure of legal process had left the city in a state of anarchy — "redress can be had for aggression but through the never failing remedy so admirably laid down in the code of Lynch." The exhortation continued:

> Are we to be robbed and assassinated in our domiciles, and the law to let our aggressors perambulate the streets merely because they have furnished straw bail? If so, let "each man be his own executioner." "Fie upon your laws"; they have no force.

The handbill ended:

All those who would rid our city of its robbers and murderers, will assemble on Sunday [the next day], at two o'clock, on the Plaza.

The handbill stirred up some excitement, but by suggesting that action be put off until the next day it actually tended to allay passions. Moreover, it was weak in that no names were signed to it. What the crowd needed most of all (as reporters noted) was a leader. The writers of the handbill refused to put themselves forward as leaders, at least until the next day.

The afternoon had worn away. After another speaker had still further soothed the crowd, it began to ooze away. People were getting hungry — and thirsty. By sunset the crowd had vanished into hundreds of twos and threes and half-dozens, snatching something to eat or downing a few whiskeys in one of the numerous saloons.

Thus fanned, the banked fires of excitement blazed up. Why wait till tomorrow? Shortly before dusk many people began to drift along the streets toward the City Hall.

As the light was failing, a large crowd had assembled, much larger than in the afternoon when many people still were working. But there was an even greater difference from that previous assemblage. The earlier one might well have been called a mob. This later one was more in the nature of a mass meeting of citizens. Though at the beginning it had neither leaders nor organization, it soon attained both, by parliamentary methods. But this is not to say that the crowd was either calm or orderly. It was neither, and at any moment might have become a mob, governed only by passion.

Present, occupying advantageous positions on the first-story balcony, were the major, most of the city officials, many of the judges, and a number of the most prominent citizens. These were men of courage; they had rallied to the point of danger

WILLIAM D. M. HOWARD

with a strong sense of responsibility, and with few exceptions they were devoted to the idea of preventing the mob from taking over.

Their first success came with the selection of W. D. M. Howard as chairman. He was one of the city's richest and most respected citizens, and had been a resident since 1845. He was a large man of fine presence, good-natured, with a touch of wit. If anyone could preserve decorum at this meeting, Howard was the man for it.

Speaker followed speaker — a judge, another judge, then the

mayor. All urged moderation and the legal process. The crowd, however, would not merely disperse without having accomplished anything. Obviously some definite measure must be taken.

At this point another speaker was allowed to address the crowd. He was well known — a big, swashbuckling individual. One would guess that as he stepped forward the crowd raised a louder cheer than had greeted the judges, and then lapsed into a stiller hush than they had granted the mayor. Even the hotheads would have grown quiet, those men whose hands were already itching for the feel of a rope. They would have recognized Samuel Brannan.

Moreover, Brannan's personal sentiments were widely known. He made no secret of them. Like Moloch in the council of the fallen angels, he was always for open war. Whatever he might say on the present occasion, those who had been calling "Hang 'em!" would know that he was one of them. The very fact that he was thus put forward as a speaker at this time was doubtless a sop to the would-be lynchers, to make them feel that they had, so to speak, a representative.

But he did not launch forth upon an inflammatory speech. Instead, he moved that a committee of twelve be appointed to cooperate with the authorities and in particular to guard and to protect the prisoners overnight.

The motion was carried, and the committee was appointed. It was composed of substantial, even wealthy, citizens, and included Howard, Payne, and Brannan himself.

The meeting then adjourned. The crowd, for the second time that day, dispersed peaceably. . . .

The committee met immediately. It floundered for a little while, committee-like, in a bog of motions and speeches. Then someone proposed that the citizens should by-pass the legal authorities by themselves appointing a jury to try the prisoners. Such a proposal might seem radical, but it was not enough for one member of the committee.

Brannan took over. If he had restrained himself when speaking to the crowd, he now let himself go in characteristic manner. His sense, and even his words, were reported:

> I am very much surprised to hear people talk about grand juries, or recorders, or mayors. I'm tired of such talk. These men are murderers, I say, as well as thieves. I know it, and I will die or see them hung by the neck. I'm opposed to any farce in this business.

He concluded:

> We are the mayor and the recorder, the hangman and the laws. The law and the courts never yet hung a man in California; and every morning we are reading fresh accounts of murders and robberies. I want no technicalities. Such things are devised to shield the guilty.

Brannan must have been speaking out of conviction, indeed, but with an eye on the record and on the future. He was, in essence, putting himself forward as the much-needed leader of those who were calling for direct action.

He can scarcely have had any hope of swaying the committee as he knew it to be constituted. Instead, the committee appointed a patrol of twenty men to guard the prisoners — another evidence that the integrity of the police force was not highly regarded.

This seemed to complete the work. Howard moved that the committee adjourn, to meet again in the morning.

Before a vote could be taken, and against the rule that a motion to adjourn is not debatable, Brannan was on his feet. He moved an amendment: *That the committee do recommend to the people that the prisoners be hung at 10 o'clock, on Monday morning.*

Apparently no parliamentary objection was raised. A vote

was taken on the amendment. Three others voted *yes* along
with Brannan. The other votes were *no,* including those of
Howard, Payne, and the other most prominent men on the committee.

The amendment being lost, the original motion was put and
carried, and the committee adjourned.

But peace and quiet did not descend upon the troubled city.
The people had been deeply stirred, and had gained no release
through action. All night the streets were disturbed. Rumors
floated about, that the Sydney ducks were abroad, assaulting
and robbing, that they were planning to burn the city. Armed
volunteer patrols walked the dark streets till dawn.

CHAPTER 4

# THE PEOPLE IN COUNCIL

*(February 23)*

AFTER THAT almost sleepless night many San Franciscans
were on the streets early to face an ominous day. By
nine o'clock a crowd was already gathering around the courthouse, though the meeting would not convene till an hour later.

Only one newspaper was published on Sundays, the *Alta
California.* Its readers found themselves cautioned, "Lynch law
is a whirlwind which once let loose may sweep down all peaceable barriers before its angry blast."

In exchanging recollections of what had happened on Saturday, people could fix upon two mysteries. First, how had the
Washington Guards thus happened to appear, as if providen-
tially, with fixed bayonets? Second, who were the authors of the
handbill?

The appearance of the Guards was due to the foresight of the
Recorder, Frank Tilford, in whose court the hearing had been
held. Since there had already been threats to hang the prisoners, Tilford seized upon the lucky chance that this was Washington's Birthday and that the Guards would be parading. He arranged that they should not disband after the ceremony, but
should be held close at hand in their armory, armed and ready
for action.

The authorship of the handbill, however, was never to become publicly known. Both its sentiments and its language suggest that Brannan was involved, but there is no certainty. . . .

While the crowd was gathering, a young man came out of the

house where he lived, and quietly began to take a walk. He was dressed in what people liked to call "his Sunday best," and he proposed, we assume, to attend services at the Episcopalian church, after finishing his walk. He was twenty-seven years old, vigorous-looking and youthfully slender. His handsome and classically regular face was distinguished by a tight lipline, which might be taken to indicate strength and self-control. Though his hair was dark, his eyes were of that pale blue which the early West often associated with men who were extremely dangerous. This young man bore the heroic name of William Tell Coleman.

Of all people in the city, few had been so little involved in the present crisis as had Coleman. He could not have escaped reading something in the newspapers, but he had apparently attended neither of the meetings on Saturday. He was extremely busy with his own business as the senior partner of Wm. T. Coleman & Co., Wholesale Dealers in Provisions and Commission Merchants. In the current newspapers the firm was advertising a large assortment of goods for sale. Young Coleman was already making money, and he was eager to get ahead.

Still, this was not a working day, and he was only human. As he walked along in his Sunday clothes, he saw many people hurrying toward the meeting-place, and he must have heard scraps of conversation which indicated the possibility of momentous events. Naturally, he picked up something of the excitement, and decided to leave off his quiet walk and attend the meeting.

He did not, however, go there directly. Instead, he turned quietly about, returned home, took off his good suit, and donned something ordinary.

This procedure is not only characteristic of the man, but it is also something of a heroic gesture. With the Sam Brannans of this world I shall take my chances, but let me never stand in opposition to a man who, about to attend what may well be a double hanging, calmly turns about and changes his suit.

So William Tell Coleman, properly attired, went and mingled with the crowd. Not being a man of wealth or a public figure, he did not take his place among the notables on one of the balconies.

Standing there, he had the advantage of being able to feel the temper of the people more quickly and more surely than could the mayor and those others on the balconies. He soon sensed that the crowd was at the point of becoming a mob.

Personally, he was not perturbed. When nature had made up her recipe for this young man, she had omitted even a pinch of cowardice. Kentucky-born to the tradition of the fearless and honor-loving gentleman, he had well proved himself on the rough-and-tumble frontier in Wisconsin, and by crossing the plains and mountains in '49. On some occasion he must have seen a mob at work, though he omits from his reminiscences any reference to it, perhaps because the memory was too painful. All that he wrote was, "I always had a holy horror for mobs and the results of their wild and hasty excesses."

He stood there, and felt the mob, beast-like, beginning to stir.

At ten o'clock, promptly, the meeting began. There is no mention, this day, of any cordon of armed volunteers surrounding the courthouse. Mayor Geary may well have concluded that he could not risk the frightful consequences of a full-scale battle, and he may therefore have decided to depend upon holding the crowd back by argument and reason, believing that the crisis had already passed.

As the first business, Brannan reported for the committee that the prisoners were safe, and asked that the committee might be discharged. *So ordered.*

By now the crowd was dense — estimated at six thousand, almost a quarter of the city's population. The people were orderly and quiet.

The speakers began. The city officials were making a good try, and their tactics of handling a crowd showed some sophistication. If there could be speeches from the balcony by respected gentlemen, talking reasonably, if everything could be dragged out long enough so that tempers could cool and people even become bored, then the situation might be saved.

A judge spoke, another judge, then the mayor again. They urged a legal trial, and spoke highly of "the propriety of calm and cool action." But, as a newspaper reported, with what may be considered under-emphasis, "which sentiment appeared to meet with general dissent."

To Coleman things did not appear to be going well. About him he noted angry glances, clenched hands, and impatient gestures. The crowd was quiet, but it was also sullen. He noted a tendency of the people to press in more closely to the building.

A cheer must have gone up as the dashing figure of Sheriff Jack Hays appeared on the balcony. Former officer of the Texas rangers, Colonel Hays was immensely popular. He too began talking. Time was dragging on — past eleven now.

At about this time, still standing in the crowd and sensitive to its mood, Coleman came to the conclusion that all these reasonable speeches were being wasted, that in the long run they were not calming but irritating the people. Sooner or later the mob would find its leader, rise, and do its ugly work. But, if there was no possibility of a legal trial, there might still be a possibility of something short of a lynching. As he wrote later, "It occurred to me that a middle course might be adopted." Thus in the cause of moderation, for the golden mean, he would make his try.

Whenever Coleman decided to act, he brought to that end a certain physical vigor, but also a moral resolution and an intensity of purpose that broke through all barriers. Even to make his way through the packed crowd was an achievement. Then he had to get through the corridor, up the stairway, and out upon the crowded balcony. Once he had got so far, he would have had no difficulty in gaining permission to speak. There was a power about this young man that no chairman would have cared to resist.

Before Coleman could have a chance, Mayor Geary himself proposed that a committee of twelve be appointed to sit with the examining justice on the next day as a jury, and that their verdict be final. Such an arrangement, though highly irregular, had some degree of legality, since it was proposed by the mayor.

In some way this motion was approved, and steps were taken to appoint the committee. Whether it would have been successful will never be known. The courts might not have accepted it, or the mob might have acted in spite of it. Coleman, for one, felt that such a course of action would not appease the people.

Then he was speaking from the balcony to the vast crowd. His words have not been preserved, though there have been attempts at reconstruction. But he was not a man with great gifts of expression. Neither was what he proposed in any degree highly original or remarkable; a similar proposal had been brought forward in the committee the preceding evening.

As Coleman himself remembered, years later,

> I proposed that those present should immediately form themselves into a court within the building; that the prisoner should be brought before them, counsel on each side allowed, and testimony be taken, and that the trial should proceed fairly, calmly, and resolutely, and, if the prisoner should be found innocent, that he should be discharged and this intense excitement allayed; but if he should be found guilty, that he should be hanged before the sun went down.

As he finished speaking, an instantaneous and universal shout of approval arose from the vast throng. The crowd suddenly sensed that here was a leader. Some unknown young man had appeared from nowhere, and in decisive words had proposed action. Here was no city father, necessarily defending caution, warning everyone as to what they should *not* do. But, even more than all this, this young man possessed that strange intensity that marks the natural leader, the one into whose hands men commit their fates.

Everyone seemed to forget that a committee had just been appointed. Instead, a new committee was formed, and it withdrew to put Coleman's proposals into writing, consider the details, and present a motion.

After the committee had withdrawn, the throng felt the impact of another force, and of another man. Certain people began to circulate a printed handbill: TO THE PEOPLE OF SAN FRANCISCO, its ink scarcely dry from the presses. Four names were appended to it, the first of these: *Samuel Brannan.* It read:

> The undersigned, the minority of the committee appointed by you, report as follows: That the prisoners, Stuart and Windred, are both deserving of immediate punishment, as there is no question of their guiltiness of crime. The safety of life and property, as well as the name and credit of the city, demand prompt action on the part of the people.

Here was Brannan's bid for quick action, after his proposal and its defeat in the committee the evening before. The presentation of a minority report of an inflammatory nature directly to the crowd was obviously unethical, but Brannan had never been noted as a man of finer feelings.

By this time so many committees had been appointed that many people were confused. Careless readers skipped the word "minority." There was again a wild rush forward to secure the prisoners. Fortunately the crowd accepted the explanation that this was only the minority report. Without the new-found confidence in Coleman, Brannan might well have taken control.

The last-appointed committee reported. It recommended

the appointment of thirteen men to be the judge and jury. In spite of the general pressure for immediate action, the trial was set for two o'clock. Coleman's other propositions were accepted, and the committee made one significant addition, that the new judge and jury should act in conjunction with the courts, if the courts proved to be willing; if not, the jury should then proceed independently. This proviso showed the great reluctance with which any break with the tradition of legal authority was being considered.

The selection of jury and judge followed immediately. Probably names were put into nomination from the floor, and election followed by acclamation. The process was brief, and no difficulties seem to have arisen — a fact the more remarkable since membership in such an illegal jury was certain to be onerous and might well be dangerous. John F. Spence consented to serve as judge — an office doubly eminent and therefore doubly dangerous.

The time was now about twelve-thirty. As already stipulated, the meeting adjourned until two. The crowd, by this time, was so large that an observer compared it to the whole population of the city.

During this recess many individuals drifted away for a short period, but the crowd as a whole did not disappear. The day was one of those balmy interludes which sometimes descend upon San Francisco in mid-winter. The weather thus contributed to bringing out a large crowd, but at the same time its soothing and beneficent character did not suggest deeds of blood.

The hour-and-a-half interval must have been hot with impassioned argument in the attempt to secure the cooperation of the authorities. Only one individual proved willing. This was Judge D. D. Shattuck, Associate Justice of the Superior Court. He thus consented, probably, for two reasons. First, he was to act as one of the counsels for the defense, and so would be, in effect, opposing any conviction by the extra-legal court. Second, having witnessed the workings of lynch law in Mississippi, he had a deep horror of it, and as attorney for the defense he would still be able to talk against it.

As the meeting reconvened at two, the physical situation was, theoretically, that the trial was proceeding in the courtroom and the people were standing in the streets outside. But the crowd had been working its way into the building. Both courtroom and corridors were jammed, so that the dense mass of men extended from the streets through the corridors and clear up to the jury-box. A rumor, a sudden excitement, or even the forward thrust of a determined few, could thus be transmitted clear through the crowd in an instant. The situation was more dangerous than ever.

In spite of the crowd's loud insistence against lawyers' tricks, the lawyers could not be silenced. Hall McAllister, a leading attorney, had been appointed counsel for Windred. McAllister stated that the evidence against his client was different from that against Stuart, and asked that the two be tried separately. The court thereupon decided to try Stuart first. The action showed that the hastily constituted court was not yielding to hysteria.

Justice Shepheard then rose, and formally protested against the case being taken out of his hands. His statement was undoubtedly made for the record and not with any hope that it would be successful.

Coleman, the new hero, then made the proposal — strangely inconsistent with his statements elsewhere — that all counsel should be dispensed with and that the case should be tried "on its merits" before the jury.

Shattuck protested, citing that he had already been appointed as counsel, and had undertaken the task.

Coleman then reiterated his position, that there should be "no lawyers with their long speeches and law from the time of Moses." His words again brought loud cheering, good evidence that the technicalities of the law were considered to work in favor of the criminal, as the common man has always believed, since lawyers began. Shattuck protested against "such a trial, or farce."

At this point, a juror simply arose, and said that the jury could not function unless the prisoners were allowed counsel. This statement was decisive, since the jury had already received the final authority.

A member of the jury now nominated Coleman himself as prosecuting attorney. This proposal swept the crowd, and Coleman was appointed, "amid a storm of ayes."

This enthusiasm resulted partly from the feeling that Coleman, not being a lawyer, would move directly, unconfused by technicalities. Actually, he had once studied law, though he had never qualified for practice.

Thus, by mid-afternoon, the preliminaries were over. One man was on trial for his life. He was being tried under the name of James Stuart. Almost everyone in the great crowd, and the two prisoners themselves, undoubtedly believed that a double execution would occur, in Coleman's words, "before the sun went down."

At this juncture, ominously, the crowd demanded the actual presence of the prisoners. Coleman opposed it, saying that the two men were safe in custody, and undoubtedly fearing that their presence would lead to mob action. He then addressed the jury, in what amounted to an arraignment of the prisoner.

Payne was sworn as witness. He had hardly got a sentence out before the counsel for the defense pounced upon him — this was hearsay testimony, and the presence of Jansen himself was necessary.

Shattuck and Coleman then skirmished about procedure, with members of the jury also making proposals. An ominous voice from the crowded courtroom interrupted, "Go on with the evidence; never mind the speeches."

Doubtless as the result of such pressure, the prosecution won the decision, and Payne was allowed to testify, both as to what he himself had seen, and as to what Jansen had said when he identified his assailants.

Another witness confirmed this testimony, and then the prosecution called to the box the officer from Sacramento who had made the arrest. At this point some excitement aroused the crowd, both in the courtroom and outside on the street. Such a tumult arose that the reporters could not hear the officer's testimony.

Other witnesses followed, as the prosecution attempted to connect the prisoner not only with the assault of February 19, but also with a murder in the mining-camp of Auburn.

The afternoon had worn away, and the winter darkness was falling. As testimony was being taken, the crowd several times grew restless, so that the wisdom of Coleman's refusal to have the prisoners present became obvious. About six-thirty there was a surge forward. Shattuck spoke to the crowd, and order was restored. Once again the clamor was so threatening that Coleman had to be summoned. The crowd was so thick that he could move only by walking on the shoulders of the thickly packed mass. He spoke briefly to the people in the street, and managed to calm them.

About seven o'clock the jury went to visit Jansen. This was the third occasion on which the injured man had been aroused and subjected to questions. This time he went as far as to say that there could not be any doubt about the matter.

During the absence of the jury, speakers from the balcony continued to talk, in the effort to keep the crowd quiet. Even so, a push was made to seize the prisoners in the station-house. Malachi Fallon, the marshal — doubtless with the aid of a good Irish brogue and a bit of blarney — talked to "the boys," and turned them back.

At last, after a restless interval of some forty minutes, the jury returned, and the court reconvened.

Judge Shattuck, for the defense, was the first to make his plea. He spoke against hasty and extra-legal trials, citing "precedents in Mississippi and other places," where people had lived to regret their mistakes. He next attacked the prosecution at its weakest point, the problem of identity. He questioned the propriety of accepting testimony from a man as badly injured as was Jansen.

Coleman then addressed the jury briefly, "stating the testimony to be fully positive."

Finally, the judge rose from his seat. First he addressed the crowd, formally and in dignified words: "Fellow citizens, will you abide by the decision of the court?"

The answer was an affirmative shout. He then made his charge to the jury.

He first declared his belief that the identity of the prisoner had been fully proved. The rest of his instructions to the jury were expressed with great candor, moderation, and dignity:

> The people have now risen in their majesty, and disdaining and disregarding the ordinary forms of law as insufficient and inadequate to mete out proper justice have constituted you a jury to pronounce upon his guilt, and to award his punishment.

He urged "caution, reflection, and deliberation." He underlined the frightful responsibility which he, along with the jury, had assumed: "We are now overriding [the courts] and making ourselves judges and jurors . . . in direct violation of the Constitution and the laws of the land." He emphasized the dangers: "Once destroy our government, and we are at the mercy of every ruffian who may have the strength to assault us." Finally, he stated that the jury had been assigned the power to hang, but that the state law made fifteen years the maximum penalty for assault and robbery.

When some jurymen protested that they should not decide the punishment, the jury was instructed to report "Guilty" or "Not guilty."

When the jury finally withdrew about nine o'clock, few in the vast crowd had doubts as to what the verdict would be, and as to what would happen to the prisoner. After an absence of ten minutes, the jury called for a further consultation with Shattuck, and Coleman was granted permission to be present.

An hour passed, and the jury did not return. Still the crowd kept their ground. Time and again the cry arose, "Bring them out! . . . Hang them!" Invariably, as a counter-cry, went up the shout "Order, order!"

During the period of more than twelve hours the crowd had been standing there, though we must think that most of the individuals must at some time have temporarily drifted away, out of sheer weariness and the necessities of nature. This long wait had failed to cool the crowd, and there were still attempts to rush the building and much shouting.

Rumors also were rife. One of these was that Shattuck, threatened with violence because of his defense of the prisoner, had gone into hiding. At this word the crowd became indignant, and cries arose: "He is but doing his duty! . . . We appointed him! . . . We'll protect him!"

At this point, Shattuck himself appeared, and spoke to the people within the courtroom, saying that he had no fears of his fellow citizens. Coleman then spoke in praise of Shattuck, for doing his duty.

Midnight was approaching. At last the jury returned. The hush fell. The foreman stated a disagreement — nine for conviction; three against.

At this wholly unexpected outcome, a tremendous shout went up, a cry of frustration. In some way, the lawyers had triumphed again! There were calls: "Hang them anyway! . . . A majority rules!"

There were even cries of "Hang the jury!" and a rush was made. The jurymen drew their revolvers, and hurried back to the shelter of the jury-room. Only after a considerable time was some degree of order restored, so that the jury could be discharged.

At this point, after so many hours of excitement, most of the crowd melted away in sheer weariness, and with them went Shattuck, Coleman, and the others who had controlled the situation. This diminution had the unfortunate effect of draining the moderates from the crowd and leaving the most determined lynchers still in it. Again a crisis swelled up, with shouts for action. The few responsible citizens who still remained found themselves forced to take the floor again. A new chairman was appointed, and he made an impassioned appeal that the crowd should abide by the decision of their own jury.

Others spoke also, and at last, about twenty minutes to one o'clock, the chairman dared to put the question, "Shall we adjourn?"

The excitement had now drained away. The vote was in the affirmative. The crowd then quietly drifted off, and in five minutes the space was nearly clear. A few irreconcilables still remained around the door of the station-house, where the prisoners were retained. They constituted a self-appointed committee to see that the prisoners were not spirited away or permitted to escape.

Thus, after thirty-six hours of wakefulness and excitement, the city at last relaxed. Even the Sydney ducks took a rest. No robberies were reported.

# CHAPTER 5

# THE DAY AFTER THE BATTLE

*(February 24)*

O N MONDAY the *Pacific News* offered an editorial upon the recent events:

> It was one of the most impressive demonstrations of the power and majesty of the people we ever looked upon, and one which will be long remembered among the important events of San Francisco.

The editor continued, the accuracy of the reference of his pronouns suffering a little, but his meaning plain:

> This was not the assembling of a mob — it was not a whirl-wind of ungovernable popular fury; but it was composed of the whole body of our citizens, of every class, and of every calling.

The editor next commented, with some exaggeration, upon "the calmness and deliberation which marked the whole action." But the affair supplied evidence, he continued, "that crime and outrage shall no longer stalk in our midst unrebuked and un-punished."

In his final paragraph he looked to the future:

> The effect will not be lost upon the courts and ministers of the law. Criminals cannot longer be suffered to escape through legal quibbles, and the facility with which straw-bail is given and received. *As yet, no murderer has been punished under our laws.* Hereafter, no criminal can go free except at the risk

of anarchy, from which we have escaped only by a forbearance
on the part of the people beyond all praise.

The other editors came to the same general conclusions. The
*Alta* advocated, reasonably but impractically, the British procedure — that the demonstration was the equivalent of a vote of
lack of confidence and that the city officials should therefore
resign. The *Herald,* as usual, looked with favor upon direct
action — an attitude which is explicable enough, since its editor
was William Walker, later to be known as The Gray-eyed Man
of Destiny and to be the most notable of the filibusters. The
*Herald* also noted:

> The exciting scenes of Saturday and Sunday were the theme
> of general conversation. . . . Little knots of talkers collected
> around and discussed the merits of the case. The opinion
> seemed nearly unanimous that the citizens had done right.

A great day for the man in the street! He felt virtuous because he had restrained his passions and kept from deeds of
blood. But also, he had proved himself a dangerous fellow who
would stand for no nonsense. Let those people at the city hall see
to it that the Sydney ducks were got under control!

But the editors, and the average man too, forgot one detail.
The law had been overthrown. Extra-legal action had actually
been taken. That a divided jury had forced the return of the
case to the regular authorities may be considered merely an accident; even the dissenting jurors had been serving in defiance
of the law.

Moreover, an acquittal by a people's court was not without
precedence and was not even highly remarkable. In recent
years, to be sure, a legend has grown up to the contrary. People
have come to think that their great-grandfathers assembled
blithely to the slogan "Let's give him a fair trial and then hang
him!" The reason for this belief is largely journalistic. By the

very nature of things the editor would give the headlines to the hanging. But anyone reading the newspapers carefully will discover, tucked at the bottom of columns, clipped from the back-country sheets, these accounts of people's courts that tried and acquitted, or turned the culprits over to the sheriff.

Still, the affair at the City Hall was remarkable enough. And the man in the street, certainly, had behaved well. He had waited hour after hour, instead of taking the quick way. He had listened to reason. He had allowed the establishment of a court which granted to the prisoner all the civil liberties practicable under the circumstances. In the end, he had accepted the established practice of unanimity for a jury-decision.

Even more praise should go to the civic leaders. To face that crowd and urge an unpopular cause took cold courage and a devoted sense of responsibility. Mayor Geary and Judge Shattuck deserve the highest regard. "Judge" Spence, in his charge to the jury, was equally outstanding, and he may thus have given courage to the three dissenting jurors.

Those three may well be considered the heroes. They kept their heads, weighed the evidence and found it shaky, and then had the courage to maintain their convictions against the pressure of the majority of the jury and in the teeth of a mob crying for blood. One of them was R. S. Watson, and a second was George E. Schenck. Both of these were merchants. The identity of the third dissenting juror was never revealed.

On the other hand, much as we may praise these three, they should not be considered champions of law and order and of civil liberties in the narrower sense. Watson and Schenck certainly — and the third juror, too, by implication — voted for acquittal because of insufficient evidence and not as a protest against the extra-legal court.

Those "little knots of talkers," however, probably spent scant time discussing Geary, Shattuck, and the three jurors. Two other men, undoubtedly, were the centers of attention.

One of these was Coleman. The *Herald* granted him special mention:

> Mr. Coleman spoke in good taste, and very sensibly. Indeed, his course throughout the entire day was characterized by firmness, moderation and judgment, and elicited the warm approbation of all parties.

In Coleman, the people already recognized a leader. How great a leader they could not as yet realize.

In noting that Coleman had spoken with "moderation and judgment," the *Herald* was almost suggesting Coleman's own later words, that he had taken "a middle course." He was thus already establishing himself as a symbol, a possible leader who would stand somewhere between the strict law-and-order party, and the "wild and hasty excesses" of the mob, which he so hated.

The second man who stood out from the recent events was Samuel Brannan. He represented the extreme which Coleman rejected. Although he had stopped short of an all-out effort to raise the mob, his position was well known. On Saturday evening, he had moved in the committee the resolution to hang the prisoners. On Sunday, his name had led the list on the handbill circulated among the crowd. Whether or not he had been responsible for the inflammatory handbill circulated on Saturday, it could be reasonably attributed to him.

Brannan had first arrived in San Francisco in 1846 as the leader of a Mormon colony, which he had brought by sailing vessel from New York. Since that time he had been a central figure in the city. He was probably its best-known person — broad-shouldered, heavy-chested, richly dressed, talkative and loud-mouthed, open-handed. People loved to tell stories about him. Even though the stories scarcely redounded to his credit, he seemed to thrive on them.

He had laid the foundations of a fortune by the plain dishonesty of appropriating the Mormon contributions, and then leaving that church. After that, he had built up his fortune by speculations, especially in real estate.

Brannan was always a kind of public figure. He had been a chief leader of the action against the Hounds. He was at his best when addressing a crowd, with his commanding presence, big voice, familiar manner, and forceful use of language. Potentially he was a rabble-rouser.

But Brannan cannot be considered really an able man. He had little record of solid achievement. He did not inspire confidence in those who associated with him. He drank too much, and he could grow quarrelsome. He was a quarter-horse, built for the sudden burst, but without the resolution for the longer race.

All in all, however, he may be taken to stand as a symbol of those who cried, "No nonsense!" and wished to cut the legal corners and act directly.

As for those at the opposite extreme from Brannan, those who would eventually come to be known as "law-and-order" men, they as yet had no one to stand symbolically as their leader. Mayor Geary was about to retire from office. Among the others were some able and courageous judges and lawyers, but no one had assumed leadership.

At the same time, one may say, this party needed no man for a symbol. Its symbol was the personification of law itself.

Moreover, what this party really needed was action. More than words or a leader, it should have a tangible record — some thieves convicted and imprisoned, a murderer legally hanged, some oiling and repairing of the almost-broken-down machinery of justice. As the newspapers pointed out, the recent events had given notice that the patience of the people would not abide forever.

On this Monday, then, after a week-end more heady than drunkenness, the streets were again quiet, and the citizens returned to work. Brannan, we may suppose, paid some attention to the buying and selling of real estate. Coleman again considered the mixed lot of goods that he had advertised for sale — 20 barrels of Carolina rice, 200 barrels of pork, along with lard, candles, 200 dozen fresh Baltimore oysters, tea, pails, axe-helves, and 1000 gross of lucifer matches.

Workmen moved into the badly wrecked courtroom, and began to put it back into shape.

Berdue and Windred, retrieved from beneath the beds where they had been hidden, had a quiet hearing before Justice Shepheard. He held them over for trial, and placed on each of them $10,000 bail. This impossibly high figure served as a rejoinder to those who had been criticizing the courts for "straw-bail" practices. Actually, the two prisoners were by this time looking upon the police as their best friends, and the last thing that they wanted was to be free on the San Francisco streets.

On this day also the city council took significant action by instituting a chain gang. Whether this establishment would be of any significance in the control of crime may be considered doubtful. It was, however, an obvious sop to those who were demanding stronger action.

Also on this day occurred an incident to which the newspapers accorded a modest few inches of space. A man, having been found with stolen goods upon him, was seized by the crowd. Immediately, as the *Herald* reported:

> A rope was procured and he was in a fair way to swing, when the crowd were induced to commute his punishment. One man had already pounded the fellow's features into a flat, but now . . . several, sturdy, honest truckmen laid upon him with their heavy cart whips and lashed him into a foam. The blood spouted at every slash over the face, and the culprit cried "murder." When the truckmen were pretty well tired out, they wrung his ears almost off, and proceeded to wash him off by pitching him into the dock. Finally however, the police took him in charge.

This incident, since it did not end in death, has been neglected by historians. Its punishment, however, may be considered more brutal — and more brutalizing to its perpetrators — than a decently conducted execution. Occurring on the very day after the City Hall affair, it stands in striking contrast, and provides conclusive evidence that Coleman's fear of the mob was well grounded. It may also be referred for consideration to those who maintain that the men who organize an extralegal court and give as fair a trial as they can are really behaving worse than a mob, since they are acting with premeditation.

# CHAPTER 6

# CITY INTELLIGENCE

*(February 25–March 20)*

ALL THESE EVENTS were occurring in that remarkable city which was San Francisco in 1851. . . . Among connoisseurs of cities, Periclean Athens doubtless stands as chief masterpiece. In slightly lower place they may rate Augustan Rome, Florence under the Medicis, and Shakespeare's London. As modern examples they perhaps select Paris of the Second Empire and New York of the Twenties. But at some point, one would think, a connoisseur of cities might mention San Francisco of the 1850's.

The city had about 25,000 people, with a drifting population of perhaps 5000 more. It was about the same size as its contemporary Chicago. In San Francisco, however, perhaps 80 percent of the population consisted of males of working age. In business transactions and work done, therefore, the city was the equivalent of one of about 50,000.

The original settlement had been on Yerba Buena Cove, to make use of that secure anchorage. The cove was now being rapidly filled in, and ships anchored farther out, but the center of the city remained at the original site.

From there it was spreading out north, northwest, and south, sprawling over the low ground, as yet not climbing far up the steep slopes. To the north it lapped around Telegraph Hill. To the northwest it reached out through Spring Valley to the base of Russian Hill. To the west, closer at hand, California Street Hill (later to be known as Nob Hill) as yet blocked the extension of streets. To the south, the city extended across Market Street to Rincon Hill.

Thus, like Rome before the capture of the Sabines, it was a city of hills, populated by men with few women. Also, if we may trust the legend, early Rome was a city of many tribes, with its full share of runaways, bandits, and refugees. So also was San Francisco.

Nevertheless the basis of its population was American, and mainly from the northern states. With this American majority the large number of English-speaking immigrants from Great Britain and Ireland mingled easily, and were rapidly becoming naturalized. Also readily assimilable and causing little problem were the numerous immigrants from the continent of Europe, chiefly French and German, and largely refugees from the revolutions of 1848.

On the contrary, the numerous Spanish-speaking people formed a resistant mass. Only a negligible number of these were from the native Californian stock. Most of them had poured in from Latin America with the gold rush, and they were chiefly Mexicans and Chileans. They congregated in a district where the Chinese were later to succeed them. Little Chile it was called before it became Chinatown.

As for the Chinese, only a few of them had as yet arrived. They were considered curious, harmless, industrious, and somewhat amusing.

Alien in everything except speech were the Sydney people, who crowded Sydneytown at the base of Telegraph Hill. That name, like Little Chile, would soon vanish, but its reality as a haunt of vice was to be continued by the later-named Barbary Coast.

If, resembling early Rome, San Francisco was a city of hills and men of many tribes, it was like Venice in being the gift of the sea. Not only was a part of the business-district built on reclaimed land, but also, literally and symbolically, the citizens

NEW WORLD MARKET

Note Chinese vendor in foreground, and the large amount of game for sale.

looked to salt water. Each of the east-west streets, from Green south to Market, ended in a long wharf extending out into the bay. Some of these wharves had stores and warehouses built up part-way along them. Derricks and cranes rose against the skyline.

Beyond the ends of the wharves, the ships rode at anchor — tall three-masters, trim clippers, little brigs and schooners, big steamers for the Panama run, small ones for San Diego and Portland, river steamboats for Sacramento and Stockton, tiny sloops and launches to carry freight to the head of every estuary and far up the rivers.

On one particular day of this year, 451 vessels were lying in the harbor — about half of them American, six Chilean, and the rest flying some European flag.

Located at the end of a long, mountainous, and almost uninhabited peninsula, the city might as well have been occupying an island off the coast. Even with the interior all its important communications were by steamboat.

The city had thus only one essential reason for existence. It was an *entrepôt* at which goods for the supply of the mining-region were landed, re-distributed and re-shipped. Everything was import business. The only export was gold.

The vicinity of San Francisco was agriculturally barren, and had no mines. Manufacturing had not yet developed. The city, therefore, was predominantly commercial, and the merchant was king.

Aside from commerce, there was only one basic industry — amusement. As the largest city in the state, it also had the brightest lights. To it came eagerly every lucky miner, and everyone who had made money by supplying miners. In San Francisco he found elegant saloons, rich gambling houses, horse-races, opera and the theater, and what was sometimes called "night-life."

Architecturally, the city consisted of hastily-constructed wooden buildings. Artistically, it offered nothing. Its intellectual life had barely begun to stir. Its opera and theater were not better than second-rate. Why then should this raw encampment of business be nominated for greatness among cities? Only, one may say, because of the astounding variety of its life, and the overwhelming vitality.

Take, for instance, those exciting events of February 22 and 23. Not only were they exciting in themselves, but also, in an ordinary city, they would have remained dominating events in people's minds for months. But in San Francisco, by Tuesday — if not, indeed by Monday afternoon — people seemed to have pretty well forgotten what had happened on Sunday.

Partially, of course, this was bad! It meant that the ordinary citizen went about his usual activities, that the officers of law-enforcement lapsed into slackness, and that the professional criminals resumed business. . . .

In this lull, then, we may consider what we may term the city's problem of "crime and lack of punishment."

In most places and at most times, we may agree, crime springs largely from economic pressure. But in San Francisco of 1851 such a conclusion is scarcely warranted. The city was new, and there was no heritage of poverty. There was full employment. On the contrary, the conclusion seems warranted, the criminals were mostly professionals, who supported themselves by robbery because they found it easier, more profitable, and more exciting, than ordinary labor. Nearly all of these professionals were the ex-convicts from Australia.

Every country recognizes its right to protect itself against the immigration of known criminals. In 1850 California had enacted a law against such immigration. But no preventive machinery had been set up, and by dozens the "ticket-of-leave men" had been boldly walking ashore from every vessel that docked in San Francisco from Sydney, Adelaide, and Hobart. Many of these men had doubtless been originally convicted for comparatively minor crimes, and were not habitual law-breakers. They became good citizens. But a considerable number of these immigrants were confirmed thieves and burglars. In San Francisco they saw much money, and large quantities of valuable goods, inadequately protected. The temptation was great, and many of the immigrants resumed the ways of life which they had followed in London or Manchester or Liverpool. As compared with tight little England, they found loosely organized San Francisco a paradise and a picnic.

There was only one difficulty, and that was the citizen himself. He was generally a young man as compared with someone who had already served out a ten- or fifteen-year sentence. He was likely to carry a weapon, and to be quick to use it. Still, with proper care, you could either elude the citizen or take care of him. As for the police and the courts, they could be handled — in fact, were laughable.

In this last conclusion, the citizens of San Francisco agreed thoroughly with the Sydney ducks — agreed, but did not join in approving. But what was to be done about it was not a simple matter, because what was wrong was also far from simple.

Like those citizens, the historian feels this lack of simplicity to be unfortunate. Single massive flaws are easier to describe and more dramatic to portray than are numerous minor ones, just as they are usually easier to rectify.

If we may compare that system of justice to one of the contemporary stagecoaches, one may say that, looking at it, anyone could see, well enough, a stagecoach and six horses harnessed to it. The vehicle was even capable of moving, though not very rapidly and only with numerous halts. Looking closer, one could notice that the wheels were wobbly, that one thoroughbrace was broken, that the whip was missing, that the brakes were faulty. As for the horses, one of them was lame, one was blind, one was dangerously skittish, and one was so old that he could not even pull his own weight.

So it was with the system of justice. . . . The police were not altogether bad, but some of them were corrupt. Lines of communication existed between the police and the criminals, and along these lines of communication money might pass. So you might hold the police off, and that would be the end of it.

If you took a chance, and went ahead without squaring the police, and could not do so afterwards, you still need not despair. If you were operating on your own, you might be in trouble. But the typical Sydney duck operated as one of a gang. The gang hired a lawyer, and the criminal lawyer (often criminal in more than one sense) was already flourishing in California. His simplest device was merely to have someone stand bail for his client. The courts were extremely easy-going in this matter. Then both the principal and the one who had stood bail for him could merely disappear.

Another lawyer's device was to have the trial postponed. This was simple enough, because the courts were always busy. After a few weeks, mobility of population being characteristic of early California, the necessary witnesses could no longer be found in the city, and the case was thrown out of court.

Or you could prove an "alibi." A lawyer did not need to go to much trouble, or to spend much money, to end up with two or three witnesses who would swear that the prisoner had been in their company at the time of the commission of the crime. The reliability of the witnesses thus testifying might be highly dubious, but the jury had difficulty in going directly counter to the testimony.

And the juries themselves were far from flawless. No representative body of citizens was impaneled for duty. Instead, when a jury was needed, there was a quick round-up of people who happened to be in the vicinity of the court. Among twelve men thus collected, a lawyer could see to it that one at least was either in his pay or was a friend of the prisoner. A hung jury was thus assured.

At a higher level, the judiciary was also questionable. The judges had merely been elected by popular vote, and they had in most cases been nominees of the political machine.

Still, in spite of all these safeguards, you might occasionally be convicted. (After all, the courts had sometimes to make a gesture.) *Nil desperandum!* In the first place, an escape from jail was no great trick. Here again, collusion with the police came in handy, though it was not essential. The rules of incarceration were slack. You could even arrange for a visit from your wife or "woman." She was not searched, and could carry you any tools you wished, beneath her voluminous skirts.

But if you lacked the initiative to escape or had bad luck, you might eventually find yourself in the state penitentiary. There was still a starting-hole. Governor McDougal worked on the principle that he should always pardon his friends, and he seemed not to have an enemy in the world. At least, as a machine-politician he claimed as a friend every man who had a vote, or had a friend who had a vote.

This mention of machine-politics indicates another complication to the situation. The administration of the city was solidly Democratic, and was integrated with that party in the state.

The machine had its influence upon the administration of justice in the usual ways. It put venal men into office, even into some of the judgeships. Needing votes, it was not too much concerned about what a man did with his spare time, as long as he voted properly and perhaps lined up a few friends to vote along with him. The machine dealt in fraud, particularly on election day. The machine also had no objection to a bit of violence in the interest of assuring a majority, and it maintained its shoulder-strikers. The partisans of the machine, thus dealing in fraud and violence, and even in robbery, were not the best agents to suppress outbreaks of a similar kind in others.

The machine also controlled San Francisco County, which was larger in area than the city. The chief law-enforcement officer in the county was Colonel John Hays, the immensely popular former Texas ranger. He was an honest man, and a bright spot in the situation.

Another bright spot was the Grand Jury. This body was not composed of hangers-on around the courtrooms, but was carefully selected, and comprised many solid citizens. Its report, that spring, was an indictment of the system of law-enforcement, particularly as wanting in night patrols and water police. It commented upon "the patent influence of money." It inveighed against the "straw-bail" system and legal technicalities. In addition, it accused Judge R. M. Morrison and Justices Edward McGowan and H. S. Brown of "gross and wanton extravagances . . . and of unfaithfulness generally in the discharge of their duties."

The situation was somewhat simplified by the resignation of Judge Morrison. In his place the governor appointed Alexander Campbell, a much better selection than would have been expected of McDougal. Judge Campbell was another of the bright spots.

In short, an efficiently managed and corrupt machine had captured the new state, and the whole system of law-enforcement was tunneled with rottenness. On the other side, the Sydney ducks constituted a large group of skilled professional criminals, organized into gangs. . . .

One would err, however, in supposing that the citizens of San Francisco were daily and hourly, that spring, apprehensive about crime. To be sure, burglaries and robberies, sometimes with violence, continued to be about as numerous as they had been before the threat of direct action in the Jansen affair. But the number of such crimes in proportion to the number of houses and businesses was not too alarming. A merchant need not expect to be robbed every week or every month, and might even go through a whole year. In addition, he could take precautions — keep a good watch, and not have too tempting a store of coin and gold dust available. Then, if he lost a certain amount of cash and some goods, he could write it off as a business expense.

As for robbery on the streets, the ordinary San Francisco merchant was a fairly tough character. With his derringer in his pocket, he had a feeling that he could take care of himself. Charlie Jansen — a nice fellow, but a bit of a softie! And really asked for trouble, the way he had failed to take precautions!

Besides, in that extraordinary city, during that extraordinary spring, there was always something new. In two weeks, the whole Jansen episode was relegated to the category of ancient history by a new excitement.

Judge Levi Parsons presided over the District Court. He

may have been honest, but was apparently, to use a common British term, an ass. He was in love with the letter of the law, and seems to have found more pleasure in quashing an improperly punctuated indictment than in convicting a red-handed murderer.

On this occasion he gave to the Grand Jury certain instructions which seemed, to many people, to infringe upon the prerogatives of that body. The peppery and fearless editor of the *Herald* so stated in his newspaper. Thereupon the judge clapped a contempt charge upon him. Thereupon the whole city rose in defense of the freedom of the press. The result was an indignation meeting, on March 9.

Coleman, at one point, addressed the meeting and reminded everyone that the courts had not yet tried Berdue and Windred. Should the citizens not do something about it? But the suggestion fell flat. Berdue and Windred — who were they? Oh, yes — but that was two weeks ago! It was ruled that the meeting had assembled for another purpose, and could not consider Berdue and Windred.

Coleman was perhaps needlessly impatient. The case against the two men was proceeding, and was even showing some strange developments. On February 26 another officer from Sacramento had taken a look at Berdue, and had declared definitely that he was *not* the Stuart who was wanted in Sacramento. A few days later, even stronger testimony came from Frank M. Pixley, who was a well-known criminal lawyer and had defended Stuart on several charges. He swore an affidavit that the prisoner was not his former client.

The question for the San Francisco court, however, was merely whether the prisoner (under whatever name) had assaulted and robbed Jansen. So, in their creaky and rickety fashion, the wheels of justice continued to turn.

Actually, even before Coleman had spoken, one action had been taken. On March 5, the Grand Jury had brought in indictments against the two men. . . .

In the weeks following the freedom-of-speech mass meeting, the events recorded in the newspapers were so varied and so interesting that anyone can see why the San Franciscan had difficulty in keeping his mind fixed upon any one problem, such as crime, or good government.

A robber, attacking a sea captain, put his hand on his victim's mouth, to prevent his outcry. Thereupon, the captain bit him severely, and the robber hurriedly made off.

A street preacher addressed a crowd on Long Wharf, and the *Alta* commented succinctly, "Considerable preaching is needed on Long Wharf."

Henry Ingles and Peter Swinson were arrested for fighting, because the latter had alienated the affections of the former's wife. Testimony indicated that the husband, returning home, had discovered his wife and Swinson, as the *Herald* put it, *"in a most interesting state.* The lady and gentleman seemed wrapt up in each other — a strong attachment evidently existed between them."

D. Burdis had his pants stolen, in a situation which may be imagined, by a "señorita."

The racing season opened on the Pioneer Race Course at the Mission Dolores.

Adrian & Story advertised a fine lot of Gallipagos terrapin, direct from the islands.

A certain Simpson accidentally shot himself with his own pistol while playing cards, and had to be emasculated.

The health of the city was reported to be good, with deaths averaging scarcely two a day.

A visiting miner, William Clarke, fell in with a pleasant fellow calling himself Captain McIntyre. The latter set up drinks, and Clarke awoke the next morning, minus $1400 in gold dust. No arrest resulted.

The clipper ship *Surprise* set a new record, arriving from New York by way of Cape Horn, after what the editor termed a *surprising* voyage of ninety-six days.

The San Francisco Literary Union announced a debate: "Are the merits of the Warrior superior to those of the Statesman?"

A new import, of new import (the punning habits of these editors are contagious), was announced, to wit, "a couple of hundred cats, designed as *mousers* for our rat-ridden neighborhood."

The proprietor of the Washington Baths was recorded to be a public benefactor, his arrangements being so nearly perfect and his charges so moderate. The *Alta* declared bathing to be "a luxury that everybody ought to enjoy at least once a week."

A big row at the foot of Broadway seemed so threatening that twenty-five policemen and the mayor himself went down to quell it. They arrived to find everything quieted, and all parties had a drink together.

Roxana Coxin was sentenced to ten days hard labor for having stripped herself naked in the street.

The Pacific Tract Society held a meeting. . . .

Against such competition the trial of Berdue *alias* Stuart could scarcely draw headlines. Jansen, chief witness for the prosecution, told his often-repeated story. The prisoner steadfastly maintained his innocence, and his lawyer attempted to set up an alibi. On March 15 the jury, after half an hour's deliberation, returned a verdict of guilty, and fixed the punishment at fourteen years imprisonment. The *Courier* reported:

> The prisoner was deeply moved at the rendition of the verdict. He shed tears freely, and fell upon his knees, his lips moving, as if engaged in prayer.

He was then handed over to an officer from Marysville, where he was to be tried on a charge of murder.

Thus, on the same evidence, the legally-constituted jury convicted, while the extra-legal jury did not. Perhaps Jansen had grown more convincing in his identification. Perhaps the legal jury felt itself under greater pressure, by threat of mob action, than did the other jury.

The trial of Windred followed quickly. Jansen testified to Windred's identity, "with nearly the same certainty as he identified Stuart." On March 20 Windred was sentenced to ten years imprisonment. In contrast with Berdue, he received the verdict "with perfect indifference."

The docket was now clear. Jansen was well on the road to recovery. He even had been partially compensated, by money taken from the prisoners, for his loss in the robbery.

# CHAPTER 7

# ALARMS OF FIRE

*(March 21–April 27)*

T HE SITUATION in the world at large, and even the situation in the United States at large, need not be here of much concern. California was so isolated that it might almost as well have been a lunar community.

Europe, in this spring of 1851, was getting back to its feet, shakily, after the revolutions of 1848. Great Britain had escaped revolution, and Victoria's reign was settling into its pattern of greatness.

As for the United States, the Whigs held the presidency. Zachary Taylor had died in 1850, and Millard Fillmore had succeeded him — a man who may well be called the most minor of the Presidents. The excitement of the Mexican War was some years in the past. The spoils, including California, had been consolidated. Most of the people considered it all to have been a glorious demonstration of Manifest Destiny, but a good-sized minority continued to think it a national disgrace.

California had come in as a state, as one result of those months of dickerings, horse-tradings, and broken ideals which had produced the Compromise of 1850. Of the three great leaders, though greater to their contemporaries than in retrospect, Webster and Calhoun were recently dead, and Clay was dying as a broken old man. Disunion, seldom as yet called secession, had been in the air during 1850, and was not forgotten. Slavery had at last come, so to speak, out of hiding, and had forced itself upon the national consciousness as the unescapable and nightmarish problem. Throughout the country the time was without leadership, statesmanship, or vision.

Only in literature was it, by exception, a time of greatness, as the country entered the second year of its most notable literary decade. In 1851 appeared *The House of the Seven Gables, Moby-Dick,* and *The Conspiracy of Pontiac.* Mrs. Stowe was working on *Uncle Tom's Cabin;* Thoreau, on *Walden;* Whitman, on *Leaves of Grass.* That only *Uncle Tom's Cabin,* among them all, would be widely read at the time, is perhaps an index of the lack of greatness in the time itself.

But, to repeat, all of this made little immediate difference to San Francisco, which lived, far off and in its own way, on the strange economy of wealth produced by digging a yellow, inedible substance out of the ground. . . .

A common charge against those who have acted against crime by direct action has been that they should have worked by legal means, that is, by elections. In the case of the citizens of San Francisco in 1851 the answer to this charge is that they did so work.

An election of the city officials was scheduled for April 28. The Democratic machine was presenting a full slate. On the other side, the Whigs were standing for reform. The chief issue was not crime, but finances.

In retrospect, this situation may appear strange. To a contemporary it was obvious enough. As against every dollar that a Sydney duck stole, some rascal at the City Hall was making away with a hundred dollars. To take only one small but significant item, at a certain point $140,000 had been expended on the construction of the jail, but some visitors estimated that not more than about $15,000 of work was to be observed after an inspection. Such wholesale plundering had brought the city close to bankruptcy.

The Whigs approached the election with great expectations, being able to rally the voters to that simplest and best of all reformers' slogans, "Throw the rascals out!" As far as crime was concerned, that could be considered as absorbed into the larger issue. If an administration was to be honest and efficient in financial affairs, one might consider that it also would be honest and efficient in law-enforcement.

On the other side, the Democrats may not even have been trying to set up a very hard fight. The administration had been a glorious one, and everyone could afford to live for a while from its profits. When the winds of reform blow hard, the experienced politician may well decide that it is best to take shelter, and wait it out. Such a tempest is not usually a long-enduring storm out of the roaring forties, but merely a summer squall. . . .

The newspapers, during the weeks before the election, continued to report the vital, vibrant, and often violent life of the city.

The steam excavator, of twenty horsepower, was reported tearing down the sand hills south of Market Street at a great rate. The excavated material was being used to fill the cove. The sight of the "Steam Paddy" was recommended as "worth seeing."

"Forty-four Mexican señoritas" arrived in a sailing vessel from Mazatlán.

Of the same interesting suggestion, the captain of the ship *Josiah Quincy* reported that while rounding Cape Horn, he had spoken a French barque bound to San Francisco. She had on board sixty young ladies from France.

Of different import, an editor noted "a whole cart load of cradles, not gold cradles, but the genuine baby rockers." The editor considered this novel sight to be "encouraging."

As if emphasizing the point, the city's first Chinese baby was born. Elegantly congratulating the mother with an echo of Shakespeare, the *Herald* declared, "Afoy-Whang has . . . done the State some service by adding to the population."

To continue the oriental theme, the first Japanese arrived. There were twelve of them, survivors picked up from a storm-tossed junk, hundreds of miles at sea. The Japanese, though unable to talk to anyone, were hospitably received and entertained, but viewed chiefly as curiosities. They did not escape an occasional practical joke, perpetrated by one of the inveterate California hoaxsters. Some of them demonstrated their artistic ability by copying pictures of their junk on stone for a lithographer.

To pick up the Shakespearean theme, the editor of the *Picayune* put the governor of Texas into his place for having opened a proclamation: "In the beautiful and expressive language of the Bible, 'the winter of our discontent' is gone." The San Franciscan pointed out that the words of the villainous Gloucester had never before been cited as Holy Writ.

The county court considered the *habeas corpus* case of Frank, a Negro, whom Mr. Calloway had seized and confined as being his slave. The judge decided against Calloway, on the ground that Frank was not a fugitive but had been brought to California, a free state, by his master, and had thus become free.

The Sons of Temperance, numbering about one hundred and being in a most prosperous condition, were reported to meet every Friday.

A riot in Boston was recorded, with a certain amount of satisfaction, as an indication that mob violence was not a peculiar California institution.

A "free fight" occurred on the road near the Mission, some fifteen participating. The races were just over, and a number of citizens were returning to the city on horseback, after a convivial afternoon. The *casus belli* was not reported, and was probably trivial. Once started, the fight became open-ended. As each horseman rode up, he leaped to the ground, and joined battle with the most convenient adversary. The *Herald* concluded, "The result was sundry black eyes, and broken heads. Nothing very serious."

During these weeks the city experienced an epidemic of what were known as "cow-hidings." An alderman, feeling his honor touched by the remarks made about him by a judge during the course of a trial, arranged for a meeting on the street, and "immediately drew a cow-hide with which he was armed, and laid it over the Judge in rather a severe manner." Another affair grew out of some remarks alleged to have been made by a certain Mr. Hinchman as to the chastity (or lack of it) of the wife of a certain Mr. Gould. The relevancy of the remarks (if they were made) cannot have been very immediate, since Mrs. Gould (like many other wives) had not accompanied her husband to California, and was reported to be at this time "a highly respectable lady of Cincinnati, Ohio." None the less, Gould confronted Hinchman, and "after a few complimentary remarks, usual on such occasions," laid on with great vigor. In a third instance, a strong-armed lady was the defender of herself, and went after an alleged traducer with a cane. When the cane broke, she "clawed him down" with her nails. (In all of these cases, the sympathy of the crowd was with the attacker, probably on the theory that he or she would not be moved to such violent action without provocation.)

A number of items kept the San Franciscans reminded that they themselves were much more easy-going with criminals than were the people in other parts of the state. Five horse thieves were noted as having been hanged near the Tuolumne River. At Cache Creek two men were hanged, but were taken down before they were dead. Each of them then received two hundred lashes on the bare back. A more general note merely recorded several lynchings in the mines. . . .

The criminal record in San Francisco itself continued. On April 1, the *Alta* pronounced, "The annals of crime are about as black as ever." But the editor thought the convictions of Stuart and Windred to be encouraging. By April 6, however, the editor had changed his mind, and was concluding that crime had declined markedly in the last three or four weeks.

He attributed this to the establishment of the chain gang — like all of his contemporaries, having perfect faith that the possibility of punishment was a great deterrent to criminals.

Street lights were installed, by private subscription, along Montgomery and Merchant streets, thus giving the honest citizen a better chance after dark.

Several robberies occurred, and one particularly heinous murder. Near the Mission, an isolated settlement four miles off, on the evening of March 26, when Captain E. M. Jarvis was walking with his wife, a man sprang upon him from behind, and plunged a dirk into his back.

Evidence was strongly enough against a man named Slater to permit the swearing out of a warrant. On the day of his examination, while he was being taken through the streets, some horsemen attempted to seize him. The assailants, believed to have been from the Mission, were beaten off. A few shouts went up, "Hang him! Hang him!" But the crowd refused to respond, and the police remained in control.

At 3 A.M. on April 13, the alarm bell pealed, and there were shouts of "Fire!" Immediately the streets were alive with volunteer firemen and anxious citizens. The alarm proved to be false. The next night about eleven o'clock, there was another false alarm. Still another one, on April 25, was possibly an election ruse, designed to break up a meeting which the Democrats were holding.

Such false alarms, on the one hand, made some people nervous. On the other hand, they lulled others into a feeling of false security. Fire had been the city's worst enemy, and the threat remained. Almost all the buildings were of wood. The water supply was inadequate. The only fire engines had to be pumped by hand, and the stream of water which one of them could send forth was pitifully small. Moreover, the season had been a dry one, and by the end of April the grass, the trash, and the buildings themselves were tinder-dry.

On April 23 occurred an event which may well have tended to swing some votes in the coming election. Eight prisoners escaped from the jail by cutting their way through a partition in the rear of a cell. Such a wholesale escape aroused suspicion that it could only have been effected with the collusion of the police. Of the prisoners who escaped, one had been convicted of rape; three, of grand larceny; three, of burglary; one, of assault. This last was Windred!

Next day, the *Alta* printed an editorial on this escape, concluding, "Truly the branches of government, judicial, aldermanic and police, are all of a piece — just good for nothing."

In such an atmosphere the elections of April 28 drew near.

CHAPTER 8

# INCENDIARISM AND ITS AGENTS —
# THE REMEDY

*(April 28–June 8, morning)*

WHEN THE VOTES were counted, the Whigs were found to have made a clean sweep. . . . The new mayor was Charles J. Brenham, who had been a popular steamboat captain. He was a man of some virtues — honest, affable, conscientious. He was lacking, however, in the essential quality of leadership.

The comptroller, treasurer, and other fiscal officers seem to have been honest and efficient, and they accomplished much toward getting the city back on a sound financial basis.

The three officers having to do directly with law-enforcement were the recorder, marshal, and city attorney. In their duties these corresponded roughly to a modern judge of the municipal court, chief of police, and district attorney.

R. H. Waller, the recorder, has left little record of himself, and so the probability is that he was neither very good nor very bad. Similarly, Robert G. Crozier, the marshal, seems to have been colorless. But Frank M. Pixley, city attorney, was a man of very decisive character. He was the lawyer who had defended Stuart and other criminals, and who made affidavit that Berdue was not Stuart. Many San Franciscans must have wondered what Pixley was doing in this gallery of reformers — unless, they might cynically conclude, it was on the principle of setting a thief to catch a thief.

The law allowed little time for a lame-duck administration. The Whigs prepared to take over the government on May 4.

They had the people's clear mandate, and had reason to hope for a successful and peaceable term of office. Then disaster struck.

The evening of May 3 was an ordinary one. As was to be expected at this season, a steady northwest wind, funneling between Telegraph and Russian hills, was sweeping across the city.

About eleven o'clock a fire started in a paint shop on the west

FIRE OF MAY 4TH, 1851

The artist has treated the subject impressionistically, and shows a southerly instead of a northwesterly wind. The view is toward the east from California Street Hill (now called Nob Hill). Telegraph Hill, with its semaphore, shows at the left. The broad thoroughfare in the foreground is apparently California Street, but the artist has shown only one street between it and Telegraph Hill.

side of Portsmouth Square, commonly called the Plaza. In five minutes the whole building was ablaze. By the time the most alert fire-company got its hose to playing, the buildings on either side of the paint shop were on fire.

A few minutes later the conflagration was out of control, and was sweeping down upon the main business-district. Soon people were figuring no longer by individual buildings, but by blocks.

Ahead of the fire raged confusion, despair, and panic. Men who had counted themselves wealthy saw all their assets go up in wind-driven flames. People strove furiously to move valuables to some safe spot. Occasionally, delaying too long, someone was caught in the conflagration. In hysteria, without apparent cause, a man shot and killed a Mexican woman.

During the hours that should have been those of darkness, the city was luridly alight. Except for the *Alta* every newspaper was burned out.

At five o'clock that morning, in the early light, the editor of the *Alta* sat down to his "melancholy duty." He wrote:

> San Francisco is again in ashes. The smoke and flames are ascending from several squares of our city, as if the God of Destruction had seated himself in our midst.

A major part of the city had already been burned. The editor continued:

> Here and there a brick building stands like a tomb among a nation of graves, yet even they in most cases have nothing but their walls standing.

By 7:00 A.M. the fire had burnt itself out, having come to the less thickly built portion of the city and to the waterfront.

Eighteen blocks were destroyed, except for an occasional fireproof building. Even the plank streets were burned. Five other blocks were largely destroyed, and many individual buildings outside of these limits. The main business-district was wiped out, and much of Sydneytown. The destruction was estimated at 1500 buildings, about three-fourths of the city, and historically-minded persons compared their disaster to the burning of Moscow at the time of the French occupation.

The victorious Whigs thus took their oaths of office to administer, not a functioning city, but an expanse of scorched earth. Demoralization was extreme. There were even many who said that the site might as well now be abandoned, and the commercial activities transferred to some better location, such as Benicia or Sacramento.

The outlying districts, however, where most of the people lived, were still intact. Most of the bank-vaults had escaped destruction. Capital was therefore available for reconstruction. Inside of a few hours, with magnificent San Franciscan resili-

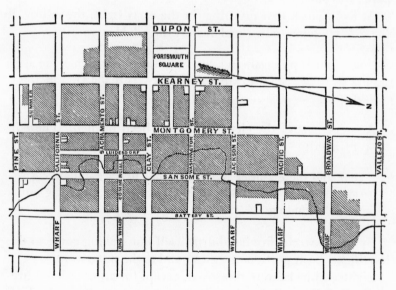

DIAGRAM OF THE BURNT DISTRICT, MAY 4TH, 1851

ency, confidence was being restored, and plans for reconstruction were developing.

The reaction of Coleman may be considered typical. Burned out and losing four-fifths of his goods on Saturday, he began rebuilding on Sunday, and was back in business, with goods from a newly arrived ship, on Monday.

Once the period of shock was over, people began to inquire as to the cause of the fire, and rumors were circulating. Could it have been arson? Several details made people suspicious. On May 4, 1850, a year ago to the day, the city had suffered its last great fire. Could this be mere coincidence? (To be sure, this present fire had started on May 3, but the correspondence was close, and most of the burning had been on May 4.) Now people remembered the recent false alarms. They learned also that there had been much looting, even of buildings which were out of the line of the flames but had been abandoned by people going to fight the fire. Could the fire have been planned by people who thus wished to have a chance to plunder? As the *Alta* commented, "Crime seemed to run riot."

Another story began to circulate, and apparently on good authority. During the excitement of February 23, friends of Berdue and Windred among the Sydney ducks were planning to burn the city, in revenge, if the two should be hanged. This story, moreover, was the more sinister in that it was reported by way of the police, and suggested that the police were in entirely too close touch with the criminals.

Only five days after the fire these rumors had so consolidated that the editor of the *Alta* could write, "but little if any doubt remains that this city was set on fire by some incarnate fiend for the purpose of robbery." The editor assumed that this fiend would be found among "the convict population." But the editor was also optimistic, noting "the hundreds of new buildings now being built all over the burnt district."

On May 12 the *Herald,* having resumed publication, declared,

"It appears now beyond doubt that the recent conflagration
. . . was the work of an incendiary." The editorial continued
with a direct accusation against the professional criminals,
and urged enforcement of the law forbidding their entry.
"This," it decided, "must be the work of the people themselves."

Only a few days later, the newspapers reported an attempt,
on May 15, to burn the Verandah, one of the principal saloons.
No longer content with the singular, the editor of the *Herald*
declared, "There is a band of incendiaries in our midst."

The very next morning, at one o'clock, the watchman at the
city hospital saw clouds of smoke issuing from an outhouse.
Rushing with a bucket of water, he saw a man run from the
outhouse and escape by the back gate. The watchman was
able, with some difficulty, to extinguish the blaze. Again the
evidence pointed toward incendiarism. "This attempt to fire
the city," wrote the editor of the *Alta,* "seems now to be a
nightly occurrence."

The citizens of San Francisco were reduced to such a state of
nerves that they hardly dared go to sleep at night. Some of
them took action by banding themselves together as a volunteer
auxiliary police, "for the purpose of preventing crime and protecting property and life in this city, from the assaults of the
assassin and the incendiary." Among these volunteers, the
*Herald* declared, were "some of the best men in the city." Cooperating with the regular police, these volunteers raised no
question of extra-legal action. They patrolled the streets after
dark, when the regular police were ineffective.

At the same time the work of restoring the city was progressing with great rapidity. By the middle of the month an esti-
mate was that three hundred buildings had been repaired or
erected, so as to be again available for habitation and business.

On May 17 the San Franciscans read some disturbing news
of direct action at near-by Napa. Hamilton McCauley had

been sentenced to death, but the easy-going governor com-
muted this punishment to imprisonment. Thereupon the citizens, in the middle of the night, seized McCauley, and hanged
him. The *Alta* commented:

> This is a horrible affair, but the fault lies with the courts,
> lawyers, judges, and politicians, who show themselves so much
> more anxious to rescue villains from punishment than to pro-
> tect the worthy, that the people have been driven to despera-
> tion.

Reading such an account, the San Franciscans might well think
that they themselves were acting in a slack manner. Moreover,
Napa was not a wild mining-camp, but was a little town in one
of the most stably settled of the cow counties.

As might be expected, however, the crisis in San Francisco
eased off. A late rain fell on May 18, and somewhat reduced
the fire-hazard. Perhaps the volunteer patrol was helping, and
fewer robberies were reported. Still, the city government
thought it worthwhile to offer a $2500 reward for the apprehen-
sion of arsonists.

On the whole, the San Franciscans had little reason to think
that the Whigs were doing any better than the Democrats had
done at law-enforcement. Considering the disaster of the fire,
anyone could see that the problem was even more difficult.
The election itself had produced some problems. Two claim-
ants to the same judgeship attempted to hold court at the same
time and place. In comic-opera fashion they leveled charges of
contempt the one against the other, and court could not convene for a whole day, until a more seemly procedure was de-
vised to settle the difficulty.

Marshal Crozier was at least doing something about the
police force, but one could question whether what he was doing
was very advantageous. He had dismissed large numbers of
policemen, and had replaced them with worthy Whigs. Per-

haps the honesty of the force was improved, but the new men
were inexperienced.

Then, with June, began an outbreak of robberies, accompanied by the dull thudding of slung-shots.

At this, even the conservative *Alta* broke down:

> Can we not catch some of these rascals? There is a flag-staff in
> the square with a block for a rope to run through. To what
> better use could it be put than to run up to its very truck, some
> of those who infest the city, setting fire to the buildings and
> robbing the citizens?

On the early morning of June 2 there was another jail break.
Nine prisoners escaped — four of them under the charge of
larceny; two, of robbery; one, of burglary; two, unidentified.
One of these men was George Adams, a celebrated burglar
among the Sydney ducks, who had already escaped three times
from custody. James Burns was also a noted ex-convict, generally known as Jemmy-from-Town.

The *Alta* commented with considerable restraint:

> It certainly appears a little singular that with three police
> officers in the station house, and two on the outside, that this
> escape should have been made. The manner in which the key
> was obtained also appears strange, and it is to be hoped that
> this affair will have a thorough investigation.

That very evening, as if the rhythm were quickening, an
alarm of fire was raised in the upper rooms of a lodging house
on the waterfront. The blaze was easily extinguished. The
police, on the scene with commendable promptitude, arrested
a Sydney man named Benjamin Lewis. Much evidence suggested that he was an arsonist, though a bungling one. Several
of his fellow lodgers were ready to testify. On the next day, a
hearing was held in the Recorder's Court. The building and
room were the same as those which had witnessed the exciting

events of February 23, since the City Hall was located in a part of the city which had not been burned. A number of witnesses appeared, and their testimony produced a strong implication of guilt. As news of the hearing circulated, more people came into the courtroom, until it was crowded. They remained quiet and orderly.

Twelve o'clock approached. A lawyer was summing the case up. At that moment a fire-engine went noisily rushing past the building. Some imaginative fellow jumped to the conclusion that the prisoner's friends had raised the alarm of fire with the idea that in the resulting confusion they could rescue him. The cry went up, "Hold that man fast! See to the prisoner!" Dozens of excited men leaped forward to seize Lewis, probably not themselves knowing whether they were trying to prevent his escape, or to take vengeance on him. The police sprang to the defense.

There was a fierce, doubtful struggle. Some of the crowd got their hands on Lewis, and almost tore his clothes off. Then the police closed their ranks, and bore their prisoner off to an inner room.

Order was restored. The case was continued in the absence of the prisoner. The lawyers in their speeches placated the crowd by emphasizing that justice would be done.

The recorder stated that he intended to refer the case to the District Court for trial. Everything was quiet, and he was about to order the prisoner's return.

Then, to the amazement of everyone in the courtroom, a great shout arose from outside the building. A crowd had collected, aroused by the attempt of those inside to seize the prisoner. Now, however, those inside came rushing out, thinking that those outside had in some way seized Lewis. At the hubbub — with no one knowing anything and everyone imagining all things — people came hurrying from all directions. Cries went up, "Bring him out! Hang him!" Within a few minutes several thousand men had assembled. The mob spirit took over, and many people were in a frenzy of excitement. The police and the city officers massed themselves at the door entering into the courtroom, and the crowd surged against them.

Again, as if in repetition of February 23, a speaker came forward. This was Colonel J. D. Stevenson, one of the best-known figures of the city. Fifty-one years old (an elderly man by San Franciscan standards) he had commanded the regiment of New York volunteers which had occupied San Francisco in 1847. He had remained in the city, and grown very wealthy. Now, to everyone's surprise, he did not attempt to calm the crowd, but harangued them in violent language, urging them on to take vengeance upon the prisoner.

To regain control, Mayor Brenham appeared on the balcony and tried to command attention. The shouting was so continuous that he could not even make himself heard. The crowd was crying "Brannan! Brannan!" Finally the mayor gained a hearing, and declared himself amazed that such a citizen as Colonel Stevenson would speak as he had and that other citizens would applaud such sentiments. He himself was thereupon interrupted with shouts and hisses.

When he still tried to speak, there were some cries of "Hear the mayor!" At the same time a tremendous and discordant roar was going up — shouts, boos, groans, hisses, catcalls.

At last the mayor was able to announce that the prisoner was no longer in the building. He again exhorted the people, as Americans and good citizens, to disperse, and not to violate the laws. The crowd, apparently not believing that the prisoner had been removed, continued to make rushes.

The mayor, once more unable to make himself heard, began to panic. The best he could do was to command the police to perform their duty, even if they perished in the attempt. The majority of the crowd continued to shout, "Hang the incendiary! Bring him out!"

JONATHAN D. STEVENSON

Loud calls then went up for Brannan, and that idol of the crowd stepped forward and spoke. As on February 22, he was less inflammatory than the crowd had expected him to be. His principal suggestion was that the prisoner should be turned over to the volunteer police. This idea was approved by acclamation.

Although such action had no legal status and was not binding upon anyone, its passing gave the people a feeling that they had done something. Besides, they had now become convinced that the prisoner had really been spirited away. Moreover, it was dinner-time. Things quieted down, and the people dispersed.

The crowd of June 3 offers interesting comparisons with that of February 23. The excitement was briefer, not more than two hours. More violent, it was equally ineffective. Again the crowd had needed a leader, and again Brannan, though speaking, had not taken the responsibility of initiating action. Again, it had been a very close thing!

But if any San Franciscan thought that the arrest of Lewis had settled the problem of arson, he was soon disillusioned. In the next few days two more fires of suspicious nature were reported. In connection with one of these another rush was made upon the Recorder's Court, causing it to suspend briefly.

The state of tension had obviously become one which no community could long maintain without some action or relief. Even the most conservative citizens had lost confidence in the machinery of law-enforcement. Colonel Stevenson, wealthy and middle-aged, had never been noted as a firebrand, and his acting as a rabble-rouser showed the pass to which things had come.

The volunteer patrol was functioning, but what was the use of its arresting a thief or an incendiary if the courts would not convict?

All over the city, this first week of June, little knots of people were discussing the problem. The men of substance were chiefly concerned, and in San Francisco that meant the merchants. There was about them, as a class, a tremendous solidity. They possessed also a considerable sense of social responsibility. They were the ones who already, by robbery and much more by fire, had been the chief losers. They were the ones who in any future trouble, would stand to lose the most. But what to do?

A mere incitement of the mob made no appeal to such men. Mobs easily get out of control; they turn upon the man of property to plunder and loot; that way is the reign of terror. On the other hand, was there any use in trying to bolster up the constituted authorities? Even the Whigs seemed to be shot through with weakness and corruption.

The term "merchant" covered a wide range of activity. It included everyone from a man who kept a small store to one who imported whole shiploads of goods. A special group, numerous and prominent in an *entrepôt* such as San Francisco, was that of the commission merchants, who primarily acted as middlemen, breaking up cargoes of imported goods and reselling them to wholesalers and other merchants, usually by auction, making their own profit from the commission exacted. Most of them speculated in the merchandise that they handled, making and losing large sums with much of the abandon of gamblers. Not only were they numerous, but also they were, as a group, particularly active, energetic, and aggressive — and, we may also maintain, public-spirited.

In any nineteenth-century American city the natural leaders were the lawyers. But now the merchants drew away sharply. Some of the lawyers, for a fee, would defend even the worst of criminals, and manage so to confuse the issue that a conviction could be avoided. Even the best of the lawyers seemed to be in and around with the corrupt system. So, in the little knots that gathered together, lawyers were viewed with suspicion, or excluded altogether.

The merchants, left to themselves, even though they were numerous enough, might have felt isolated. But, even after excluding the lawyers, they could find allies. Physicians, for instance, seemed to have a sensible attitude. And ship-captains! With as many as two hundred American ships anchored in the harbor, some of them remaining for long periods and many in the coasting trade, San Francisco was full of ship-captains — vigorous, bluff, and hearty fellows, required to enforce the laws on their own, often by strong-arm methods, once the ship was at sea.

Groups were forming, and one group interlocked with another. In conversations men were noting which other men seemed trustworthy, courageous, inclined to be aggressive. Leaving such a session one might say, "That's a good man! He has good ideas."

June 8 was a Sunday. The *Alta* was the only newspaper published on that day, and so it was assured a wide reading. It contained an article headed "Propositions for the Public Safety." An editorial comment introduced it: "The annexed communication is from one of our most respectable firms and is worthy of the close attention and consideration of every citizen." Glancing at the end, the reader would have seen that the communication was signed only with the pseudonym "Justice," but since it was from "one of our most respectable firms" it must originate from some businessman, or more than one. The communication filled half a column, was well written, and was very far, in tone, from anything that could be called rabble-rousing. Its opening offered almost a touch of unconscious humor. The writer, whose chief desire was apparently for a quiet life, was especially perturbed that his strength was "worn out in nightly watchings," and that he was not able to "obtain the rest so necessary to qualify him for the arduous and exciting life we all lead."

He went on to make definite proposals, admitting that "the remedies I am about to suggest may not be strictly in accordance with law." He believed, however, that "we must be *a law unto ourselves,* and there are enough good men and true who are ready to take hold."

He proposed, first, "to establish a committee of safety." The duty of this committee would be "to board, or cause to be boarded, every vessel coming in from Sydney, and inform the passengers that they will not be allowed to land unless they can satisfy this committee that they are respectable and honest men."

He next proposed "to appoint a committee of vigilance say

of twenty men, in each ward." The duty of these committees would be "to hunt out these hardened villains." Having been identified by the police, the villains would be summarily banished from the city, on pain of death. If they proved to be recalcitrant, they were to be shot down "like dogs."

The author did not pretend to know how all this could be worked out, and merely stated, "I leave the details to others."

These proposals, taken as a whole, were so extreme that they might be called a program for a revolution. Even such a term as Committee of Safety had strong revolutionary associations. "Justice" really proposed that a group should band together and replace the constituted government, at least in so far as the administration of justice was concerned. Moreover, the movement was to be associated with an abrogation of the ordinary processes of law. Accusation by a policeman was to be the equivalent of conviction. There would be no appeal, and anyone resisting would be shot down.

One would think that such propositions could arise only from some irresponsible firebrand. Actually the author, as he later confessed himself to be, was R. S. Watson, a prominent commission merchant, a man noted throughout his life for responsibility and integrity of character. That he could even momentarily have been constrained to write as he did was an evidence of hysteria which had seized even the most stalwart citizens under the long-continued strain of listening for still another alarm of fire.

Watson himself, on February 23, had been one of the three jurors to vote for the acquittal of Berdue. He had thus upheld, in an almost quixotic way and at personal risk, an accused man's right to have a fair trial and to be considered innocent until proved guilty. But on June 8 he was for shooting a man down like a dog without any trial at all.

Nevertheless, we should not think too badly of Watson, or merely write him off as a good man gone to pieces. His communication was remarkably moderate in language, even when radical in idea. It made no cry for vengeance upon some particular individual, such as Lewis. Moreover, Watson was the first to lay down, however hazily and amateurishly, a definite mechanism of action, just as he also seems to have been the first, in the current crisis, to record the term "committee of vigilance." He did not merely advocate "Something ought to be done!" Instead, like a businessman organizing a new firm, he calmly declared, so to speak, "This is the first step we should take toward achieving our end." He did not shriek, "Let's hang the villain!" Instead, he proposed, "Let's form an organized group." And, for American citizens, the formation of such a group had been a matter of familiar practice ever since the *Mayflower* passengers organized to sign their compact.

Moreover, though Watson first put the words on paper, many others had already been voicing much the same ideas in conversation. He became the spokesman of all these others. Rarely, therefore, has a single brief piece of writing brought quicker and more decisive results. As Watson himself put it, years later, he had touched a powder-train already laid.

# CHAPTER 9

## QUOUSQUE ABUTERE, CATILINA, PATIENTIA NOSTRA?

*(June 8, afternoon–June 10, evening)*

GEORGE J. OAKES was a partner in the firm of Endicott, Green, and Oakes, merchants. James Neall, Jr., was a dealer in lumber. They lived near each other in the almost suburban area just south of Market Street. Each was a rather average member of the merchant class, not outstanding in either wealth or prestige.

That Sunday morning each of them, we may suppose, read the *Alta,* including "Propositions for the Public Safety." In the afternoon, as neighbors do, they got together and talked. On that day, when two serious-minded San Franciscans began to converse, there could be only one chief topic — the situation. The two neighbors decided to do something about it. First, they would go to see Sam Brannan.

Even on a Sunday, you were likely to find a San Franciscan businessman in his office, especially if he lacked a wife to maintain a home for him, and few San Franciscans had wives — except in the East. Brannan's office was at the northeast corner of Bush and Sansome streets, a block beyond where the great fire had burned itself out.

He was there to receive Oakes and Neall, and with him was his clerk, Wardwell. A clerk was a very special attachment to a man of business in those days. Though he might be an attendant in a store, he more generally was a secretary, bookkeeper, and general assistant. Sometimes he was a young man on his way up, learning the business.

SAMUEL BRANNAN

Oakes and Neall explained why they had come. Brannan was quick to take up the idea. He had been trying for weeks, even months, to get the people to take some direct action.

At the present moment the three men did not need to decide exactly what should be done. The next move was obvious. They must increase their numbers. The way to do this, also, was obvious. They would hold a meeting, next day, at the California Engine House. Oakes was a member of the company, and so the room was available to him.

But it would not be a public meeting. There had been enough mob scenes. Those masses of people might be swayed this way or that way, might just as likely do the wrong thing as the right thing, and had always ended by doing nothing at all. Instead, Brannan, Oakes, and Neall would here and now give to Wardwell the names of some men whom they knew to be "reliable." Then Wardwell would write each one of these men a note, formally inviting him to attend the meeting.

These notes could hardly have been better timed. By this date the volunteer patrol was proving its worth, and was rapidly teaching men to act on their own in making arrests, that essential preliminary of law-enforcement; many men who received notes were already acting with the patrol. In addition, little groups had come to some general understanding about the need of action, so that to send a note to one man meant that the information was at once transmitted to three or four or half a dozen.

Moreover, on Monday morning there was already the suggestion of another crisis. A San Franciscan, reading the *Alta,* could bristle up at the heading ANOTHER ATTEMPT TO FIRE THE CITY, and could read the editorial summation:

This could not possibly have been the result of accident, and it is now rendered positive and beyond a doubt, that there is in this city an organized band of villains who are determined to destroy the city. We are standing as it were upon a mine that any moment may explode, scattering death and destruction.

With a classical gesture the *Alta* also offered an editorial, "QUOUSQUE ABUTERE, CATILINA, PATIENTIA NOSTRA?" The editor, indeed, did not wholly trust the Latinity of his readers, and explained:

With equal provocation our citizens might propound the above question of Cicero, to the miscreants who infest our city — "how long will you abuse our patience?"

With regard to taking action, the editor asked another and highly significant question, "Gentlemen, do you wait to catch accomplished burglars in the act?" thus implying that indirect evidence would have to be accepted. Continuing his rhetorical questions, in Ciceronian manner, he then went through a roll of recent criminal cases, asking what had happened in each instance. In still another question the editor inquired of the San Franciscans, "Have they no spirit, no indignation, no life, energy, character?" Finally, at last in the positive, he declared roundly:

> If we are willing to let the felons burn us up, let us say so, and the sooner it is done the better. Men that have no resentment ought to be abused and kicked by villains and cripples and everybody else.

Thus called a coward in his own newspaper, a man might well be prodded to action.

Other such stimulation was not wanting. On this same day the comma-loving Judge Parsons committed what seemed to the righteous-minded citizens to be two separate outrages. First, he declared the present Grand Jury to be no longer legally constituted, and in effect he abolished it. No criminal cases could be tried until a new Grand Jury was in session, and this could not be until after July 1. The city was thus condemned to be without a criminal court, at a time when all facilities for housing arrested persons were dangerously and inhumanely crowded.

In addition, Judge Parsons quashed an indictment against Lewis the alleged arsonist, the man whose case had aroused the riot. Though Lewis had not been tried, the case against him was strong, and he had become the threatening symbol of lawlessness. Again the courts were failing to function, and the order-loving citizens seemed to have little recourse but to take things into their own hands.

A highly indignant group must therefore have assembled in response to the notes sent out by Brannan's clerk. Probably some forty were present. They were solid men of business — mostly merchants. There was some discussion of the problems of the time; there was a decision to continue with the organization already begun. It was arranged to meet again, that very evening, in one of Brannan's storerooms. During the afternoon a committee hastily drafted a constitution.

In the evening the group, as yet nameless, reconvened in the storeroom. It was a cheerless place, long and narrow, poorly lighted, low-ceilinged; the rough boards of the walls were hung with white cotton cloth, dingy and streaked with water-marks from the winter rains.

By now the group was larger. Probably more than a hundred attended this meeting.

The proposed constitution was read. No one, knowing Americans and meetings, would be indulging in a wild flight of fancy to suppose that there was then some discussion, and that motions for various changes of words and phrases were made, and some of them carried. Apparently, a final paragraph was added.

The constitution was then adopted. Presumably there was a unanimous vote. In any case, a negative vote would have meant nothing. The obvious step for anyone objecting to this constitution was merely to break off his connection with the group at this point.

Next, a committee must have been appointed to prepare a fair copy of the constitution in a suitable book so that members could affix their signatures. The meeting for the signing of the constitution was set for the next evening in the same place.

The constitution thus hastily written and adopted is not a document of much literary merit. An awkward shift from third person to first person suggests the fumbling work of a committee.

Perhaps as a result of the absence of lawyers there was a certain looseness of language. For instance, at one point the word-

ing is that the bell shall be rung "until ordered stopped," but
no stipulation is made as to who is empowered to give this
order. Though the language was generally straightforward, it
included some phrases of that half-biblical and half-legalistic
phraseology which to people of that era seemed to make documents more binding — for instance, "do unite," and "to do and
perform."

The signers pledged themselves, in the preamble, "to sustain
the laws," and in the second paragraph, to aid "in the execution
of the laws." This offer of support to the constituted authority
is of importance, even though it was qualified by the statement
that the signers would support the laws "when faithfully and
properly administered." Everyone, however, knew that this repeated statement would probably be nothing more than a gesture.

The real business was set forth in the last words of the preamble, "we are determined that no thief, burglar, incendiary,
or assassin shall escape punishment, either by the quibbles of
the law, the insecurity of the prisons, the carelessness or corruption of the Police, or a laxity of those who pretend to administer
justice."

After the preamble followed five numbered paragraphs, "to
secure the objects of this association."

The first paragraph stated awkwardly, "the name and style of
the association shall be the Committee of Vigilance for the protection of the lives and property of the Citizens and residents of
the City of San Francisco."

This famous term probably stood in the original text. But
there was some discussion of the name on the floor. "Regulators" was proposed, but this suggested the infamous Hounds of
1849. "Secret Committee" was another bad suggestion which
met with no favor. "Committee of Safety" and "Committee of
Public Safety" found some supporters. But "Committee of Vigilance," with its suggestion of watchfulness, defensive rather
than offensive, was the favorite, and was unanimously adopted.

Although given a new currency by this action, the term had been circulating in American usage for twenty years. It had even been already used in California for organizations more or less resembling the one now organized in San Francisco. In spite of being thus vaguely known, the term apparently had no strong suggestions either for good or for bad. Its adoption on June 9 was probably the direct result of its use by Watson on the preceding day.

The second paragraph stated that there should be a room where a member or members should be in attendance day and night, to summon the Committee at large if any situation warranted such action.

The third paragraph stipulated that when these members had decided to call the whole Committee, they should do so by striking two strokes upon a bell, followed by the pause of one minute and then two more strokes, and so continuing. A blank was left after the words "upon a bell situated." Apparently everyone knew that one of the fire bells was meant. (This blank was never filled in, an indication of how little attention was paid to the constitution once work was really begun.)

The fourth paragraph declared the decision of the majority of those present to be binding upon the whole Committee. Added here were the strong and significant words

> those members of the Committee whose names are hereunto attached do pledge their honor and hereby bind themselves to defend and sustain each other in carrying out the determined action of this Committee at the hazard of their lives and their fortunes.

We should note "pledge their honor." By the conventions of the time, only gentlemen possessed honor. This was not, we may note again, an open meeting. Its individuals were present by invitiation. Just how some of them — Brannan, for one — might be entitled to rate as gentlemen, may well be argued.

Nevertheless, there was significance in the fact that they so considered themselves and that they used the word "honor." And that term, in those days, was far from being an empty abstraction. Honor was then very real, and a gentleman was expected to be ready to die in maintaining it.

Although the wording was not close enough to be presumptuous, this paragraph faintly echoed the Declaration of Independence, "we mutually pledge to each other our Lives, our Fortunes, and our sacred Honor."

The fifth paragraph stipulated the customary officers to be chosen monthly. The short term suggests that the framers of the constitution envisioned only a short life for their organization.

A final paragraph, not numbered, and therefore perhaps added in the meeting, established standing committees on finance and qualification. The final words were, "no person shall be admitted a member of this association unless he be a respectable citizen and approved of by the Committee on qualification before admission." The Committee was thus to remain as it had begun. If it was not quite a gentleman's club, neither was it to be a sweeping of the streets. You could join only by invitation.

In practice, like many constitutions, this one meant little. The failure to fill the blank as to which bell should be struck may be taken as significant. As with other organizations in history, the Committee of Vigilance was to find its importance in what it did, not in what it stated it was going to do. . . .

The next day was June 10. If any further stimulus was needed, it could have come from an editorial in the *Courier*. Driven to an extremity of feeling by the thought of the people who perished in the great fire, the editor wrote:

> Where the guilt of the criminal is clear and unquestionable, the first law of nature demands that they be instantly shot, hung, or burned alive.

That evening, with such editorial advice fresh in their minds, more than a hundred men met in Brannan's storeroom. Almost without exception, they cherished personal grievances. They had been robbed or burned out or had suffered otherwise.

The constitution had now been copied into an ordinary account book about eight by twelve inches in size, bound in paper-covered boards. The paper was light blue in color, faintly lined. At the left-hand edge of each line, someone had neatly written numbers, so that each man as he signed would receive a number. Vertical lines had been ruled on the pages, and the three resulting columns were labeled: *Name — Place of business — Place of residence.*

The signing began.

The first dozen or so can all be identified, though in some instances vaguely. They may be listed individually, to give some idea of the type of man who formed the Committee.

1. S. E. Woodworth. Still a young man, he had served briefly as an officer in the Navy, and had arrived in California in 1847. In that spring, he had led an expedition for the relief of the Donner Party, and had done badly at it. In San Francisco he had been active in various kinds of business, and had done well. A fellow member of the Committee described him: "Selim Woodworth was a remarkable man. He was a great overgrown boy in some things; a man of a great deal of ability too in some other things; a good fellow, honorable to a fault." It was like him, we may think, to press forward and be the first to sign.

2. S. Brannan. By rights, many would have said, his name should have led the list. No man, at this point, was more responsible for the Committee than was he.

3. E. Gorham. Little is known of him, but a few years later he was one of the firm Gorham and Jackson, commission merchants, and that may already have been his business. Known as Captain Gorham, he had presumably either had some military experience or been a shipmaster.

SELIM E. WOODWORTH

4. Fredk. A. Woodworth. This was Selim's brother, more recently arrived in California, of a firm of shipping and commission merchants.

5. Geo. J. Oakes, commission merchant, whose conversation with Neall on Sunday had set the whole movement to going.

6. Frank S. Mahony. He also was a commission merchant.

7. Francis E. Webster. He also was a commission merchant.

8. R. D. W. Davis. Once more, he was in the auction and commission business.

9. Jas. C. Ward. He was the partner of Robert Wells, who later signed as #30. They were, though the repetition is monotonous, commission merchants. This Ward was a solid char-

acter, to be distinguished from the diminutive and peppery George Ward, #62.

10. Wm. N. Thompson. He was a dealer in lumber.

11. Wm. H. Jones. He was an auctioneer, involved in the commission business, and a man of considerable standing in the city.

12. R. S. Watson. As the author of "Propositions for the Public Safety" he might well have stood higher on the list of signers. He was another of the commission merchants, and a man of much standing in the city.

13. C. Winter. As a bookkeeper, he was the first who might be considered a private in the ranks. Possibly he followed his employer into the battle, and that employer may have been George M. Garwood, #50, who gave the same address.

14. Edwd. A. King. Known as captain, he was a former ship-master, and had once served as harbor master of San Francisco. His actual status in 1851 is uncertain. He may have been engaged in business.

15. George Mellus. He was a wine merchant.

16. James B. Huie. A well-known auctioneer, and a prominent man, he had signed, along with Brannan and two others, the inflammatory handbill circulated among the crowd on February 23. He had also served as foreman of the Grand Jury shortly after that time. Known as "Colonel," he was older than most of the others, probably in his middle forties.

17. W. A. Howard. Called Captain, he was one of the several shipmasters who signed. As outward mark of his calling, he wore a "navy cap." He was a man of the utmost vigor and impetuosity.

18. J. D. Stevenson. The colonel's big and bold signature filled two lines, so that no one could be #19. He was one of the best-known men in the city, and one of the wealthiest. His sudden outburst, urging the crowd to take direct action against Lewis, the alleged incendiary, was fresh in everyone's mind.

And still the signers pressed forward — too many to be listed individually, many of them not even to be identified . . .

It would now have been about eight o'clock. By one of those coincidences of timing which sometimes lend to historical events the quality of melodrama, certain happenings now began to occur about five-minutes' walk from the building where the signatures were being affixed to the constitution. A shipping agent, named George Virgin, came ashore from a steamboat, and walked to his office, which was located on the second floor of a building at the base of Long Wharf. He had with him about a thousand dollars, which he had collected in the way of his business. In his office Virgin had what was usually called a safe, though it was actually more like a heavy cashbox. It was about fifteen inches square, made of iron. Even empty, it must have weighed well over fifty pounds. In the daytime, Virgin kept his cash there, and he frequently had large amounts. In the night, however, he did not trust such protection. So, this evening, he took his money downstairs, and put it into the more secure safe of a saloon.

While he was doing all this, the building was being kept under observation. A certain man, called Simpton, had watched Virgin go into the building, and was now watching to see him come out.

Simpton, a rough-looking fellow, was tall, heavily muscled, and a magnificent physical specimen. He had no difficulty in keeping watch, for, as the summer twilight faded, a magnificent full moon lifted over the Contra Costa hills. The sky was cloudless. The evening was one of those rare balmy ones which San Franciscans occasionally experience.

Simpton was a native of London, and had arrived in San Francisco by the Sydney route. His motives, in thus watching the building, were not those of a guardian angel.

His plans were well laid. In the last few days, he had several times visited Virgin's office, under the pretense of purchasing a steamboat ticket. He had observed the safe and the money in it. He had decided that with his great strength it was not beyond his carrying away. So he now had with him a large sack, formerly used for transporting coffee. But to carry the safe all the way back to Sydneytown would be laborious, and might also subject him to suspicion. He had moored a boat at the end of Long Wharf. The boat, we may suppose, was tied up in such a way that a single jerk on the rope would release it. The oars, also, would have been placed ready for a quick getaway. He would have preferred an ordinary foggy evening, but the set-up looked too good, even so, to suggest a postponement. . . .

Men were continuing steadily to sign the constitution.

46. Stephen Payran. He was a copyist by profession, and the elegance of his signature testifies to his skill. Perhaps he continued with that work in San Francisco, but he would have little time for any other work than that of the Committee during the next few months.

53. R. S. Lammot. He was a young man in his twenties, definitely on the rise. A conveyancer and notary public, he had recently got into politics, and had received his reward by being appointed clerk of the Board of Aldermen. He was commander of a squad in the volunteer police. But he is chiefly important because he wrote dutiful letters to his parents back in Pennsylvania. From them we learn how a man actually felt to be a member of the Committee of Vigilance. And, first of all, one should note that Lammot (or, Lamotte, as he spelled it later), was gratified that he had been selected. It was a little as if he had been elected to the right club.

57. G. W. Ryckman. With a partner he owned the New World Building, and income from this investment may have carried him through a summer when he was destined to earn no other money.

58. A. Jackson McDuffee. Signing just after Ryckman (and perhaps not by coincidence, since the two had much in com-

mon) was McDuffee. He may have had some background of experience in police work, for he was to serve as sergeant-at-arms, the Committee's only paid member.

62. Geo. R. Ward. Diminutive in stature and compensating for it every hour of the day was George Ward, a great brandisher of pistols and sometimes a little ridiculous, but a good man to have on your side.

71. Isaac Bluxome, Jr. In 1849 he had been captain of a company against the Hounds. He had organized the Washington Guard. Now he was serving in the volunteer patrol, and was a commission merchant, of Bluxome and Co.

72. G. E. Schenck. Signing just below Bluxome (and again this may not be mere coincidence, for the two were much alike) was another commission merchant. He had been one of the three courageous jurors who voted for the acquittal of Berdue. None were to exceed him in conscientious service.

95. Edgar Wakeman. The shipmaster of shipmasters, "Ned" Wakeman was widely known. Lately he had gone into steam, and was taking the *New World* back and forth to Sacramento. The amiable Alonzo Delano, San Francisco's first man of letters, praised the efficiently-run boat, and described its captain as a "gentleman." Gentleman he might be, but Wakeman was also a shipmaster, who had risen to the top in a hard trade.

96. Wm. T. Coleman. Thus, almost at the end, came the name that in the long run was destined to be the most famous of them all.

98. A. Wardwell. Brannan's clerk, one can imagine, had stood by the table, supervising the signing. Now with the line almost exhausted, he put his own name down, thus following, like many another clerk, his master's banner.

Five more signatures, and then they stopped at line 104. Since Stevenson had used two lines, only 103 could be counted as members.

By then it must have been nine o'clock, getting late for businessmen who had to start the day early. There was still some work to be done. They elected Brannan as president, and Bluxome as secretary. Since there might be a sudden emergency, they set a countersign to be given before anyone should be admitted to the rooms. The word was "Lewis" — another indication that the Committee was organized largely to meet the threat of incendiarism.

Apparently at this time, also, Colonel Stevenson felt called upon to make a speech. Having been born on the first day of the first year of the century, the colonel was one of the oldest men present, and he felt a sense of responsibility. He might even have been having some ugly second thoughts on the whole matter. So he put on his severest military manner, and warned these young fellows in their twenties that this was a very serious business, and that every man must face up to the responsibility and do his full duty. Apparently he was pompous, or at least appeared so to the eyes of youth.

So everything was over, and the meeting broke up. Some members were appointed to remain at headquarters, since the constitution so stipulated. Some others undoubtedly lingered, talking things over. The prospect was exciting. But, actually, there was as yet no definite scheme of action laid down. In effect, 103 men had created a Committee of Vigilance, but they had very little idea just what they were going to do with it.

# CHAPTER 10

# GREAT EXCITEMENT

*(June 10, evening–June 11, 7 A.M.)*

ABOUT THIS TIME Virgin emerged from his office, and started home, as was his custom. Thus came the opportunity for which Simpton was watching.

Having given Virgin time to get well away, the big Sydney man entered, and set to work. He began to pry at the door of the office with a chisel, but he had to work quietly, because a bookseller occupied the adjoining room.

And now Virgin, who had not gone far, paused in his walk. He had recollected something that he must still do at the office. He turned about, and started to return.

Simpton got the door open, and entered. Virgin drew closer. Simpton bodily picked the safe up, put it into the sack, and turned and left.

As he was descending the stairs, he met Virgin. They passed, Virgin merely considering the lumpy sack to contain books from the bookseller's.

Simpton, realizing his bad break, got to the street, and made for the end of the pier as rapidly as he could under his heavy burden.

Virgin, passing through the forced door, saw at once that the safe was gone, and realized what he had passed on the stairway. He hurried to the street, and raised a cry, "Stop thief!" In the brilliant moonlight, the big Simpton was clearly visible, awkwardly running toward the end of the pier with the bulky and heavy burden on his back. A number of men joined in the chase, among them several of the boatmen who made their living by rowing people back and forth between the wharves and the ships.

Long Wharf stretched out a quarter-mile. Simpton had a good start. Without abandoning his booty, he reached the end of the pier, leaped into his ready-waiting boat, and was off. Only half a mile to the north lay Sidneytown, a safe refuge.

The boatmen, hallooing like hunters, ran down the stairway and into their own boats. But painters had to be cast off, and oars shipped. As professionals, they might be able to row faster than Simpton could, but he himself was powerful, and soon the boatmen, still shouting the alarm, saw that they had no chance.

Then another boat showed up, off to one side, but ahead. In it was a young boatman named John Sullivan, returning from having taken a fare out to a ship. He was a little fellow, but game. Hearing the shouts, and sensing the situation, he swung about, and intercepted.

Cleanly trapped, Simpton reacted quickly. He stopped rowing, and dumped the safe into the bay. As Sullivan came up, the towering Sidney man threatened violence, but the little boatman, unshipping one of his oars, threatened to knock the big fellow into the bay. Soon the other boatmen arrived.

Back at the wharf, the boatmen first pounded Simpton's face for a while, thus giving him something by which to remember the evening, even after he should be acquitted by a jury, or have broken from jail.

Other boatmen went out with some long-handled tongs which were used to dig oysters. With these they located the safe, and brought it up, sack and all. Thus they not only restored Virgin's property, but also supplied material evidence.

The pursuit and capture had caused some commotion, and a number of people had come to see what was happening. Among them was David B. Arrowsmith, who was, we may suppose, a member of the volunteer police. He took Simpton in charge, to turn him over to the authorities. The fact that no regular policemen appeared on the scene may or may not be of significance.

As it happened, Arrowsmith was also a member of the Committee, having just signed as #25. Psychologically, however, he had not made the adjustment, and he did not realize that the Committee might have an interest in the prisoner. In fact, this capture of an accomplished burglar in the very act was the precise stroke of luck which could scarcely be expected.

As it was, Arrowsmith took Simpton by one arm, and the original captor, Sullivan, took him by the other, and they set out walking to the police station.

But this was not Simpton's lucky night. First there had been the moonlight; second, Virgin's change of mind; third, Sullivan in a position to intercept. And now, George Schenck, #72, also aroused by the commotion, came along.

He was a man for quick decisions. Hearing what had happened, he said to Arrowsmith, "You are a member of the Committee of Vigilance. Why not take him to the Committee rooms?" The best that Arrowsmith could do was to yield to the stronger will, saying, "If you say so, I will." Schenck was firm: "I do say so. He is the first man we have got since we organized. Let me have hold of him, and we will go right along."

Schenck replaced Sullivan, and the trio changed direction.

At the Committee rooms, they found a number of members, including Oakes, the redoubtable Ryckman, and McDuffee, the sergeant-at-arms. Along with Schenck, a group of stronger men could scarcely be found in the Committee.

Immediately they took the responsibility of calling a general meeting. Oakes hurried off to one of the fire houses and just before ten o'clock he firmly struck the bell with a billet of wood. Another stroke, and then a pause! Most of the citizens of San Francisco came to the alert, already nervous with alarms of fire.

Another stroke and another! And then, the members of the Committee recognized the signal.

They began hurrying through the streets, toward the rooms. Hundreds of other aroused citizens, sensing the direction of movement, began to converge toward the same center. The police came to the alert.

At the door a guard barred the way, demanding identification and password. Some outsiders tried to gain access, from curiosity or mere excitement, but not knowing the word they were refused.

Soon eighty members, out of 103, had assembled. Of the others, Colonel Stevenson was later accused of cowardice. Most likely he and the other absentees had merely gone to sleep and were not awakened, living far enough away to be out of the range of the bell.

Inside the rooms, no one knew just what to do. Everything had happened so suddenly that the members were not mentally prepared. They had not even established any procedure for a trial.

The prisoner was held in another room while the discussion raged. Some were for turning him over to the authorities, some, for an immediate trial; some, for delay. Everything hung in balance.

Then Captain Howard, the shipmaster, strode forward. With a fine gesture, he took off his sailor's cap and slammed it down upon the table, saying, "Gentlemen, as I understand it, we came here to hang somebody."

The sudden plain-spoken words swung the balance. The decision was immediately made, not to hang the prisoner, but at least to try him. A court was organized, with Brannan as presiding officer, and the members as a whole acting as jury. Schenck was assigned as prosecuting attorney. The prisoner had no counsel, but was allowed to conduct his own defense.

Several witnesses were called, Virgin in particular. He established not only the theft itself, but also premeditation.

The prisoner himself proved to be his own worst witness. To begin with, he gave his name as John Jenkins, a palpable and almost arrogant *alias,* since that name would be for an Englishman practically John Doe. He gave the name of one witness whom he wished to have summoned, but what anyone could have said would seem doubtful. This man, however, when located, refused to come, saying that he did not know the prisoner. Jenkins (to use that name, since he was tried under it and has generally been known by it) could put up no defense, having been caught in the act. He refused to answer questions. Silence might have been his best defense, but he was abusive and profane. He as much as defied the Committee, individually and collectively, to do anything to him. Seemingly, as everyone thought, he expected to be rescued at any minute, either by the police, or by his friends, the Sidney men.

Outside, the city was in a turmoil. Sounds of a rising mob may well have penetrated to Jenkins's ears. Twice Captain Ben Ray of the police knocked at the door, demanding the prisoner. Each time he was merely put off, being told to wait for a while.

Everywhere, in and out of the building, rumors were running. . . . The Sidney ducks were making ready for a rescue. David Broderick, the local political boss, rallying his henchmen to the cry of law-and-order, "was out with all his strength." The mayor had called upon the military companies to assemble. This last, indeed, would be only a cause for laughter. The military companies were private clubs, and some of their prominent members were also members of the Committee.

Inside, the tide of feeling was setting strongly against the prisoner. The very fact that he was a Sydney man told heavily against him.

The preliminary discussion, the organizing of the court, the assembling of witnesses, the taking of testimony, had consumed nearly two hours. Midnight was approaching. At last the chairman called for the vote of the members in their self-assumed capacity as jurymen.

The vote stood — for conviction, unanimous; for death, unanimous.

Yet, even then, there were doubts. A policeman, eavesdropping momentarily at an opened window, heard a voice, which he thought to be Brannan's, crying out for a new trial. The death penalty must have seemed too severe to some members. Even though there was a recent California law permitting that penalty for robbery, the small value of the theft was a confusing issue in this case. But again, the small value was a mere accident; the thief had thought he was making a big haul.

Yet the Committee had little choice. They had no way to imprison anyone. Flogging, in most of their minds, rated as a more cruel punishment than death. Once the prisoner cried out, "Shoot me like a man; don't hang me like a dog!" But, between shooting and hanging, there was no real choice.

About midnight the bell of the California Engine House began to toll ominously. Word spread through the waiting crowd that this was the signal, and that the mysterious conclave had voted death to the prisoner.

At this last moment Brannan, who had so often called for vigorous action, weakened in his resolution. Ryckman spoke to him, almost contemptuously: "You had better go out of here and rally the mob."

At a quarter to one Brannan went out, accompanied by another member. He climbed to the top of a mound of sand, and addressed the large crowd. Here, at last, he was in his element. He told that the prisoner had been tried and convicted and that the execution would take place on the Plaza within an hour. He called upon the people, as they valued the importance and the gravity of the occasion, to make no disturbance or attempt at interference. He promised that the Committee would conduct all things to the satisfaction of the citizens in general. Already the Committee had sent a request to a clergyman to come and assist the unfortunate man in his preparations for death. Then, with characteristic effrontery, Brannan put the question to the assembled people whether the action of the Committee was satisfactory. A tumultuous cry of affirmation rose, some "noes" mingled with it.

In the pause that followed, a voice in the crowd cried out, "Who is the speaker?"

Hundreds must already have recognized Brannan, and his name was given.

Another voice called, "Who are the Committee?"

But the crowd itself answered, sending up the cry of "No names! No names!"

Then a large number of people moved off toward the Plaza, to get good positions there. Many, however, remained where they were, to see the prisoner brought out.

Inside, the argument had continued for a while about immediate or delayed execution.

Coleman spoke out, and he was not a man to be easily argued down. It would be, he said, "not bold, not manly . . . to hang him at night, in such hot haste." Such action, he thought, would subject the Committee to "an undeserved imputation of cowardice."

The argument about hanging "at night" was technical rather than real. The moonlight was so bright that anyone could be recognized as well as by daylight. The other arguments had some strength, but Coleman could get few supporters.

He faced a combination of opponents. Some members were shaken and nervous, and so thought that the best chance was to finish the business before opposition could consolidate. Other members, like Ryckman and Wakeman, were equally courageous as Coleman, and had less regard for what other people might think of them.

Jenkins had at first refused any chance for spiritual aid. Later, perhaps realizing that he might as well play for time, he said that he would like to see someone of the Church of England. The Reverend Mr. Flavel S. Mines, an Episcopalian, was summoned.

Jenkins continued to be arrogant, profane, foul-mouthed, and abusive. He even managed to get under the skin of the usually imperturbable Coleman. Finally, Coleman dropped his objections to an immediate execution, having, in any case, no chance of prevailing.

Final operations began. Wakeman, Schenck, and Coleman (three more determined and efficient men could not have been selected) were picked as a committee which would, in Coleman's words, "make arrangements." Watson remembered that he had a large supply of manila rope in his store, and he and Coleman went off to procure a sufficient supply of that necessary article.

The distance from the rooms to the Plaza was about half a mile. To take the prisoner so far through the streets was risking a rescue. He could just as effectively have been hanged from one of the windows of the building where he already was, or even inside it. The planned march was aimed at public impression, and the risk was a calculated one. A hanging in the Plaza, even by moonlight, would have a hundred times the effect of something privately conducted, and the spirit of the crowd, in their response to Brannan's question, was encouraging.

The clergyman, having arrived about one o'clock, was now closeted with Jenkins, laboring valiantly against his opponent Satan. Unfortunately, Jenkins seemed always to ally himself with the enemy. Mines prayed at great length, and then tried to inspire the prisoner with thoughts of contrition. But rarely has a worker labored in a stonier field. Jenkins uttered only "exclamations of indecency, revenge and blasphemy." Mines continued to plead.

Time was passing, and every quarter-hour gave an additional chance for Broderick's men and the Sydney ducks. At last Ryckman pressed in upon the minister: "Mr. Mines, you have taken about three quarters of an hour, and I want you to bring this whole business to a rapid close. I am going to hang this man in half an hour." The minister withdrew, confessing that he had accomplished nothing.

Everything was ready. Outside, the friends of the Committee, who formed a large majority, had organized to help as an additional escort. At the Plaza, some of them had also been at work.

This old village-square had been the center of the original settlement, and still remained, symbolically, the focal point. At its northwestern corner stood the squat Old Adobe, a relic of Mexican times, the oldest building of the city. At the end of the Adobe abutting on the Plaza a heavy cross-beam served to brace the roof. Wakeman, Coleman, and Schenck had picked this beam as the gallows. Wakeman had been chosen to act as hangman.

In the Plaza towered a flagpole, a perfect 110-foot Oregon fir, sent to San Francisco as a present from the citizens of Portland, Oregon. On this flagpole those who sympathized with the Committee, ignorant of the other plans, now rigged a block with a rope attached.

A little before two o'clock the doors of the Committee room opened. The members, each armed with a revolver, came out, and formed a solid column. The men on the outside held to a long rope which would enable them better to hold position against a rush and would impede anyone attempting to break into the column. Four abreast and twenty deep, they began the march up Sansome Street. At the middle of the column walked the gigantic prisoner, his arms pinioned, a man at either side holding him. Behind him followed little George Ward, flourishing a big revolver, and calling out to Jenkins, as they started, "If the police attempt to seize you, we will blow your head off, sir." At this Wakeman was heard to mutter, "Take the pistol away from that boy, or he will hurt somebody."

There was no great crowd in the street. Many men had already gone ahead to the Plaza. North on Sansome Street, two blocks, went the death-march; on California, to Montgomery; then, by Montgomery, to Clay.

They walked through a region laid waste in the great fire — a fire that might have been set, they believed, by friends of the man who now walked in their midst. They passed ruins and half-built structures, rising gauntly in the moonlight. A dozen people had died in that fire, burned miserably. The friends of this man had plundered ruthlessly, and perhaps he had plundered with them. Such thoughts helped keep their resolution firm.

All was quiet, almost hushed. They marched along streets eerie with moonlight. Ahead, in the Plaza, the crowd was quiet; so still it was that a man asleep in a house there was not even awakened.

And now, turning up-slope into Clay Street, the leaders of the column could see the open space ahead, where Clay came into the Plaza at the corner of Kearny. There, rumor was running, would be the point of danger, where the Sydney men would make their attempt at rescue.

The column came there, and the Sydney men made their rush, but it had little force behind it. Knocked somewhat out of order, the eighty men with their prisoner debouched into the open space of the Plaza. It was thronged with hundreds of men, many of them hostile to the Committee. Police officers mingled with the crowd. From a cart Broderick harangued the people, urging them on to rescue the prisoner. His chief strong-arm men, "Dutch Charlie" Duane and Ira Cole, were there to help.

Now, by some error, the column headed toward the rope hanging ready from the flagpole, and not toward the Adobe.

As the column pressed through the crowd, its ranks disintegrated more. In a rush of rescuers, officers Noyce and North, bold men, ducked beneath the rope, pushed into the column, and laid hand on Jenkins. Noyce felt a pistol thrust against his own breast, and almost screamed. "For God's sake, stop! Are you a Christian?" He heard the warning, "I'll blow your heart out, or let go of the man." Then Noyce felt two more pistols, and pulled away. North also backed out before leveled pistols.

Seeing in what direction the disordered column was heading, some people cried out not to hang the man from the flagpole, that such an act would be desecration. Possibly the cry was a ruse of the opponents, to cause more confusion.

In any case, the column — by then scarcely more than a clump of men — changed direction and headed for the Adobe.

From all sides came the rush of police officers and Broderick's men. To balance them, friends of the Committee, men who had never heard of signing the constitution, sprang into the melee. As in a nightmare, someone was calling, "Napoleon, Napoleon, come here!" Broderick, struggling in the mass, heard an excited voice: "To hell with all the courts, let's take care of ourselves."

Police Captain Ben Ray pushed in and seized Jenkins, but fell back when one man thrust a pistol against his head and another threatened him with a club.

Wakeman, acting as sheriff, knew that the moment of crisis had come. He slipped the noose over Jenkins's head.

From the flagpole to the Adobe was a long 125 feet. The column was breaking down into a wild swarm of struggling men. Revolvers were out everywhere. Jenkins was down. Wakeman and a dozen others pulled at the rope around Jenkins's neck, and the opponents in their excitement, with small regard for consequences, pulled at his feet. But the men of the Committee and their friends were the more numerous, and swept ahead.

In moments of wild confusion and uproar Jenkins was dragged bodily along. Someone threw one end of the rope across the beam. A score of men hauled away, and he was swinging. . . .

HANGING OF JENKINS ON THE PLAZA

The representation of the crowd was rather beyond the artist's capacities, but he did his best to be accurate, even to the depiction of
four women — a detail not elsewhere recorded. The prominent figure
on the cart is probably intended for Broderick.

The time was ten minutes past two. Even after Jenkins was
hauled up, Officer Noyce pressed forward with a knife to cut
the rope. The members of the Committee closed up, and beat
off all attempts. George Ward and others were making show of
their revolvers. Several policemen, in spite of declaring themselves officers, were roughly handled.

Captain Wakeman, imagining himself on shipboard, was bel-
lowing for a belaying-pin to make the rope fast. Finally he tied
one end of it to the porch railing.

As men realized that Jenkins must be dead, the melee died
out. The reporter for the *Herald* left, to get the news in for an
early edition. Writing at half-past two, he noted, "He is probably dead at the time of writing this." An hour and a half later,

he concluded the account: "Four o'clock — he is still hanging — dead."

By this time, the crowd had melted away. Many members of the Committee continued to watch so that friends of the hanged men could not take the body away. (Whether they felt like Roman soldiers is not recorded.)

At last, when daylight had come and the full effect of their example could be known to the city, the guards too went home. At seven o'clock the coroner came and took the body. . . .

Thus died the man who chose to give his name as John Jenkins, and has so been generally recorded. He also passed as Simpton. What was his real name is uncertain.

In San Francisco, he once kept a disreputable drinking-house called the Uncle Sam. He lived well, being quoted as saying, "We drink nothing here but champagne." Mrs. Connolly was his woman.

As the story ran, he had been transported to Australia at an early age. Thence he came to San Francisco. A long way it was to travel — three-quarters of the circuit of the globe — to end it all, dancing on air, in the bright summer moonlight.

Yet he too was one of us, and there is even a little that we can admire. He died in the best traditions of crime. He cursed his captors and asked for no pity. He refused to sneak into heaven by a last-minute repentance, and said, "I want no goddamned parson!" Instead, he asked for brandy (a gentleman's drink), and tossed it off. He asked for a cigar too. Then he tipped his chair back against the wall, and coolly puffed away. As they took him through the streets, he was still smoking it. His friends who watched must have been proud, seeing him make a good end. Some said that the cigar was still in his mouth when they pulled him up.

Who knows? Except for some little accident years before, John Jenkins might have been hauling at the rope, not the one hauled upon.

# CHAPTER 11

## CORONER'S INQUEST ON THE BODY
## OF A MAN CALLED JOHN JENKINS

*(June 11, 7 A.M.–June 13)*

H AVING TAKEN the body, the coroner set about impanel-
ing a jury for the inquest. With this action the bizarre
chaos of the night seemed to end, and the inexorable forces of
the law to resume control.

In that light of day the members of the Committee, hag-
gard for lack of sleep, must have looked at each other a little questioningly, and many of them may have had second
thoughts. Those men were of many kinds, and a species *Homo
vigilans* cannot be catalogued and described. Some of them
were bold and reckless to the point of irresponsibility. Others,
we can only suppose, were timid, merely sucked into the swirl-
ing current. A few of them may have been sadists, or men with
a lust to kill. A few were veterans of Mexico or of Indian
fighting. Most of them, however, were men who had grown up
in peaceful ways of life. They could never have imagined
themselves, a year before, doing the deed which they had just
perpetrated in the moonlit Plaza.

Only one of them, that day, committed his thoughts to paper,
and that was young Robert Lammot in a letter which he began
"Dear Mother." That he had some doubts seems clear, and
would be natural enough. He wrote that he had participated,
but added, "I do not think that I ever was bloodthirsty." He
took some comfort also in having been a minor actor, who "did
*not* fix the noose around his neck, nor haul upon the rope."
But Lammot showed no real remorse, and gave no sign of weak-

ening in his resolution to be a loyal member of the Committee.

Yet, that morning, he and many another might well have been uncertain and afraid. San Francisco had, overnight, become a city split between two hostile factions. No one knew the strength of either of them, or the degree of violence that a hot-headed individual might precipitate.

On the one side, the hard core consisted of the Committee itself. Though small, it had the inestimable advantage of the solidity that comes when determined men, already organized, find themselves bound together as the consequence of an overt act. Moreover, at this time, their secrecy was of great importance. Rumor exaggerated their numbers, and a man could not utter words against the Committee for fear that he might be speaking to one of its members.

Another great advantage of the Committee lay in the support of all the important newspapers.

The third source of strength was a wide public sympathy, though no one as yet knew just how dependable this sympathy really was. But, certainly, in the course of the preceding night, most of the crowd had supported the Committee.

On the other side was arrayed the legally constituted government, with its power and prestige, in all its chain of command — from city, to county, to state, and even to nation. In close and inalienable alliance with the government was that strong group of citizens, the lawyers. A large portion of the public would certainly tend to support the established authority. Curiously, also, the government could count upon the support, in a sense, of the criminal classes — particularly, of the Sidney ducks.

But the Law-and-Order party (as it came to be known), though it looked formidable, was badly divided. Certainly there could be no formal alliance between the agencies of law-enforcement and the Sidney ducks. The federal government was far away, and the state government was lacking in armed forces, and unlikely to attempt intervention. The individual city and county officials might personally approve of the Committee, though officially they could not take such action. In fact, the real strength of this party, the vigor of the counterattack, rested in one man. Though trying to minimize the opposition to allay his mother's anxiety, Lammot put the matter not too badly, that the opponents were "a few lawyers, two judges, some policemen, and David C. Broderick."

Broderick was a man whose strength of character was only rivaled by its complexity. . . . Born in 1820 of Irish immigrants, he had grown up in one of the tougher districts of New York City. He fought his way, often literally, toward power. As ward-heeler, saloon-keeper, and Tammany leader, he made money and gained power in local politics.

In 1849 he went to California, and soon was successful. In 1851 he was president of the State Senate, political boss in San-Francisco, second only to Senator Gwin in the Democratic state machine, and known everywhere as a ruthlessly efficient and unscrupulously powerful leader.

But there was another side. In private life Broderick was puritanical, almost ascetic. Though uneducated, he was widely read, and intellectual. Moreover, his whole life is a refutation of that facile generalization that power corrupts. With every step upward and the greater power that he attained, Broderick became more of a statesman, more of a responsible leader. By 1851, already fairly well along, he was even showing a tendency toward being a man of principle.

Without this assumption, indeed, one is at a loss to discover why Broderick opposed the Committee. The Whigs were in office in San Francisco. A Democratic politician would naturally seize this opportunity to embarrass the rival party. Instead, Broderick threw all his great power into what was really an alliance with the Whigs in combatting the Committee.

In contrast stood Senator William M. Gwin. Even more

powerful than Broderick, he was first and always a politician, and he reacted to the situation as an astute politician should. He spoke no word and raised no finger, not being forced to do so. He took no stand, and lost no votes. Though his state was shaking with violence, its senator did nothing. Anyone considering Gwin's lack of action would have been justified in concluding that the federal government would remain neutral. . . .

San Francisco was a strong-stomached city. On this day, a continuous line of people, including women and children, passed through the so-called dead-house, noting the hanged man's magnificent physique, the still-visible marks of the pounding that he had taken at the hands of the boatmen, and the deep indentation in the neck. No one laid claim to the body.

In general, the sense of shock at the hanging was the less because almost everyone accepted the normality of capital punishment, which was integral, not only to law, but also to religious tradition. The Old Testament set the death penalty freely, and often specified death by stoning. The New Testament, in spite of its horror of the Crucifixion, accepted the idea of crucifixion.

Moreover, as in the instance of the two thieves executed on Golgotha, people were familiar with the idea that other crimes than murder might justly be considered capital. In particular, a California law of April 2, 1851, made highway robbery and grand larceny punishable by death, at the discretion of the jury. . . .

At one o'clock the inquest began. A jury of respectable citizens was soon selected. Called as witnesses were three police officers who had participated in the struggle on the Plaza. Though recalling much in detail, they displayed a failure of memory as regarded names of people. Officer Noyce flatly refused to answer certain questions. He had reason to believe, he stated, that there was in the city a secret committee or inquisition, and that he would be in danger of his life if he testified. Anyone, he continued, was likely to be seized and carried before a secret tribunal.

On the motion of a juror the court was cleared, and Noyce testified, believing that what he said would not get to the Committee. (Actually, the Committee's files contain a summary of his testimony so detailed that we can only think the clerk of the court to have been highly favorable to the Committee's cause. One should also note that the Committee not only refrained from taking Noyce's life, but also paid him no attention at all.)

Another witness was J. L. Van Bokkelen, who declined to answer many of the questions on the grounds of incriminating himself. In reality, he was one of a number of citizens who had become involved in the struggle though they were not members of the Committee. (He would soon join, as #173.)

That afternoon at four o'clock the Committee prepared to meet its first test of public support. A large meeting assembled in the Plaza, which only fourteen hours before had been the scene of the hanging. J. F. Hutton, selected as chairman, spoke vigorously from the porch of the Adobe, where Jenkins had been hanged. On the grounds of the necessity of the situation, he whole-heartedly supported the Committee. Cries then arose, "Brannan!" and "Coleman!" Neither of them, however, proved to be present.

Someone from the crowd thereupon moved that the meeting should sanction the proceedings of their fellow citizens in executing Jenkins. When the chairman called for ayes, a tremendous shout arose. On his call for noes, only one or two men called out, and the crowd hissed them strongly.

Then one of the lawyers, H. K. W. Clark, courageously took the stand, and boldly declared to the crowd that he had answered "no." He would tell them why he had thus voted against "endorsing a cold-blooded murder."

At these words a trememdous storm of hissing arose, and cries of "Down with him! . . . Drag him out! . . . Hang him!"

Clark, with an aplomb that still further enraged the crowd, stood gently waving his hat, waiting for them to get quiet. At this, some of the crowd rushed upon him, dragged him down the steps, and with difficulty were kept from doing him serious harm. Eventually the chair managed to restore order.

The meeting, after the passing of a motion to reassemble on the next day, adjourned with three cheers for the chairman and three more for the proceedings of the previous night. As the crowd dispersed, Clark was again roughly handled and his coat torn.

In the evening session of the inquest the chief witness was Broderick himself. Under oath, he boldly identified by name six individuals who had taken an active part in the hanging. . . .

On the next day, Thursday, the struggle continued. The Committee scored first, with the appearance of the morning papers. These printed a statement by four members of the just-dismissed Grand Jury, who emphasized the critical nature of the situation and the breakdown of law-enforcement. The papers also printed editorials favoring the Committee. The *Alta* used the heading "The Execution of Jenkins," thus avoiding such derogatory words as "lynching," and even "hanging." The editorial summation suggested that the newspaper had better sources of information than the coroner's jury had as yet uncovered:

> The trial and conviction of Jenkins was not the act of an inflamed and excited mob — his case was adjudged with calmness and deliberation, his guilt fully established, and the penalty of death imposed by a set of men respected and esteemed by their fellows, asuming a responsibility imposed on them by stern necessity, with a full perception of their accountability to their fellow men and their Maker. Who but he shall adjudge or condemn them? We dare not.

The editor took exception only to the "secrecy observed in the deliberations" — by which he may have meant merely that he would have liked to have a reporter present.

The papers also published the coroner's statement that the hanged man's pockets had contained $218. Here was another evidence of the respectability of the Committee. Whatever you might say about its members, they did not stoop to picking pockets.

In the morning session of the inquest, the first important witness was the lawyer Hall McAllister. Allying himself with Broderick, he identified several persons who had participated in the hanging. Next, Brannan took the stand. He had the proper combination of self-assurance and a ready tongue to make a good witness. Although he refused, on constitutional grounds, to answer certain questions, he talked with remarkable frankness about what had happened. While never quite admitting that he had participated in the trial, he made it clear to everyone that he had been present. He used his position as witness to propagandize, making such statements as "the object of the association is to assist the law and administer justice." He objected to giving names because "it would endanger their lives in consequence of threats made against them." He stated that he himself had received a warning that he would not live ninety days.

The last witness of the morning was John S. Eagan, #42. The difference between his testimony and Brannan's was so great that it can scarcely be explained except by the assumption of a sudden change in the policy of the Committee. While Brannan had refused to give names, Eagan identified several members, including himself.

The next trial of strength came at the reassembling of the citizens in the Plaza at five o'clock. The previous meeting had been wholly pro-Committee, but Broderick had seen to it that this one would not be so. He himself was present, and his men were strategically scattered in the crowd. As Alonzo Delano put it (and he was usually a fair-minded reporter), Broderick was there "backed up by a gang of rowdies and gamblers." After a resolution supporting the Committee had been offered, Broderick began to address the meeting, "strongly condemning the proceedings of those who have taken the law into their own

hands." No sooner had the drift of his sentiments become evi-
dent than a hiss arose from the crowd, to be offset by cheers.
The speaker was assailed with encouraging shouts of "Go on!"
and with threats of "Hang him!" and "Pull him down!" Some
people made a rush for Broderick, and his friends came leaping
through the crowd to his defense.

Hoping to allay the near-riot, the chairman put the question,
and loud shouts went up on both sides. The chairman declared that the resolutions had passed, and Broderick declared
that they had lost.

After order was restored, another speaker addressed the
meeting and adjournment followed — again with the stipulation that the meeting would reconvene the next afternoon.

The evening saw decisive action by the Committee itself —
unless, indeed, the action occurred during the day, and thus
caused the difference in the testimonies of Brannan and Eagan.
The Committee, by unanimous vote, issued a public statement.

In general, this statement recapitulated the objectives of the
Committee, as stated in its constitution, and called for public
cooperation. Much more important, to the statement was appended a list of 183 names.

The names were declared to represent "a portion of the
Committee of Vigilance lately established." Literally, this was
true. As nearly as can be ascertained, the membership at this
time totaled 186, so that only three members were omitted.
The members thus signing were "unwilling that the names of a
few of their associates should be selected by the Coroner's Jury
as the principal actors in the trial and execution of Jenkins."
These signers declared themselves "equally responsible for the
first act of justice that has been dealt to a criminal in San
Francisco, since California became a State of our Union."

The closing words were a rejection of future secrecy, except
for "such matters as would tend to defeat the object for which
we are associated."

The statement grew both out of confidence and out of anxiety. By this time the Committee could count upon strong popular support. Therefore, it could assume responsibility with some confidence. On the other hand, the procedure of the inquest and the attitude of Broderick were alarming, and suggested that a few of the members might at any moment be arrested.

Appearing in the newspapers of June 13, the statement effectively undercut the attempt which Broderick and his allies were making, through the coroner's jury, to split the Committee by pinning murder charges on a few members — thus perhaps causing those individuals to leave the city and forcing the Committee as a whole to disband.

The jury announced its verdict in the early afternoon, declaring that John Jenkins had come to his death by strangulation "at the hands of and in the pursuance of a preconcerted action on the part of an association of citizens, styling themselves a Committee of Vigilance." The verdict named nine persons as "implicated by direct testimony," including Brannan, Wakeman, and T. K. Battelle. This last, as it happened, had not been a member at the time of the hanging.

At this point the verdict would necessarily have stopped, except for the recent action of the Committee in forcing the issue by publication of the names. The verdict therefore continued that "the following members [are implicated] by their voluntary avowal of participation." The whole list of names then followed.

In the afternoon what we may call the usual meeting in the Plaza was anticlimactic. The chairman began by stating that "since reading the names of the Committee of Vigilance, he was satisfied that there was no necessity of any further meetings, and he felt perfectly safe in entrusting his interest in the hands of that committee."

He thereupon moved an adjournment. A motion, however,

was then made "that the people should consider the Vigilance Committee as their agents and sanction their proceedings." This motion was lost, apparently being considered unnecessary and possibly embarrassing to the Committee. The meeting then adjourned quietly — this time, without any arrangement for reconvening.

In the evening the Committee held another meeting, and unanimously passed a brief resolution, which referred to "the invidious verdict rendered by the coroner's jury." The resolution reiterated the joint responsibility of all the members, and the same list of names was appended.

Undoubtedly the members were pleased with the success of their maneuver. By refusing to leave a few of their fellows in the lurch, they had performed a somewhat heroic act, one calculated to gain them much popular sympathy. By their declared numbers and by the prestige of their individual members they gained a practical immunity. He would be a bold city attorney who would have warrants sworn for the arrest on charges of murder of 183 citizens, all of them respectable, most of them well-to-do, some of them among the most prominent men in the city. From this time on, the fact that the Committee comprised "the best people" was frequently emphasized. The *Alta* declared public sympathy for the Committee to be so strong that "riot and bloodshed" might result if any attempt should be made to arrest the hangers of Jenkins. . . .

With June 13 a critical period thus came to an end. Early Wednesday morning the Committee had taken violent action. It had then been forced to stand on the defensive. By Friday evening, however, if it had not won a complete victory, it had at least repulsed the counterattack.

The time, moreover, had been far from lost in other respects. By having ascertained, under stress, that it had strong support both from the newspapers and from the public, the Committee had the better established itself. Moreover, it had developed organization, tested leaders, and considered future policy. For instance, the public statement went back directly to Watson's "Propositions for the Public Safety," but showed a very significant change. Watson had declared that any persons refusing to leave the city after due notice should be shot down like dogs. The statement merely declared that such persons should "be compelled to depart."

Very significant was the rapid growth in membership during this period when to join the Committee might have seemed to put the noose around one's own neck. In these few days the numbers almost doubled, and thus approached two hundred. Moreover, there had been no general appeal for membership. The Committee, although it was to some extent forced to accept the sponsorship of the general populace, still considered admission only on an individual basis. A member could recommend another man, and then this recommendation must pass the scrutiny of the Committee on Qualification.

The approximately eighty members who were admitted during this period maintained the same standards of character and personal status that the original members had possessed. They included merchants and their clerks, shipmasters, and at least one physician.

A few of the new members were of some notability. . . . J. Thompson Huie, #108, was the son of James B. Huie, #16. J. F. Hutton, #117, a commission merchant, had been the presiding officer at the public meeting of June 11; he may not at that time have been a member of the Committee. Henry M. Naglee, #132, was a prominent banker; of more importance in the present connection, he was a graduate of West Point, and had been the captain of the First California Guard. Napoleon Smith, #168, was a merchant, whose unusual first name explains the fact that someone at the hanging of Jenkins was calling out for Napoleon. James Dows, #170, was a saloon-keeper and liquor-dealer; the admission of a saloon-keeper is of interest in view of the fact that the Committee seems to have excluded gamblers; but Dows, as a wholesaler, might be counted as a merchant. James King of William, #186, who had distinguished himself from other James Kings by adding his father's given name, was a banker and a man of considerable standing in the city. F. Argenti, #187, was a banker; according to a contemporary listing, he was the richest man in San Francisco, being rated at half a million.

Though the whole list included many names of distinction, those of King and Argenti bestowed some special prestige. They bore the highest numbers of any members signing the statement. The suggestion is that their friends already in the Committee made a special effort to enlist these two in time to have their names appear. . . .

By this time the hanging of Jenkins and the existence of the Committee had been impressed upon the consciousness of everyone in the city. One of the most isolated was Martha Hitchcock, who was living quietly in a boarding house with her husband, Dr. C. M. Hitchcock, and caring for her baby daughter Lily. But even she, writing a long letter to her sister on June 13, interrupted her disquisition on family matters:

> By the way, a man was hung the other night in the Plaza, for stealing — served him right, I think, for the place is full of convicts from Sydney — there is scarcely a night that there is not an alarm of fire; and people are positively afraid to go to bed — nothing but Lynch law will put an end to it.

Even men who preferred merely to go about their own business could not ignore the situation. Such a one, William K. Weston, wrote to his wife, "I have worn a revolver and belt with heavy dirk for some days."

Another resident to be affected was the British consul, George Aiken. On June 13 he forwarded a sharp note to Governor McDougal, causing the royal lion to utter a dignified growl at the unauthorized hanging of a British subject. He also reported the affair to Lord Palmerston in London. . . .

During this critical five-day period, to re-emphasize, the most important action of the Committee had been the issuance of the signed public statement. Although it may originally have been conceived as nothing more than a maneuver to counter Broderick, it was actually much more than that. By thus assuming responsibility for their actions, the members differentiated themselves from the participants in a lynching. By openly announcing themselves, they transformed their organization from a secret cabal or a possibly sinister conspiracy into a large public group, partaking — as the *Alta* at once pointed out — of the nature of a revolutionary party.

Thus, by Friday evening, the Committee had cleared its flanks, and could at last resume its own attack upon the Sydney men.

# CHAPTER 12

# THE VIGILANCE COMMITTEE AT WORK

*(June 14–July 1)*

A SALUTARY EFFECT of the hanging of Jenkins was soon patent. On June 16 the *Alta* noted, "There has been scarce a robbery since." It added that "the pilferers, the slungshot men, the lifters of safes," many of them known to the police, were steadily leaving town. Two days later the *Herald* stated, "This city is more free from crime than it ever has been within our recollection."

With criminals no longer active, the Committee itself was transformed. Its originators had envisioned it in terms of violent and even desperate action. Thus, on Tuesday morning, it had closely resembled a lynching mob. But, by Saturday, it had become a busy bureau of investigation.

Numbering now about two hundred members, the Committee was too large to function effectively as a unit, and its daily meetings were discontinued. General meetings were still held on occasion, but they were concerned chiefly with the consideration of reports. Direction was now entrusted to the officers and to the elected Executive Committee.

This latter body, numbering 21, met almost every day. It initiated action, planned the work, and issued instructions to officers and sub-committees. It was chiefly composed of men who had helped found the Committee — such as Brannan, Coleman, the Woodworths, Oakes, Watson, Schenck, Huie, and Bluxome.

The officers chiefly directed the day-to-day work. A. Jackson

McDuffee, sergeant-at-arms, was on duty almost continuously at the rooms. He kept order there, stationed a door-guard to insure that only members could enter, and maintained a watch over prisoners.

Jacob L. Van Bokkelen, Chief of Police, organized the street-patrols, which were maintained both day and night. He supervised arrests. He reported to the Executive Committee on the information obtained.

The colorful Captain Edgar Wakeman was Chief of Water Police. He maintained boat-patrols to prevent crime along the waterfront. He was also charged with the inspection of ships entering the harbor.

The ordinary member reported for duty daily, and might spend several hours patrolling the streets or performing some work of investigation.

A pressing problem was the need for better quarters. The original room, donated by Brannan, offered no facilities for the detention of prisoners. Moreover, the dignity of the Committee called for adequate headquarters. In spite of the scarcity of empty buildings in the recently burned city, a committee of three soon located a suitable room. Since the Committee was unincorporated and had no legal entity, five members, as individuals, signed the lease on June 17.

The new quarters were on the west side of Battery Street between California and Pine. The rent was $400 monthly. The space consisted of a single large room, sixty by eighty feet, on the second story. It had been designed for storage purposes, and two heavy beams projected outward from above its windows into the street. These were designed for the hoisting up of goods, but there was a sinister suggestion about them.

A builder was immediately hired to make alterations. Two smaller rooms were partitioned off — one for the accommodation of prisoners, another for meetings of the Executive Committee. The builder also installed a privy. Benches and other furniture were provided.

These preparations took time, and throughout most of June the Committee got along as best it could in its original quarters. During this quiet period the membership continued to grow; by the end of the month, it approached five hundred. This mere increase in numbers, in the face of official opposition, strengthened the position tremendously. Six times as numerous as the little group which had hanged Jenkins, the Committee now totaled a block of votes too large for any politician to ignore, and in its control of wealth and influence it was vastly more important than in mere numbers. (A comparably sized group in San Francisco of the mid-twentieth century would have to total at least 15,000 persons.)

Among the new members were some notable figures. J. F. Spence, #244, had served with distinction as presiding judge during the trial of February 23; he was at once elected to the Executive Committee. W. D. M. Howard, #287, who had also been prominent in the Jenkins affair, was a leading citizen, and was captain of the Washington Guards. Eugene Delessert, #439, was a well-known member of the French colony, and a prominent banker. Samuel Fleischhaker, #349, may be taken as a representative of the Jewish merchants; Pedro Carrillo, #401, was a member of the old Spanish-Mexican aristocracy. William M. Eddy, #400, calls for special mention, since he held public office, as county surveyor, and yet did not consider this a bar to joining the Committee. Dennis Janvrin, #486, was a customs inspector, and therefore a federal officer. Probably, also, other revenue officers were among the new members.

At the same time, the democratic base was somewhat broadened by the admission of several members from the "mechanical trades." Thus we have John T. Smith, #209, carriage-maker; Hugh McGrath, #225, carpenter; Thomas Morris, #236, marble-cutter. Of particular interest is John Sullivan, #269, who was the boatman responsible for the capture of Jenkins. He was one of several boatmen to become members at this time, doubtless to facilitate the work of the Water Police.

Sullivan himself immediately fell under suspicion. A memorandum from Van Bokkelen stated of him, "Knows too many men of bad character — would recommend that he *be not trusted too much.*"

The work of these two weeks was unspectacular. Basically, there was a great amassing of information, especially necessary since the police offered no cooperation. The idea that known criminals could be easily spotted was soon proved false, and the Committee set itself to the tedious task of adding fact to fact. The partially preserved records for these two weeks, all laboriously set down in long hand, fill a hundred pages of printed text.

One aim of this investigation was to pinpoint centers of criminal activity, and the Committee focused its attention upon what were known as "cribs." These were cheap roominghouses, with some associated prostitution, which were the hangouts of the Sydney men.

At a meeting of the Committee on the evening of June 16 a list of suspicious characters was presented. Action was taken against James Hetherington and William Burns, "both keepers of Cribs, the resort of felons & burglars."

On the following day each of the men received the succinct notice, "You are hereby warned to leave this city within five days. By order of the Committee of Vigilance."

Neither man accepted the situation supinely. Burns appealed for a hearing, and was granted one. He made a long statement, but failed to convince the Committee that his character was benign.

Hetherington took another course by appealing to the city authorities for protection. The recorder, however, was either unwilling or powerless to combat the Committee. Hetherington retired to a house at North Beach, and was still there when his time of five days ran out.

The Committee thereupon mustered in strength, its leaders

apparently heeding the principle that if a display of force becomes necessary, it should be so overwhelmingly displayed as to make force unnecessary. More than two hundred strong, in regular formation, fully armed, the Committee marched to North Beach, and took Hetherington into custody. Eventually both he and and Burns were returned to Australia.

During these weeks, members of the Committee appeared conspicuously at some of the trials being conducted in the criminal courts, but took no action, other than to observe. The newspapers generally considered that such observation would aid in the proper determination of justice.

As was only to be expected, numerous reports and accusations poured in, from sources more or less reputable. Sometimes the Chief of Police investigated, and sometimes he even made arrests, holding individuals temporarily for questioning. The Committee, however, soon adopted the policy that it could not assume responsibility for the general administration of justice.

On the one hand, the Committee was not concerned *de minimis,* as in one case, which took only one line in the record: "John McDonald — Drunk — Discharged." On the other hand, the Committee decided not to become involved with even serious crimes if these appeared to be of a wholly private nature. Thus, one evening, in a sordid quarrel over a prostitute, Samuel Gallagher drew a pistol and spattered the brains of Lewis Pollock over the threshold of the girl's room. A patrol picked Gallagher up immediately, and brought him in. The Committee, however, turned him over to the city police.

On the evening of Sunday, June 22, a disastrous fire swept over some dozen blocks of the city which had escaped destruction in the fire of May 4. Hysteria and mob-violence broke out along with the flames. The police shot down two men as looters. Mobs beat two men to death, and injured several others. The patrols of the Committee labored to maintain order, and saved the life of at least one individual who was being attacked by a mob.

Arson was again suspected, but could not be proved upon any individual, though several were arrested and questioned. A few days after the fire the Committee posted notices offering a reward of $5000 for information leading to such a conviction for arson. Doubtless some of the wealthier members underwrote the reward.

During the fire one of the patrols had arrested a man for looting. He turned out to be a Mexican, named Justo Reyes. Being tried, he was convicted of having carried off some clothing, but the case was not a flagrant one. He was sentenced to be publicly flogged and to leave the city.

To mitigate the punishment, the knots were removed from the cords of the cat. Reyes was tied to the tail of a cart in Battery Street on June 24, and received his punishment. He bore the flogging stoically. When unbound, he put his shirt on, and left. The *Herald* commented:

> It was exactly the kind of punishment suited for such an offense, and the discrimination displayed by the Committee in this case, gives proof of their moderation and sound judgment.

One must remember, when considering this incident, that flogging was a recognized punishment in several states. Moreover, it had just been abolished as a means of enforcing discipline among the jolly tars who constituted the United States Navy. Nevertheless, the general sentiment in the Committee seems to have been against flogging as a punishment.

A more serious involvement of the Committee with the fire was not without its humorous element. . . . Felix Argenti, already mentioned as #187, was a wealthy banker of Swiss origin. As might be expected of such a gentleman of continental background, he had a friend. Her name was Angelina Duclos.

Her house happening to lie in the path of the flames, she bargained with Peter Metcalf to remove her goods to a place of safety in his cart. Metcalf, according to Mlle. Duclos, took four loads of furniture and wearing apparel, but delivered only three loads of furniture and not all of the wearing apparel. None the less, he insisted upon his payment of $50.

Mlle. Duclos complained to her protector, and Argenti was wrathful. Here was an example of looting — just what the Committee was trying to prevent! Quickly rallying a dozen comrades, including several members of the Executive Committee, Argenti proceeded to Metcalf's house. Refused entrance, he entered forcibly, threatening violence. Mlle. Duclos, being of the party, assisted in the search and claimed several articles as her own.

An enterprising firm of lawyers immediately realized that they had caught a wealthy man in an embarrassing and probably illegal situation. On Metcalf's part they brought a suit against Argenti for $25,000. Inevitably the Committee was involved.

Though this suit was probably nothing more than an ordinary attempt at shake-down, it may to some extent have sprung from a desire to harass the Committee, whose enemies, though silenced, were far from being annihilated. They had been repulsed in their direct attack; they continued their campaign by more subtle means.

On June 17, a handbill was circulated through the city. It was anonymous, being signed merely "Many citizens." It vilified the members of the Committee in violent terms, and called for another meeting to express disapprobation of the Committee's actions. The mayor stopped circulation of the bills, on the ground that they would lead to a breach of the peace and might result in armed conflict.

A few days later there was a flurry of excitement when "a number of good American citizens" received by mail a notice which was signed THE COMMITTEE, and marked by a seal. One of these read:

> Sir:
>
> The most eminent physicians of this place have decided that the climate of San Francisco is very injurious to your constitution. It is due to you that we should inform you of the fact and request that you will seek a place more congenial to your health, feelings and disposition, before Wednesday next.
>
> By order of<br>THE COMMITTEE

One recipient of this notice was Colonel G. F. James, well known as a lawyer who had defended criminals. There was therefore a certain plausibility in the situation, so that James probably had a few moments of rage, indignation, and possibly fear. A little examination, however, would have shown that the seal was nothing but the imprint of a Mexican dollar, and a re-reading of the notice, in its laboriously facetious language, would also have suggested the reality, that it was nothing but a hoax.

Quite possibly, none the less, it was partially serious in intent; in times of confusion, any additional confusion may work to someone's advantage. The Committee did not deign to take official notice of the hoax, but merely authorized the newspapers to state that the Committee always served such notices to the individual personally, and never through the mail.

Much more serious, and much more sophisticated in its method, was the infiltrating of the Committee which occurred during these weeks. As nearly as can be made out, three or four men (possibly more) managed to gain membership, with the object of acting as spies and informers. Obviously the Committee on Qualifications could not be expected in all instances to be sufficiently well informed upon the background of those applying for membership.

During this period, moreover, some of the opponents set in action a complicated plot — that is, indeed, if the interpretation which the Committee itself put upon the incident is to be trusted. . . . There was in the city a Negro named Ben, who was apparently somewhat deficient mentally. Although California was a free state, Ben allowed himself to be kept in a condition of practical slavery by his mistress, Mrs. Margaret Robinson, who treated him very badly, even beating him.

On June 28 the city police arrested Ben on the charge that on June 22 he had set fire to a house and thus started the recent conflagration. That same evening, inexplicably, the police released him. He was thereupon rearrested by the Committee. He repeated the confession which he had already made to the police, that he had set the fire, at the order of Mrs. Robinson.

After full investigation of both Ben and Mrs. Robinson the Executive Committee reported its conclusion that the whole affair had been an attempt at frame-up "which was hoped in the excited state of this community would induce this Committee to arrest, hastily try & condemn the person [Mrs. Robinson] against whom he [Ben] testified."

About this time the Committee proved itself remarkably up-to-date in scientific methods by employing a daguerreotypist to photograph such individuals as were considered worthy of being kept in a permanent record. Since the daguerreotypist charged six dollars per person (the equivalent of about twenty-five dollars a century later), the expense was far from negligible.

By and large, during this quiet period, the Committee vastly improved its position. Though remaining officially the Committee of Vigilance, familiarity soon reduced it to Vigilance Committee in common speech. Similarly, a member came to be known simply as a "vigilante," a Spanish word for "watchman," pronounced in four syllables but otherwise preserving no trace of its Spanish origin.

Paradoxically, much of this improved position of the Committee arose from the fact that it was doing so little. The great mass of citizens could now be sure that there was to be no reign of terror. Such accusations as "Inquisition!" " Star Chamber!" "Secret tribunal!" fell flat. Although the list of new members was not published, there was little secrecy, because anyone could see unmasked members on patrol or entering the headquarters.

The relationships with the city and county governments, though necessarily anomalous, were raising no special problems. When the mayor suppressed an anti-Committee handbill and the county surveyor was a member, there seemed to be little cause for fear. Moreover, one member felt confident in reporting, "the Sheriff & his officers are with us *Heart and Soul.*"

With public acceptance of the Committee thus steadily improving, many people must have noted with interest the newspaper announcement:

A sermon, suggested by the Execution of JENKINS on the Plaza, will be preached by Rev. T. D. Hunt, TO-MORROW (Sabbath) morning, in the First Congregational Church.

The Reverend Mr. Hunt preached on June 29, having in his congregation no less redoubtable a vigilante than James King of William. Doubtless there were others too, unspecified.

Hunt developed his sermon from the first chapter of Exodus, particularly the verse, "But the midwives feared God, and did not as the king of Egypt commanded them."

The application to the hanging of Jenkins was clear. In the final test, the devout man and the good citizen must make his decision, as did the Hebrew midwives, not according to man-made law, but according to his own interpretation of the law of God, that is, by his own conscience.

"When a government does not protect," thundered the preacher, *"there is no government."* Logically, he concluded, "Such rule is just cause for revolution."

Hunt, the Presbyterian pastor of a Congregational church, feared that word "revolution" no more than had his predecessors who had cried out from Presbyterian and Congregational pulpits against King George in 1775. His whole sermon, in fact, was an excellent exposition of the Protestant theology which throws the responsibility for action upon the individual. At no point did Hunt actually counsel anyone either to join the Committee or to oppose. Instead, he said, in effect, "Consider the matter, and make your decision according to what seems to you to be right."

A number of the gentlemen who had heard the sermon arranged to have it printed as a pamphlet, and distributed. One of them, P. W. Van Winkle, joined the Committee, soon afterwards, as #554.

Hunt's sermon buttressed the Committee's position by providing religious and philosophical support. Though San Francisco of 1851 was not a city much devoted to the practice of religion, there were a number of small congregations. Their ministers occupied a position of prestige, and their pronouncements upon matters of right and wrong bore much weight. The Reverend Mr. O. C. Wheeler of the Baptist church also preached a sermon supporting the Committee.

By the end of June, moreover, the Committee's position was much strengthened as the result of the establishment of similar organizations elsewhere. As early as June 13 the Committee had taken action, inviting such collaboration. The response had been immediate, and now there could be no attack in San Francisco without consideration of how Sacramento and Marysville and other towns would react. . . .

Nevertheless, by this time, any well-wisher of the Committee would have had much cause for worry. Such a movement can thrive only on activity, immediate need, tangible results, excitement — and danger! No volunteer organization can flourish on a regime of steady and monotonous routine. The Committee had scarcely been at regular work for a week before McDuffee was forced to complain about members who failed to report for duty. The Sydney men, by leaving the city and by temporarily renouncing their ways of crime, were managing to ruin the Committee more effectively than if they had stayed and fought. Unless it could find more to do than it had been doing lately, the Committee might soon shrivel and die from inanition.

CHAPTER 13

IMPORTANT ARREST
BY THE VIGILANCE COMMITTEE

*(July 2–July 3, afternoon)*

CALIFORNIA STREET HILL, much of it overgrown with brush, encroached upon the city from the west. Streets had not yet been laid off on its steep slopes, but a few small houses had been built there, affording their occupants a panoramic view eastward, of the city, the harbor with its ships, the broad bay, and the distant hills of the Contra Costa.

In one of these houses lived two workingmen, James Adair and Wesley Diggins. About noon on July 2, they discovered that someone had broken into the house, and robbed it. Certain circumstances suggested that the thief might be planning to return, and therefore would still be lingering in the neighborhood. Hastily rallying some others to their help, they began to search through the clumps of brush where someone might be hiding.

They soon met a man who was merely walking along. After questioning him as to whether he had seen anybody carrying a bundle, they asked him what he himself was doing there. He said that he had come from the Mission and was on his way to North Beach. At this reply the searchers were immediately suspicious: "A damned pretty way to come from the Mission!" Asked where he lived, the man said that he lived at North Beach but he would not tell where or with whom, except that they were friends of his.

The condition of the man's clothing also aroused suspicion. His coat and pants had wrinkles in them, as if they had just been taken out of a trunk, and the shoes were not dusty, though he stated that he had worn them while walking from Sonora more than a hundred miles away.

Adair, who was the leader of the group, was nonplussed. There was nothing to connect the stranger with the actual robbery. But the man was evasive and was pretty certainly lying. In the end, as Adair put it, "I mentioned the suspicious circumstances to him, and requested that he should come down and give an account of himself to the Vigilance Committee." The man agreed, even saying, according to one account, "I am anxious to see that far-famed Vigilance Committee, and I will go with you with pleasure."

At the rooms the prisoner was searched. No property belonging to Adair or Diggins was found on him. He was carrying a revolver. Also, suspended inside his shirt, was a Bowie knife with a fourteen-inch blade. But the carrying of such weapons was so customary that no one was much impressed.

Some members of the Executive Committee were present — Brannan, Schenck, and both the Woodworths. They conducted a systematic, routine inquiry. Adair, Diggins, and two others made statements, which were written down. The prisoner was allowed to conduct a cross-examination of each of these witnesses.

The prisoner also made his own statement, beginning, "My name is William Stephens — born March 3, 1819, at Brighton, Sussex, England." He declared that he had left England early in 1849, and journeyed to California by way of Panama. For identification, he gave the name of the ship on which he had arrived in San Francisco, and also supplied the names of its officers. He had then gone to work in the southern mines.

As for his recent movements he told what seemed to be a straightforward story. He had arrived in the city on the preceding evening, having walked, as he had already stated. He had made contact with a friend named Kitchen, who had taken him to a private house at North Beach. "There was a female in the house; her name I decline mentioning." In the morning, he had walked out to the Mission, and returned over the hill, "thinking it was the nearest road." He gave the names of a few people who might identify him.

Further questioned, he added some detail. He considered the road over the hill to be as good as the other road, having traveled it before. He gave no sign of recognizing the name Frank Pixley — that of the city attorney, who was widely known as a defender of criminals before he had attained a public office.

In appearance and actions the prisoner made a good impression. He was in his early thirties, bearing himself erectly, of more than average stature, with high forehead and aquiline nose. An observer summed him up as being "of a highly intellectual cast of countenance." He was auburn-haired. As the custom was in California, he had a mustache and beard. The latter was short, and gave him, to one observer, a resemblance to the conventionalized portraits of Jesus Christ. He spoke well, with an English accent. His motions were described as "very uncommon, being as quick as those of a wildcat."

The questioning had been inconclusive. Granted that the prisoner was a suspicious character, there was nothing to connect him with the robbery on the hill, or to identify him with anyone for whom the Committee was searching. His mentioning the woman doubtless stood him in good stead. His questioners were men of the world, and would realize that a man who was thus involved might wish to be vague about his movements. They would think the more of him for shielding the woman.

Frederick Woodworth suggested that they might as well let him go. The situation hung in the balance, when Schenck had another idea. He was impressed at the condition of his prisoner's clothes, which were certainly not those which a man had worn while walking all the way from Sonora in the hot July weather. A man who was telling one lie was probably telling other lies. Schenck suggested that since it was evening already, the Committee might as well keep the man overnight. Stephens himself apparently raised no objection. Accordingly, as Schenck wrote, "He was given his supper, and put into the prisoners' room with some thirty or forty others, Sydney ducks, who had been arrested, some to be deported, some to be tried for other offenses."

After that everyone seems, literally, to have forgotten about William Stephens. There was, indeed, much else to remember that evening. The tempo seemed to be quickening at last.

On that day the first Sydney men, four of them, had been deported. The Committee, having investigated and sentenced them, arranged for their passage, and put them aboard the *Crescent City* for Tasmania.

Still more conducive to forgetfulness about Stephens was the startling change in the Executive Committee. Brannan, who had been its president from the beginning, was out. Lacking his original initiative, the Committee might never have been organized. He had rendered much good service, but his period of usefulness had ended. A headlong starter who flagged quickly, reckless rather than brave, likely to weaken in the emergency, a heavy drinker, lacking in subtlety — he was through, though he still remained briefly as a member of the Executive Committee.

His successor in the key office was Stephen Payran. . . . Little is known about him. He had been a professional copyist in Philadelphia, and the many beautifully written documents which he prepared for the Committee bear visible evidence to that calling. He came to San Francisco in 1848. His business there is not known, but he must have been considered a man of stability, since he was among the first who were asked to join the Committee. Being able to devote several months to working without salary, he must have had some business that assured him an income. Still, he was a man of no special prominence in the city on that night when he had signed the roll as #46.

Yet there was something about him that gained him immediate election to the Executive Committee, and he soon became one of its outstanding members. Whether he had previously had experience in police work is unknown. More likely, he was only making use of native abilities. Well into his forties, he was older than most of the others. He was fearless, and devoted to the objectives of the Committee. He was an able administrator, but his greatest practical talent, for the ends of the Committee, was at interrogation.

He was not without his faults. He could be autocratic. Like others of the Committee, he sometimes drank too heavily.

Be such things as they may, the replacement of Brannan's loquacious bluster by Payran's cool shrewdness made the Committee both much more efficient and much more dangerous.

This day was also a busy one because of an inspection, by a small committee, of the still-uncompleted county jail, at the invitation of Sheriff Hays. He paid the visitors every attention, showed them the disgraceful condition of the premises, and explained the gross wastage of money under the previous administration. The curious fact came to light that Argenti, a member of the Committee, held a mortgage on the building. The sheriff's hope was that the Committee would take an active interest in finishing the jail and undertake to raise the money by subscription. With such cordial and hopeful arrangements thus established, the members of the Committee were justified in thinking that the sheriff would not be eager to make any move against them.

On the next day, July 3, an important event for the Committee was the inauguration of the new Grand Jury. Judge Campbell, in his charge, lashed out in an attack on the Committee as extra-legal and dangerous. Ironically, five of the jury-

men thus admonished were members of that body. One of them
(W. B. Peake, #97) had signed the manifesto of June 13, so
that his connection was publicly known.

But even more important for the Committee was what happened in its own rooms. According to Schenck's report, "as we
were busy with other matters, the new prisoner was over-
looked." Why he did not demand his own release is uncertain.
Perhaps he had decided that his best procedure would be to
keep inconspicuous.

At two o'clock the guard was changed. The new watchman,
assigned to stand at the door of the prisoners' room, was John
Sullivan, the little boatman who had captured Jenkins and who
had aroused suspicion because he seemed to know too much
about criminals.

On taking his post, Sullivan opened the door and peered into
the room, out of curiosity. He recognized the new face, and
called out, "Halloo, Jim! How did you come here?"

The new prisoner did not respond, and looked blank.

Sullivan reacted sharply, calling out, "You needn't pretend
not to know me! I know who you are. I worked for you six
months at Foster's Bar."

He closed the door, and spoke to Schenck, who again happened to be on duty: "Mr. Schenck, do you know who you have
got here?"

"Who do you mean?"

"Why, you have got 'English Jim,' or Jim Stuart, the man who
murdered the sheriff of Auburn, and I was present when he was
about to be lynched at Marysville, when the rope broke and he
escaped. I knew him well, as I worked for him six months, and
there is no mistake about it."

At these words the whole course of events altered. The Committee, which had been almost drifting, entered upon a period which was to be fatefully purposive. . . .

From the beginning, a central problem had been of basic

interest. Was there some great organized gang among the Sydney men? If so, who were its leaders? How could information be obtained? Some people even had the idea that this gang, especially by the aid of fire, might be planning a kind of overthrow of society with a universal looting, as in the sack of a city.

In this connection the Jansen case remained of special interest. It had caused vast disturbances, and threats of arson had been associated with it.

Now having laid hands on the man believed to be Stuart, the Committee could, for the first time, grapple with this central problem.

Still, the Committee moved with caution. Their procedure with Stuart was in sharp contrast to their procedure with Jenkins, only a few weeks earlier. The change was an evidence, not only that the astute Payran had moved into a position of power, but also that other members were learning some sophistication in their approach to the highly complex problem of crime. Many of them must now have realized that in hanging Jenkins with such precipitation they had thrown away their luck. They might at least have kept him for a few days, questioned him, tempted him with thoughts of pardon, broken him down by long-continued interrogation — and thus possibly have learned a great deal about the whole criminal world of San Francisco.

In contrast, the proceedings in the case of Stuart moved with a meticulous deliberation. The only immediate action was that of Schenck. He hurried out and found Watson, his fellow dissenting juror in the Jansen case. The two of them, having never believed in the Berdue-Stuart identification, were delighted at the suddenly revealed proof that would free an innocent man. They immediately got a message off for Marysville, where the unlucky Berdue was being held in jail.

# CHAPTER 14

## STUART *ALIAS* BERDUE CONVICTED ...
## THE MURDER AT DOWNIEVILLE

*(July 3, afternoon–July 5, afternoon)*

B Y ONE of the numerous coincidences that haunted this summer, Schenck and Watson sent their message off to Marysville at the very time when the case had gone to the jury. Long before a steamboat could thread its way up the tortuous courses of the rivers, the verdict would already be in.

The trial, as trials went in those days, was a long one, lasting five or six days. The charge was that James Stuart had murdered Charles Moore. The murder had occurred on October 7, 1850, with the motive of robbery. The victim had been killed by a charge from a shotgun.

Whether Stuart had committed the murder failed to become the real issue at the trial, since both prosecution and defense accepted it. The defense put its effort into establishing that the defendant was not Stuart.

Each side was able to array an impressive number of witnesses to testify, on the one hand, that the prisoner *was* Stuart, and, on the other hand, that the prisoner was *not* Stuart. The defense was able to present two magistrates before whom Stuart had been tried. Both these men were of unimpeachable integrity, and both had enjoyed an excellent chance of observing Stuart. Both of these witnesses swore positively that the prisoner was not the same man. Moreover, they specified details in which the prisoner differed, as in being at least two and a half inches shorter, and in having eyes of a different color.

Even such testimony, however, failed to trouble the prosecution much. The general opinion had already been established in the community that this man was the murderer, and should not be allowed to escape.

In the course of the testimony three definite physical traits were attributed to Stuart. If the prisoner could be shown to possess these traits, his identity with Stuart, if not absolutely established, would be highly probable. On the other hand, if the prisoner should lack even one of these traits, he could not be Stuart. The judge considered the testimony good enough to permit the prisoner to be put to the test.

1) Stuart had "a ring of Indian ink around one of his fingers, and marked with Indian ink between each thumb and forefinger." Probably the testimony referred to some kind of tattooing, possibly for identification.

The prisoner was examined, and found to have such markings.

2) Stuart had "a stiff middle finger on the right hand."

The prisoner did not have a stiff right middle finger. The examiners, however, went farther, and discovered that the middle finger on his *left* hand, though not exactly stiff, was somewhat deformed.

3) Stuart had "a rather long scar on his right cheek."

The prisoner, having been shaved, was found to have no scar on his cheek, but to have a scar, of about the length described, commencing on the right side of his jaw, and running down the neck.

The defense would seem to have passed the examination triumphantly, but the urge toward conviction was still too strong. Though two of the three tests showed the prisoner not to resemble Stuart, the prosecution was able to make it seem the contrary, by emphasizing the somewhat similar peculiarities.

The jury was out for a considerable length of time. Finally, late on the evening of July 3, it returned a verdict of guilty — as much as to say that the prisoner actually was Stuart. At this time the message had already been sent that Stuart was in the hands of the Committee in San Francisco.

On the next day Berdue wrote a long letter to a friend in San Francisco. It is the letter of a man without hope, utterly beaten down by misfortune. This despair was well based, and he might, indeed, have believed himself singled out for persecution. Five months before, an officer from Sacramento, whose memory for faces obviously was not an accurate one, had taken Berdue for someone else and had arrested him. Since then, though innocent, he had barely escaped being lynched, had lain for week after week in loathsome and unsanitary jails, had had all his money confiscated, had been convicted for assault and received a heavy prison sentence, and had finally been convicted of murder. Yet at no time had the evidence against him been good.

At the time of writing his letter, Berdue had not yet been sentenced, but he had every reason to believe that he would immediately be condemned to death. He was too despairing, however, either to protest his innocence or to bewail the injustice that had been meted out to him.

> Understand me, I don't mean to say that I had no evidence against me because I had a many that swore I was Stuart, but most all of these persons only knew Stuart slightly. Though those who swore I was not him all said they knew him well.

He signed himself, "Yours truly, but very unfortunate, Thomas Berdue."

So we may, for the time being, take leave of him. That he was unfortunate, we must admit. His case is a demonstration that legality does not always ensure justice, any more than illegality always ensures injustice. Berdue had received justice only once, and that was from an illegally constituted court. He had twice been tried in legal courts and convicted unjustly. Thomas Berdue should be a reminder that legality is not enough. . . .

Berdue dated his letter "Marysville jail, July 4th, 1851." That was the glorious Fourth!

On that day Independence was celebrated in Downieville as was to be expected — that is, almost everyone got drunk.

Downieville was a large and prosperous mining-camp. Perhaps as many as a thousand miners made it their center. Like many other mining-camps, it was not incorporated, and existed almost without government. It was merely a part of Yuba County, which had its county-seat at Marysville, fifty miles to the southwest. A deputy sheriff covered that end of the county, but he could not be in Downieville much of the time. The camp had no special celebrity either for crime or its suppression. A year before, on the Fourth, the miners had flogged a man for knifing another man. The incident was said to have had a good effect upon the manners of the community.

The citizens were no different from those of other mining-camps. They were Americans, with a heavy sprinkling of other nationalities. They were almost all young men, vigorous and generally hard-working, inclined toward recklessness — as you would expect of people who had left the civilized world and gone to California after gold.

On this day there was to be a special treat. In fact, the occasion was going to put Downieville on the map for the first time. The concentration of voters in the vicinity had become sizeable. Therefore, John B. Weller, a rising political figure, had found it worthwhile to journey all the way to Downieville as a Fourth-of-July orator. The citizens had erected a speaker's stand for him in the little open space which was known as the plaza.

The oration and the attendant ceremonies occupied a couple of hours; after that most of the citizens continued with the serious business of the day.

Among them was a Scot named Cannon. As a subject of Her Majesty, he had no occasion to be celebrating this particular holiday — in fact, rather the contrary. But any sensible man knows that a good occasion for taking a drink should not be missed because of a technicality. Cannon was a big and handsome fellow, jovial and friendly. Perhaps he had been a sailor, for he had somewhere picked up a knowledge of Spanish.

By nightfall, Cannon and half a dozen cronies were magnificently drunk. When they finally decided to set out for home, the world seemed an incredibly fine place. Naturally, then, it seemed an excellent idea to make a lot of noise as they went along, and to bang on windows and pound on doors. Soon they came to a house, or shack, where a Mexican gambler lived, with his "woman," named Juanita. (No one ever bothered to record what the gambler's name was, or what Juanita's last name may have been. In fact, no one can be quite sure that she was Mexican, and she was sometimes called merely "the Spanish woman.")

Cannon and his exuberant companions had some kind of incident at the gambler's house. Apparently the door, being flimsy, did not resist their knocks upon it, and fell inward. Cannon fell with it, part way into the house. One imagines a torrent of indignant and excited Spanish from the bed, Cannon apologizing in what Spanish he could muster in his drunkenness, and his companions laughing.

Then they went on their way home. It was nothing! The gambler and Juanita went back to sleep. If you lived in a place like Downieville, you could not be concerned at trifles.

But something lingered in Cannon's mind. It may have been some image of Juanita. Probably he had seen her before, and was conscious of her. There were almost no women in Downieville, apparently not even a reasonable quota of prostitutes. So you were likely to notice what women there were — especially one like Juanita.

In all the descriptions she stands out clearly — the prototype of the young Mexican beauty. Her age was given as twenty-three. She was small and slender, but — as the miners' phrase ran — "well set up." Her black hair hung in two thick braids. Her dark eyes flashed. She was vivacious and quick-tempered, with the hint of passion there.

She was no prostitute, but fell in that in-between class. Californians recognized the three kinds. There was the wife, or other respectable woman. There was the whore. In between there was one who was generally called merely "woman." She lived with a man, and took care of him, much as a wife did. But she was not married.

Spanish can make the same distinction between *esposa* and *puta,* with *mujer* somewhere in between. Though no one ever proved that Juanita was not married to her gambler, the chances are that she was not *esposa.* She might, for that reason, be the quicker to resent being classed as *puta.*

On the next morning, which was July 5, poor Thomas Berdue awoke in Marysville jail, expecting to receive his sentence of death on that day. That same morning, very early, Cannon was on his way to the gambler's house again. One friend was with him.

Cannon's condition has not been recorded. Perhaps he had a terrible hangover. But, if so, why was he out at all? More likely, he was continuing his drunk into the second day. In that case, he may not have had a very clear idea why he was going to the gambler's house. Or did he think of it as Juanita's house?

Later his friends said that he went there to apologize for the trouble of the preceding night. Such procedure might have seemed very reasonable to the good-hearted drunk. But, we should also remember, Cannon was probably a man who was starved for women. Such a man might form the attractive idea that Juanita was available, if one offered enough.

Cannon knocked at the door. The friend stood a little way off. Not knowing much Spanish, the friend could only stand by.

The gambler and Juanita came to the door. Spanish spouted back and forth. There was obviously an altercation. The friend could not understand, but he caught the ugly word *puta* from Cannon's lips.

Juanita was gone from the doorway for a moment, and then back, one hand held behind her. She was hot with the anger of the insulted woman.

The hand flashed out from behind her in one fierce stroke, and she drove a long knife through Cannon's breastbone into his heart.

Cannon's friend took the word, and other friends began to rally. Soon, from somewhere, in some way, the threat of the mob came to Juanita. Taking alarm, she went for refuge to one of the saloons, probably the one where her man dealt cards. That was the wrong thing to do. It was flight, and flight eggs the hunters on.

The hunt was up! Men nursing hangovers staggered out into the blinding sunlight of that July morning. *She stabbed him!* Men dropped their shovels by the sluice-boxes, and hurried to town. *That Spanish bitch!* Men in the second day of drunkenness came reeling out of saloons. *Hang her!*

Faceless men, already a mob, took the gambler and Juanita from the saloon, and into the plaza.

No one paid much attention to the gambler. He had not struck the blow. Besides, he may have been a poor-spirited fellow, not worth bothering about. But as for Juanita — her spirit flared and flamed.

They tried her in the plaza — if it could be called a trial. The speakers' stand of the day before, they utilized as a courtroom. The cries were all "Hang her!" "Hang her!" "Give her a fair trial and hang her!"

It was very strange! Usually a mining-camp overflowed with a sentiment about a woman, even though she might be a prostitute. By all the odds, the crowd should have been crying "Self-defense!" or "She was defending her honor!" True, she

was a Mexican. Her skin was somewhat dark, with her share
of Indian blood. But that should have been counted only against
the man. An American generally had a soft heart for a señorita.

Must we not rather think of the five hundred men, sex-
starved, and against them that one provocative woman, fighting back with her cat-like anger, driving them farther and farther into madness, by the sight of this woman whom they held
captive but could not possess, and could not humble?

Someone with a little thought of propriety rigged a rope
around the area where the trial was to be held, to keep the
crowd back. They elected John Rose to be the judge, and he
could not swear the witnesses, but he told them that they must
tell the truth, "just as if they had been sworn." Twelve men
formed the jury, and William Spear acted as public prosecutor.
There was a young lawyer wearing spectacles, who undertook
the defense. His first name is unrecorded, but his last name
was Thayer, and he came from Nevada City. One would like to
identify him as well as possible, for he was a brave man.

The trial lasted for some hours, the necessity of transla-
tion slowing things down. The gambler was soon acquitted.
The fact that no one was much aroused about him raises the
thought more strongly that something about the woman herself
was driving that mob of men to madness and the lust to kill.
There was no dispute about the central fact of the stabbing.
Juanita and the gambler claimed that Cannon had used abusive
language. Even if he had done so, would that justify murder?
In any case, at no time was there any question about what the
verdict would be.

But the mob did not want to wait so long to get their
hands on her. More than once they rushed against the ropes to
seize and hang her, but the "judge" and the "prosecuting attorney" cried out to restrain them, calling on them to remember
their own wives and mothers and daughters, and to give this
woman a "fair trial."

At last Thayer started his speech for the defense, but someone knocked away the barrel he was standing on, and his hat went one way and his spectacles another, and he himself was tossed along over the heads of the thickly packed mob, being pummeled, until he was let down to the ground and kicked, and that was the end of the defense.

Here and there in the mob an individual man caught the horror of it. A few of them planned a rescue — or so they claimed later. But they were helpless in the mass. John B. Weller, men said, looked on from the balcony of the hotel, and made no move. A slight slur lay upon him for it ever afterwards, even though it did not keep him from being United States senator and governor of California.

There could be no summing up, once the counsel for the defense had been beaten and kicked. The jury went out, and came in again. The verdict was "Guilty."

Then another brave man, who was Dr. Cyrus D. Aiken, took the stand in the face of the mob, and played what should have been the trump. Juanita, he declared, was three months pregnant. They could not hang her, and the child with her.

But this was no ordinary mob to melt sentimentally at the thought of a baby. Its drunken and inflamed men were not stopped at the words of a single doctor. They appointed a committee of three, not including Dr. Aiken. These other three were said also to be doctors, though four doctors for a camp like Downieville would seem to be more than enough. In any case, the three examined Juanita, and declared Dr. Aiken to be wrong, or lying.

Dr. Aiken was given twenty-four hours to leave town. Quite possibly, indeed, he had been lying, in a desperate attempt to turn the tide. Curiously, no one has recorded what Juanita said about it. She does not seem one to hide behind a pregnancy, particularly one that did not exist.

By then it was three o'clock. They gave Juanita an hour. No priest attended her. Probably there was no priest in the camp. If they had given her twenty-four hours, they could have got a priest. But the mob was in no such mood. Probably she did not care much. The Indian blood does not need a priest for the dying.

Her gambler was acquitted now, gone somewhere. She sat alone — silent, defiant.

During that time, they rigged a scaffold on the bridge. It was a convenient place, where many people could see. They fixed a plank for her to stand on. The plank was four feet above the level of the bridge, and a ladder led up to it. Two ropes supported the plank. The noose dangled from a higher cross-beam.

Then they came to take her. But if they thought she would weaken, they knew little, those *gringos,* of how a Mexican woman can die. She had put the thought of death behind her. Now she must be concerned, not that she must die, but that she should die well!

She was wearing the dress of her own country; on her head, a little straw hat.

Then, strangely, the spirit of that mob was so strong that it seemed to sweep Juanita along with it, so that she became a part of it. No longer did she seem its victim, but rather its spirit, as if the votaries were bearing some priestess to the sacrifice.

So she went toward the bridge, chatting and smiling as if she walked with friends. Five hundred men and Juanita, they were gathered by the river.

Alone, unfaltering and unaided, she climbed the ladder. She stood on the plank, and the swift waters flowed beneath her, and the dark-forested mountains rose up around.

Standing there, she saw a familiar face in the crowd, and she took off the little straw hat and threw it to that man, crying, "Adiós, amigo!"

Then she put the noose around her own neck, with a fine

sweep of her hand pulling away the two heavy braids of her black hair.

She stood there alone, no man supporting her. Two men were there with hatchets to cut the ropes. Another stood ready with a pistol to fire a shot for the signal.

They tied her hands behind her, and bound a rope to hold her skirt around her ankles, for decency, on a day when there had been little decency. They asked her if she had anything to say, and she said no — but she would do the same again, if so provoked. Also she asked to be properly buried.

At last they put a white handkerchief over her face, and the two men raised their hatchets. The last thing she did was to call out clearly, "Adiós, señores!"

Thus she played well that last great scene, which all men and women play at the end, though few play it so well, or to such an audience and in such a setting as she.

There, in a glory, died Juanita, at the hands of what one man called "the hungriest, craziest, wildest mob" that he ever saw. "Hungriest" is a strange word to apply to a mob, but perhaps would imply something of sexuality. We cannot escape such a thought, considering that it was five hundred men against one woman — and a beautiful and stirring woman, who fought and defied them, and provoked them, to the very end — and finally died in the great tradition. . . .

If the conviction at Marysville represents legality without justice, the hanging at Downieville may be said to represent justice without legality. At least, there was some justice if we accept the common standard of retribution and a life for a life. Juanita had killed Cannon. To be sure, she was a woman, and she probably had some provocation. But to be a woman and to have some provocation does not give anyone a license to drive a knife into a man's heart. That hungry, crazy, and wild mob at Downieville was perhaps the worst ever to be recorded in California. Its hanging of the one who may be considered the proper person is nothing more than accidental. Such a mob can just as easily hang the wrong person.

A flood swept the bridge away, but could not sweep away the memory. In the quiet village by the rushing stream there lingers still a little haunting recollection of "the Spanish woman."

# CHAPTER 15

# THE CASE OF JAMES STUART

*(July 5, afternoon–July 8, 10:30 P.M.)*

THE STORY of Juanita illustrates the striking differences between a mob and the Committee of Vigilance. At Downieville the individuals rose after the crime and with the already-conceived intention of taking vengeance upon a particular person. All the actions — arrest, trial, execution — were taken while emotions were at white heat. But even in the case of Jenkins, the Committee had not organized especially to "get" him. Except in so far as he by his actions during the trial aroused some antipathy, there is no indication that the members were wrought up about him. Certainly they were not wrought up to the point of being unable to give a fair trial. In the case of Stuart the contrast with the procedure of Downieville was even more striking. . . .

During the forty-eight hours while such dire events had disturbed Marysville and Downieville, San Francisco had remained quiet by comparison. But the situation was developing rapidly. There was no immediate announcement about the capture and identification of Stuart.

On the Fourth, when Berdue was writing his hopeless letter from jail and while the citizens of Downieville were getting drunk, most of the San Franciscans also celebrated. The Executive Committee, however, put in a heavy day's work, meeting for three hours in the morning, and again in the evening from eight until midnight. Payran acted as chairman, but Brannan was present. The chief business was "Examination of prisoner

Stephens." Though he had been identified only on the preceding day, four more witnesses, in addition to Sullivan, had already been collected. One of these had been a deputy sheriff, who had had the prisoner in custody, the preceding summer.

The investigation was conducted with a considerable regard for good procedure. Frederick Woodworth acted as counsel for the defense. The prisoner confronted the witnesses, and asked questions.

The witnesses stated postively, and strongly, that they knew the prisoner. They testified that they had known him as James Stuart, or English Jim.

The prisoner denied knowing any of these people. He himself answered questions cooperatively. Still refusing to give the woman's name, he elaborated a little upon his movement on the morning before he was captured. He had a cousin, he said, at the Mission, named John Stephens, who worked for a baker.

Two members of the Executive Committee took to their horses, and made a quick trip to the Mission, visiting the only two bakeries there. They discovered no trace of any John Stephens. At one bakery, however, they had a surprise. The people told them *"that yesterday a man called upon them, as coming from the Vigilance Committee direct, who told them: everything we knew!!!"*

The three exclamation points were warranted. This was the first clear indication of treachery.

Moreover, that very evening, the sergeant-at-arms reported that J. P. Muldoon (#317), David Earl (#264), and Thomas Norris (#236) were "injurious," and subject to disciplinary action. The Executive Committee moved to refuse these three admission to the rooms until final action could be taken. To make matters worse, C. H. Welling (#237) was exposed, on this same day, as an absconder.

Although their meeting did not break up until midnight, the Executive Committee again came to order at nine on the morn-

ing of July 5, the indefatigable Payran once more in the chair.
The first important business involved recognition of the value
of the prisoner: "Ordered that the Chief of Police procure Irons
suitable to secure the Prisoner Stephens."

The Committee then hired a carriage for four, and filled it
with the prisoner and three of its own members. The others
took saddle horses, and followed the carriage inconspicuously
in pairs "so as not to create any public surprise." Their object
was, "in the matter of Stephens to procure further Evidence and
accomplices." They apparently made investigations at the Mission, but there is no record of their findings — probably because
the attempt was unsuccessful.

In the afternoon the examination was resumed. Five men
testified that the prisoner, on one occasion during the last winter, had been a passenger aboard the steamboat *New Star*. He
had been accused of stealing some gold dust, and some of the
witnesses left no doubt that they considered him to have been
guilty.

The Committee also brought three policemen to look at the
prisoner. How they picked out these particular officers is doubtful. Most likely, the three were notorious for having criminal
associations. One officer did not identify the prisoner, and the
testimony of the two others has not been preserved.

Probably on this same day was the incident of Frank M. Pixley, the notorious defender of criminals who had been chosen
city attorney in the "reform" election of April. At the time of
the Jansen affair, he had come out strongly against the identification of Berdue with Stuart, stating that he had defended
Stuart on two occasions, and knew him well. He was therefore
a man to be consulted on the present occasion. Since Pixley was
an important city official, and considered a very slippery character as well, the approach required tact. Payran, Bluxome, and
Van Bokkelen, the chief of police, made the attempt. As Bluxome reported:

We went out and found Frank Pixley. Van Bokkelen was the spokesman. Said he, "Pixley, will you say, on your word of honor, if this man is the man whom you have defended time and again in the lower courts?" "I will, gentlemen," said he. Van Bokkelen administered the oath, if it could be called an oath. We all went into the prisoner's room with Frank Pixley. The man was chained by his wrists and legs. He was sitting on a long bench, and the moment he saw Pixley, he thought his deliverer had come. He stood up, and we saw that they recognized each other, and Jake said to Pixley, "Is that Stuart or not?" Said he, "You have no authority to ask me any questions; you are an illegal body." The others heard what was going on through the thin partition, and when Pixley answered in this way, called out "Hang him! Hang him!" We had ropes and tackle all ready, and Jake just pushed him down the stairs, or he would have been hung. The people were angry with him because he defended all the thieves.

Undoubtedly Bluxome exaggerated — trying to tell a good story, years later. There is no contemporary suggestion that the Committee was ever close to such precipitate action, which would have been disastrous to itself. A few unrestrained youngsters doubtless cried out, and Van Bokkelen may have hurried Pixley out to prevent the possibility of accident; the discipline of the Committee was far too strong to make any such action likely.

But Pixley was aroused. That very evening he applied to Judge Nathaniel Bennett of the state Supreme Court for a writ of *habeas corpus* commanding Van Bokkelen "to produce the body of one Stevens, alias Stuart, by him wrongfully held in custody." The judge refused to grant the writ, declaring that the application must be made in open court.

A conveniently placed informant quickly relayed this information to the Committee, evidence that each side had by now broken the other's security.

On this day the Executive Committee was in almost continuous meeting, with morning, afternoon, and evening sessions. Everything seemed to be exploding at once.

Alexander Wright, having confessed being a former convict, was pronounced "a dangerous character," and ordered to leave the country. . . . The excitable Brannan declared himself to be insulted by the conduct of the sergeant-at-arms, McDuffee, and demanded that the Committee investigate. . . . New evidence of treachery cropped up. A member complained that he had observed W. F. McLean, #539 (and therefore a recently admitted member), engaged in an improper conversation with two policemen. . . . Brannan, finally, not satisfied with the steps being taken, sent in his resignation as member of the Executive Committee.

Most of all, the Metcalf-Argenti case was hot. Though the general meeting that evening was concerned with certain other matters also, its chief interest focused upon that legal case.

The first action was to appoint a committee of three to wait upon Metcalf and his lawyers, to request them to withdraw the suit. The second action was to pass a resolution supporting the Committee's right to search. The Committee asserted its privilege, "where we have good reason to believe that we shall find evidence to substantiate and carry out the object of this body, and further deeming ourselves engaged in a good and just purpose, we intend to maintain it."

Of these two actions the first was foolish and even naïve, unless it may be supposed to contain a veiled threat. In that latter case also it was foolish. Metcalf and his lawyers did not withdraw his suit, and the relations of the Committee with the public suffered considerably.

The second action, that is, the resolution maintaining the right to search, gave a good talking-point to the opponents, and shocked many people who had supported the Committee's work. For the first time there was significant opposition in the newspapers. But the action was probably inevitable. If the Committee had assumed the prerogatives of the police and the courts, so that it could hang a man, it could scarcely stop short at the much less radical action, forcible searching of premises.

Yet, with a remarkable inconsistency, the public which had supported the Committee in the hanging felt some degree of shock at the policy of search.

On July 6, the story broke in the papers that the committee had arrested "a man suspected to be Stuart." On this day the general Committee met once, and the Executive Committee twice. Much business was transacted.

The Executive Committee, humanely moved by word that Mrs. Goff had just given birth to twins, gave a two weeks' extension to Goff, a Sydney man who had recently been sentenced to deportation.

The Executive Committee considered a communication from William C. Graham, #152, against W. F. McLean, #539, elaborating on the charge already made, to wit:

> No. 152 states that this mg about 2 o'clock, found No. 539, standing at the door conversing with two Policemen & heard him say that it was a damned infernal shame the action of the Vigilance Committee in the case of Goff. It was a damned imposition & one he would not submit to — and farther stated, that McLean said the day they go to put their decision into execution, that he would have the Boys about & release him.

Convinced by this statement, the committee suspended McLean, and the sergeant-at-arms noted in the margin of his *Book of Names,* "not to be admitted."

The general Committee transacted some routine business, and on the motion of Joshua Norton, #339 (later to be locally famous as "Emperor" Norton) resolved:

> That no criminal shall be sentenced until he or she shall have an opportunity of pleading guilty or not guilty, and of signing his or her reason why judgment should not be passed.

In the minutes of these meetings there was no reference to the case of "Stephens," though by this time most of the members must have known what was up. Probably the decision had been made that the less said the better — in view of the generally leaky situation. Nevertheless, the investigation proceeded steadily.

Every day the Executive Committee, or some portion of it, brought the prisoner in for an examination. Since he claimed innocence, he could not well refuse some degree of cooperation. He was encouraged to make whatever statements he would, and then the members questioned him. Witnesses were introduced, some of them brought from as far off as Sacramento and Marysville. The prisoner himself was encouraged to introduce any witnesses whom he might think helpful to his case. The testimony was carefully written down.

Gradually, as more and more testimony was introduced, the prisoner found himself forced into corners and having to revise and to elaborate his own story, thus becoming more deeply enmeshed. Eventually his contention that he was not Stuart came to be an obvious bit of pretense. . . .

July 7 was equally busy. The Executive Committee met at noon, and again in the evening.

The deliberations were enlivened by a bit of melodrama, when Spence presented a scrap of paper, which was nothing less than a message-found-in-a-bottle:

> Whoever takes this up, I hope they will be kind enough to come and rescue a poor Female, who is kept as Prisoner on board of the *Izette*.

The committee, not lacking in gallantry, immediately sent two members to the rescue, but the message proved to be a hoax.

One hundred members were reported as being in arrears with their dues — another melancholy evidence that even a Committee of Vigilance is subject to human fallibility.

Captain Wakeman, chief of the Water Police, was reported as having proceeded to the Farallones, some thirty miles off the Golden Gate, presumably because of a report that those rocky islets were being used as a rendezvous for thieves.

Metcalf's lawyers replied to the Committee's letter — in high indignation, intense self-righteousness, and scathing language — declaring that they would by all means continue the suit against Argenti.

At some time during the day, Pixley formally sued a writ of *habeas corpus* against certain members. The Committee, which seems to have had its agents in most places, apparently heard of this action. Such knowledge would account for the otherwise strange action of Payran. He addressed a communication to the sergeant-at-arms, giving instructions as to how a meeting of the Executive Committee was to be called in his absence. Though the situation was critical, Payran was apparently expecting, for one reason or another, to be absent.

As far as "Stephens" was concerned, this day may well have been the critical one. The Executive Comittee had got hold of Joseph Hetherington (not to be confused with James of the ilk) and had persuaded him to turn informer.

Hetherington was a shady character. So shady was he that the failure of the Committee ever to take action against him suggests his having bought immunity at the price of giving information. His identification of the prisoner with Stuart was of little importance; others had already testified to the same effect. But Hetherington gave the names of Stuart's associates — Kay, Briggs, Whittaker, Arrentrue, and even Earl, who had managed to become a member of the Committee itself and had been already accused.

Also mentioned in the statement were Mr. and Mrs. Hogan, and it may be that the prisoner had been forced to name Mary Ann Hogan as the "woman" with whom he had spent Tuesday night.

Hetherington also gave information about the most audacious project of all, although Stuart was not directly involved in it. This was the plot to rob the custom house, where the vaults usually contained funds upward of a million dollars. The Sydney men planned to rent a near-by building and then to tunnel to a point beneath the vaults. Though the project was never developed, the knowledge of the plan still further convinced most San Franciscans that a vast conspiracy threatened their city.

Not only was Hetherington's statement of immense value in itself, but also it permitted the examiners still further to break Stuart's defense, by allowing them to mention names and otherwise to show that they knew more than he supposed them to know.

At this time, then, Payran and his committee moved in for the kill. . . . There is in the official papers an enigmatic and carelessly-scribbled document, suggesting a first-draft or a mere memorandum. A single sheet, it bears only its date of filing, on July 9, but was undoubtedly written a day earlier. The document reads like a communication to the general Committee:

> From information rec'd by the Executive Committee they are satisfied that the prisoner Stuart will implicate and *convict* at least ten [?] persons and make a full confession of all the details and of all knowledge of the various scoundrels now in this country upon this condition that he be handed over to the authorities of the County wherin he is charged with committing the crime of murder and so forth and that he will remain in our custody untill he does this and if he fails to convict at least ten [?] persons he will remain under our control as he now is.

The document is so illegibly scribbled that either "two" or "ten" incriminations may have been intended, though "ten" is more probable.

Most curiously, to this informal and impersonal document is

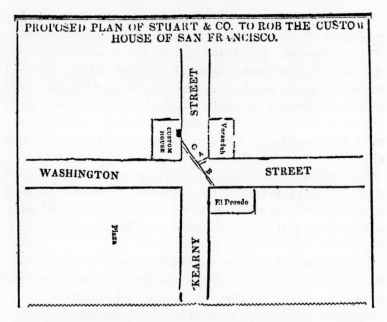

PROPOSED PLAN OF STUART & CO. TO ROB THE CUSTOM HOUSE OF SAN FRANCISCO.

The above cut illustrates the plan that was proposed to rob the Custom-house in this city as developed by the confessions of Stuart implicating himself, Morgan, Whittaker and others.

It was the intention of the gang to lease or purchase, if necessary for the accomplishment of their purposes, the Verandah at the corner of Washington and Kearny streets, and dig a tunnel or passage way under the ground in the direction A, then continue the same *drift* at the same time in the direction C, under the vaults of the Custom House, and B, in the direction of the El Dorado. When all was completed, the money in the vaults of the Custom House were to be abstracted, conveyed along the lines A and C into the Verandah building. It was then their intention, which proves the deep, damned villainy of the project *to close up entirely the passage A,* and the passage B leading to the El Dorado being left open, would naturally throw suspicion upon the occupants of that establishment, while the real felons would escape. This whole "project" establishes the cunning of the villians. It was a deep laid scheme, but fortunately inoperative.

[Author's note: This plan appeared originally in the *Pacific Star.* No file of that newspaper is extant, but this clipping has been preserved in the Committee scrapbook, now in the Bancroft Library.]

appended the signature "William Stephens." Actually all that he thus signed was a statement that the Executive Committee held certain beliefs!

Everything suggests improvisation. Perhaps they wrote such a document, and showed it to the prisoner, saying, "We shall present this to the Committee, and give you this chance!" And the prisoner may unexpectedly have agreed. Then someone said, "Sign now!" striking when the iron was hot. Out of order as it all is, a later action suggests that the Executive Committee consummated some such bargain and felt bound by it.

By this time the prisoner must have been breaking, though he still signed as Stephens. He must also have realized that some of his confederates were "peaching," and that he might as well get whatever benefit he could by confessing.

On the other hand, the bargain granted him little. The statement required "a full confession," and there was little possibility that the prisoner would present one. The Committee had enough evidence available to know how much of the truth he was telling. In addition, the Committee may even have wished to turn him over to Yuba County, under certain conditions. The authorities of that county, having just got a conviction for Berdue, were not at all happy at the prospect of admitting that they had made a mistake in identification. To save the innocent Berdue, as an incompleted document in the files indicates, the Committee was prepared to hand over the guilty Stuart in exchange.

July 8 opened in excitement. Judge Bennett had granted the writ of *habeas corpus*. Four men were specifically named, and the choice of these names indicates how well Pixley, and probably the city in general, knew the inner workings of that body which was sometimes reviled as being "secret." Specified were Payran, president of the Executive Committee; Van Bokkelen, chief of police; McDuffee, sergeant-at-arms; W. H. Jones, one of the marshals.

Doubtless a runner got to the Committee rooms in fast time. In any case, Sheriff Hays loitered. He was not in any hurry to serve this writ upon gentlemen who were showing so much interest in his uncompleted jail. At the rooms, a meeting was suddenly called, "in consequence of a writ of Habeas Corpus granted by Judge Bennett of Supreme Court — in the case of Wm. Stephens, alias Jim Stuart." It was a scratch meeting. Not even one of the regular officers was available to preside. The question must have arisen as to whether they should actively oppose the sheriff. Milder counsels prevailed. The members mentioned in the writ were merely granted permission to retire from their duties until one o'clock the next day, at which time the writ would have expired. Under the circumstances discretion was certainly the better part. Pixley, in fact, had committed a technical error. By issuing the writ against the four members, and not against the body of Stuart himself, he permitted a comparatively easy evasion. The four members could merely keep out of the way. They could be certain that Sheriff Hays would not work himself very hard at detecting them.

After that first touch of excitement the day may have dragged a little. The Executive Committee met, spending most of its time on routine matters.

But also, as the afternoon wore away into the evening, there must have been a sense of expectation, of something uncertain and momentous about to happen. Sheriff Hays had visited the rooms, and solemnly searched, and found — not one of the four persons named in his writ. That evening the general Committee met, for the second time that day, with its new president, Selim Woodworth, in the chair. Most of the business was routine — but not all!

At one point the sheet on which the minutes were recorded has been torn clear across. The assumption must be that something indiscreet was written down, and then ordered to be expunged — and expunged so well that we shall never know what it was.

Immediately after the tear come the notation:

Report of Ex Com in regard to Stewart *accepted* & resolution
accompanying same *carried*

No text of report or resolution is preserved — unless, indeed,
the report was the enigmatic statement with the signature William Stephens. In all probability, this interpretation is correct.
In that case, the resolution would be one in which the general
Committee accepted the terms as proposed by the Executive
Committee and accepted by the prisoner. Robert Lammot, writing a letter the next day and so probably echoing what had been
said at the meeting, declared that Stuart had said "nothing
would save him, yet he would confess, and leave it to us if his
revelations were worth his life."

The meeting adjourned. About 10:30 P.M., the Executive
Committee met in special session. All minor business had been
cleared; the great event could begin.

Thirteen members were present, including Schenck, Coleman, and the ever-faithful secretary, Bluxome. In the absence
of Payran (in hiding to avoid the serving of the writ) Selim
Woodworth presided.

*Moved and carried:* that Mr. Spence conduct the examination
of Prisoner Stephens, and any question which the Com: may
wish to ask Prisoner, shall be done on paper thro Mr. Spence.

Just four weeks had passed since the hanging of Jenkins, and
again the moon rode high. Inside the room the lamplight illuminated the faces of the prisoner and of the thirteen men
pledged to stay until the confession should be ended. Bluxome
sat at the table, his pen ready. The command came to bring
the prisoner in.

The pen began to scratch: "Vigilance Committee Room, July
8th, 1851, 10 ½ P.M."

Next he wrote, as if a herald were reciting his lord's many

titles, "Confession of James Stuart — alias English Jim — alias James Campbell — alias William Stephens — alias James Carlisle —"

Then the voice began speaking, and the pen scratched on, recording the words, into the night.

CHAPTER 16

CONFESSION OF HIS GUILT!

(*July 8, 10:30 P.M.–July 9, 5:00 A.M.*)

THE CONFESSION BEGAN: "My true name is James Stuart." Yet even in that first statement he probably lied, for in a situation even more conducive to truthfulness he afterwards declared that his real name was not Stuart.

The pen in Bluxome's hand traced the words, "I was born in Brighton, Eng." Then, to be more exact, he put "Sussex Co.," above the line with a caret.

"I left Eng. about 16 years of age for the New South W. — I was transported for life — on a charge of forgery."

One may note the ruthless severity of English law in 1835 as applied to a juvenile offender, but one may also note the charge of forgery, a sophisticated crime, suggesting either great natural ability or long apprenticeship.

So, off to Botany Bay! Yet, the bite of the law proved less fearsome than its bark, and after six years he received some kind of pardon. He spent five years in Adelaide, and then made his way (possibly against the terms of his pardon) to Peru.

"I was on the Coast of South America 2 or 3 years," he said, being vague about time in many of his statements. Then hearing of the discovery of gold in California, he set out like everybody else. He started a little late and lost time on the road, and did not arrive in San Francisco until April, 1850.

He went immediately to the mines, locating at Foster's Bar, a booming camp halfway between Marysville and Downieville. He tried various small enterprises — mining, keeping store, operating a ferry. On a certain occasion, as he said, "I hired one John Sullivan."

Luck went against him — or else, he was just not the sort of man to do well at business. During some four months he seems to have remained honest.

Toward the end of the summer he bought a house, and found a trunk full of clothes in it. He appropriated the clothes also, and wore some of them.

By this time he was running out of money. He went to a gambling house to try to recoup, and lost $200 in a night. Deciding that he had been cheated, he resolved to get even.

That night he stole gold from the gambler, to an estimated value of $4300.

But he was not, these days, a lucky man. He was charged with having stolen the clothing in the trunk, and in giving surety he paid out one of the gold-specimens which he had stolen from the gambler. Early in October he was arrested, sent to the county seat at Marysville, and tried. "The mob this night wanted to hang me — the Judge swore in about 60 men to protect me." (So much furor about a robbery committed against a gambler seems peculiar; in reality, Stuart at this time was probably under trial for the brutal murder of Charles Moore.)

Apparently by the connivance of the sheriff, he escaped, saving his neck, but forfeiting his money to the sheriff.

To aid his escape, he stole a horse. This horse he rode to Sacramento, and then sold.

He was warming to his story now: "I remained in Sacramento about 2 weeks — I got acquainted with three Americans & one Sydney man — who lived by stealing horses & I sold them for them — the names of the men were Dab, James Peet, and John Griffith."

The pen wrote down the names. Close to midnight now! Bluxome sat at the table. The other twelve were listening. Stuart was talking freely, and there was no need for questioning.

As they looked at the prisoner, it was not without respect, even some admiration. He was not a hulking brute, like Jenkins. Instead, he brought to mind such adjectives as "genteel," and even "polished." He talked well, and was certainly intelligent. After all, he had first been convicted as a forger, and forgers are aristocrats among criminals.

From the time of his flight from Marysville, we can scarcely do better than to adopt the conventional phrase, "He devoted himself to a life of crime." In Sacramento he became the leader of a small gang, but that city soon become too cramped for his operations.

"We then came to San Francisco — John Edwards told us there was a vessel here with considerable money on board — Jim Burns, Alias Jemmey from town came down with us — Jemmey robbed a Spaniard of about 30 oz. when we were coming down from Sacramento City — we divided the money between us — The same night by information of Edwards, we went on board the *James Caskie* and robbed her — we had hard fighting — the Capt. became desperate — we left him nearly dead — in the fight the Capt.'s wife came out with a sword — I took it from her — I acted as Capt. of our boys."

After a few days he returned to Sacramento, to engage in card-playing, traffic in stolen goods, and robbery. "I was arrested for house breaking, I employed Mr. Frank Pixley — he got me out of the scrape by the false swearing of Old Jack — He agreed to get me out of the scrape for 20$ but afterwards told me I must give him 50$ more — which I did — I told Mr. Pixley I was guilty of house breaking."

He was arrested again for robbery and confined in the prison brig. Soon he was in deeper trouble. "A Constable came down from Auborn and identified me as the man who shot the Sheriff at Auborn — two or three hours another Constable came on board from Forster's Bar and recognized me as the man who had committed the murder near Forster's Bar."

Pixley stood by his client, and pronounced the warrant of the Marysville sheriff to be invalid. The sheriff set out to get another warrant. Stuart paid Pixley $730, and that night (if by arrangement, he did not so state) he escaped from the brig, and got out of town.

By now it was December, and about two months had passed since Stuart had robbed the gambler at Foster's Bar. In that period, by his own confession, he had committed a dozen serious crimes, and one can only suppose that he had conveniently forgotten some others.

With Marysville and Sacramento thus grown too dangerous, he went to San Francisco, where he found refuge in the congenial environment of Sydneytown. Stuart's native abilities soon made him the leader of a redoubtable gang. Notable among them was T. Belcher Kay (*alias* Count Peri, Thomas Keyes, Billy Gibson, and Singing Billy) who was leading a Jekyll-and-Hyde career — being at once a public official, Warden of the Port, and a fully devoted criminal. Another remarkable fellow was Sam Whittaker, whose career in some ways resembled that of Stuart himself. Behind these leaders loomed a formidable group of professional criminals and thugs, such as Bob McKenzie, John Edwards, "Old Jack" Morgan, Big Brummy, and James Burns, the picturesquely nicknamed Jemmy-from-Town. Several police officers were in close alliance. There was also at least one woman, Mary Ann Hogan — though her husband kept himself clear.

Throughout the winter, this gang operated vigorously, and proceeded from success to success.

By now the teller was engrossed in his story. Years later, Coleman remembered the strangeness of it:

He went through the whole range of his many rascalities, gave vivid descriptions of his adventures, entering with great zest into the details, and it was curious to see his eye brighten and twinkle, and a smile play round his facile countenance, when describing his best successes and recounting his best jobs. He threw off all restraint or reservation, and felt that he was bringing to light a brilliant record that had heretofore been necessarily kept in the dark.

Now, at last, the true story of the Jansen robbery came out. Stuart himself had been the second man to enter. He stated, simply, "I hit him on the head with a slung shot and knocked him down."

The listeners may have had some difficulty in associating that deed of blood with the politely talking figure who now confronted them. Another paradox was associated with his next words. The gang, it seemed, was disturbed that the wrong people had been arrested for the crime. "We did not wish to see them hung, as they had nothing to do with it — we all agreed on Sunday night that if they hung them to burn the town down." There seems no doubt that the Sydney ducks considered themselves, in this connection, to have been motivated by the very highest moral principles, and to have acted as men of honor.

About the beginning of March the gang had bad luck, and some of them were arrested. Stuart went to Oregon by ship, and then came back to San Francisco in April, saw Mary Hogan, and decided that he would do better to go on to Monterey. Some of the gang had been involved in a big operation at robbing the custom house there, and they were under arrest. They might need help in getting clear. Stuart appeared as witness under the name Carlisle. "Sheriff Roach recd a gold watch and $700 in Cash. Juryman Morrison also recd $100 — Dennis McCarthy also recd $100 for false swearing." Apparently someone refused to stay bought. The lawyer thereupon "told me to go down and let them out of jail — went down and *busted* the jail open."

Then, "after seeing all friends off," Stuart headed for the
southern mines, the only convenient region that he had not as
yet worked.

Apparently, however, he was getting jumpy at this time. Or
else, he was thinking too much about Mary Hogan in San
Francisco. Seeing two men who knew him, he decided that he
would have to leave. By now it was June, and the Committee
had taken over in San Francisco. The Sydney men were leaving
the city in droves. Yet at this time, Stuart headed back.

Perhaps it was mere ignorance of the true situation. Perhaps
he thought that by doing the unlikely thing, he would be safer.
Perhaps it was Mary Hogan. (Yet even now, he did not mention
her name.)

His confession paralleled very closely his original statement
as to what he had done upon his arrival in San Francisco. . . .
Having walked from the southern mines, he came into the city
on the evening of July 1. At the El Dorado, one of the chief
gambling saloons, he found William Kitchen, a minor member
of the gang. Kitchen took him to Mrs. Hogan's. Next morning,
he went to the mission, planning a robbery. To keep from being
recognized, he avoided the main part of the city in the daytime,
and returned by way of the hill. The last words of his confession were those of irony, uttered with such vehemence that
Bluxome underlined them, "was arrested *doing nothing.*"

The confession totaled about four thousand words. As Stuart
spoke, Bluxome wrote the words down in longhand, legibly and
with few abbreviations. Bluxome must now and then have
halted to rest his hand, and there would have been other breaks
to establish the spelling of proper names, and to ask for the
repetition of words which had not been clearly heard. The
transcription cannot have been finished until close to three in
the morning. But the work was not yet complete.

No sooner had Stuart ended his narrative than someone
(probably Spence) asked him a question about his involvement

with the theft of gold dust on the steamer *New Star,* particularly as to when it happened. Stuart replied readily, "some time in Jany or Feby." And then he went on to volunteer more information.

> Rode down with Smith, from San Francisco to San Jose and Santa Clara, for the purpose of getting the gold and silver from the Churches. Could not find any golden images tho I attended mass regularly.

During the confession, we may suppose, the various members of the committee had jotted down memoranda of points on which they would like more information. These questions then seem to have been put into the hands of Spence. Almost a hundred in all, they were of various kinds. Some of them merely tried to obtain further information. Some of them, to which the Committee already knew the answers, were tests of the prisoner's veracity. Some were aimed to surprise the prisoner into further admissions. Others may have attempted to trap him into inconsistency.

The questions uncovered little of importance. Perhaps by this time both the examiners and the prisoner were so tired that they could accomplish little.

"Have heard hundreds remark here that the day would soon come when this country would be taken by the Sydney people." Such a statement gave support to the opinion that the criminals were attempting some major stroke.

"We should certainly have fired the town in three or four places, had the men arrested for striking Jansen been hung." Again, by conceiving arson as a deed of honor, the prisoner demonstrated the twisted mentality of many of the Sydney people.

"Mrs. Hogan's house is a crib for stolen property; she wears my daguerreotype; she knows all about our motions." So, at last, it was out! In reply to a direct question mentioning her name, he had acknowledged it. But the daguerreotype was his own contribution. He knew that he was not without rivals, and the thought of the daguerreotype might have made him feel that he, after all, was closest to her.

A single brief sentence followed, and one that must be credited to the prisoner's few good deeds. It was the attempt to protect a man who seems to have been uninvolved or not greatly culpable. So he added, "Mr. Hogan is innocent."

The moon had set, long since. The night had passed. The light of the morning sun poured in at the window. Weary and heavy with lack of sleep, they made ready to leave. It was over!

CHAPTER 17

# THE IMPENDING CRISIS

*(July 9, 5:00 A.M.–July 11, 9:15 A.M.)*

I N THE JARGON of gold miners, the Committee had "struck
it rich." After weeks of patient digging, their reward was
a resplendent pocket of nuggets. Yet, as so often, along with
achievement came more responsibility.

The members of the Executive Committee now faced the
problem of studying and evaluating the confession. As to its
general authenticity, no one seems to have doubted. Stuart had
confessed some twenty-five crimes, and there was no reason to
suppose that he had done so for the pleasure of telling the story.
Besides, the Committee was already possessed of much information from other sources by which they could check the details
of certain crimes. On the other hand, there was no need to think
that the confession was complete. Stuart might have been involved in many misdeeds of which he had not told, and might
have been associated with many people whom he was shielding
by not mentioning.

Even if not complete, the record of crime was large. Stuart
had operated from October until June, but there had been
several periods when he had been lying quiet. During his periods of operation, therefore, he had been committing, on the
average, one major crime a week. Most of these involved robbery, but in the press of committing that crime and covering
up afterwards, he had apparently become guilty of burglary,
forcible entrance, assault, suborning of witnesses, jail-breaking,
receiving stolen goods, resisting an officer, — and, probably,

murder. He himself did not confess the last, but mentioned
being accused of two different murders. A third one, also, was
charged to him by one of the witnesses. Two of these were
doubtful, and evidence on them would probably have been impossible to collect. The third, however, was that of Moore, for
which Berdue had just been convicted. Demonstrate that Berdue had been mistaken for Stuart, and the guilt was already
proved legally.

The confession also established the existence of an organized
gang, of which Stuart was — at least, in his own opinion — the
leader. This gang had once been ready to burn the city. At
times it had apparently even thought of a kind of general overthrow of society, after which the Sydney men would be left
triumphant, to plunder as they would.

Of the utmost immediate and practical value, the confessions
supplied the names of twenty-three men and one woman, who
at various places, but chiefly in San Francisco, had acted with
Stuart. Two of these men had died, and some had left the state.
But there would still be a chance to run down the others. Finally, Stuart had implicated several officers of the law, including
two policemen, two sheriffs, and Frank Pixley.

This confession, as the members of the Committee themselves
knew from the beginning, was only the unsupported statement
of an egregious rascal, not even taken under a valid oath, or in
the presence of officials. No court would accept it as evidence.
But it was a document of inestimable value for detective work
and for public relations. A judge or a lawyer might not be impressed at reading it, but the ordinary citizen would be.

Having evaluated the confession, the members of the Executive Committee should, as their next move, set out to lay hands
upon those whom Stuart had named.

On this morning of July 9, however, the Committee found
itself thrown upon the defensive, in spite of its great success
in obtaining the confession. During three weeks the Law-and-

Order party had been reduced to impotence, and almost to silence. Now, by means of writs of *habeas corpus,* Pixley had hampered the Committee by forcing four of its most prominent members to go into hiding. Pixley was undoubtedly motivated by personal reasons. He may still have considered Stuart to be, in a sense, his client. Certainly, in one way or another, money was to be had from Stuart and his associates. Moreover, any confession would be very likely to implicate Pixley. He would rest easier when Stuart was out of the hands of the Committee and "safely" in the city jail.

Moreover, some of the newspapers were urging the Committee not to resist the writ. The term *habeas corpus,* though most citizens would be hard put to it to define what it might mean, had a kind of mystical or almost religious significance. To "resist *habeas corpus*" suggested a nameless horror. As in the matter of the search of Metcalf's house, we have the anomaly that the citizens generally supported the Committee in hanging a man, but were doubtful about the right to hold a man in custody. During the day, the situation developed — quite literally — some elements of cloak-and-dagger mystery, and at the same time did not depart entirely from farce.

At ten o'clock the Supreme Court convened, and Sheriff Hays reported that he had been unable to serve any one of the four writs. Stronger instruction was then put upon him to produce the desired individuals when the court reconvened at two.

In the interval the policy of the Committee changed. Perhaps it was decided that Sheriff Hays should not be made to look ridiculous. Perhaps the purpose was to improve public relations by some degree of cooperation with the court.

In any case, Hays was able to report at two o'clock that he had personally served three of the writs and that Van Bokkelen, McDuffee, and Jones were present in court. As counsel, they had E. Gerry Austin, a prominent lawyer, and he presented affidavits for his clients that "they had not in custody the body of James Stuart, neither had they at the time the writing was served upon them."

Since they made this affidavit by advice of counsel, it was presumably defensible from a legal point of view. It was also defensible from the point of view of the average citizen, for obviously Stuart was in the custody of the Committee, and not of any single member. Certainly no single member would have been allowed to surrender him.

Pixley, expressing high indignation, began to make an affidavit challenging that of Van Bokkelen. Such an action would have led to a charge of perjury, but Austin countered neatly. He asked for a postponement so that he might prepare a defense against such new and unexpected charges. This was a maneuver of a sort which Pixley had often used to defend criminals, and there was at least poetic justice in its being used against him.

Postponement, however, was the last thing that Pixley desired. Given a delay, the Committee might hang Stuart or he might tell — no one would know what.

Pixley, therefore, shifted his attack by asking for a new writ, directing the sheriff to "search, take, and bring" James Stuart himself.

Again, there is every reason to believe that the sheriff did not discommode himself by hurrying. A runner got to the Committee rooms in plenty of time for action.

The Committee had more than one course of procedure open under the circumstances. At a few taps on the bell, armed men would have converged upon the rooms, in force strong enough to halt anything the sheriff could raise, while "English Jim" could be, with all proper ceremony, hanged from one of the projecting beams of the building. Some members of the Committee would probably have favored such a course of action.

As it was, the decision was reached, not to resist, but to evade. A small committee, to take charge of the prisoner, was quickly appointed. It included two members of the Executive Committee, those stalwarts Bluxome and Oakes. Bluxome himself, years later, told the story:

> I borrowed a long cloak, and slouched hat, and Oakes and I dressed Stuart up in them and took him to Endicott & Oakes's building on First St., between Market and Mission. We showed him two pistols, and said to him, "If you attempt to run, we will shoot you." We put him down cellar there. When Endicott went home, we placed a guard over him. Endicott came back, and said, "This won't do. I am a city official [alderman], and have taken oath to support the government." . . . Rube Maloney, who was also a member of the Committee, said, "I will take him." Rube kept a woman here. He said, "I will put him in my house." So we walked him up there to his house. . . . About 12 o'clock down came Maloney, and said he could not keep him any longer, his woman had got frightened, and would not have him there. We sent a guard and took him to some other place, and he was shifted round to keep him away from the Sheriff.

In spite of thus being involved with the prisoner, the ubiquitous Bluxome was back acting as secretary for the meeting that evening. There was much important business, though nothing with respect to the principal case other than the brief resolution that "Report of Ex Committee in case of Jim Stuart be accepted."

Brannan's resignation from the presidency was accepted; a proper vote of thanks was tendered him; Selim Woodworth was then elected to the office.

Brannan himself moved that the two vacancies in the Executive Committee should be filled. One election went to Colonel W. C. Graham, #154, who had already rendered much service. The other, more portentously, went to Garret W. Ryckman, #57, who was steadily to assume more and more importance in the conduct of affairs.

At this meeting, also, the Committee, for the first time, took formal action to purify itself. W. F. McLean, #539, had been suspended by executive action a few days earlier. David Earl, #264, had fallen under suspicion as early as July 4, and had been definitely implicated as a criminal in Hetherington's statement. The meeting took action: "Resolved: The following gent be expelled from this Committee — David Earl, W. F. McLean."

This treachery in the ranks led to another action:

*Resolved:* that no member of this Committee shall speak of any business that shall come before this meeting, and any member who does shall receive 12 lashes and be expelled from this Committee.

At a meeting of the Executive Committee, that same evening, Payran was back in the chair, the writ of *habeas corpus* against him having expired. The chief action of the meeting was to issue orders for the arrest of Mary Hogan and others who had been implicated in Stuart's confession. . . .

The next day, July 10, was busy, but was quiet — curiously quiet — as far as the case of Stuart was concerned. The men directing the affairs of the Committee were moving with all proper deliberation. At the time of the hanging of Jenkins, they had moved rapidly, against the counseling of Coleman. The results had been somewhat embarrassing, and the members of the Committee had been taunted with being "midnight murderers." This time, even though they might run some risk by delay, they were determined not to hurry.

One reason for especial care was that the report of the hanging of Juanita had reached San Francisco. A brief account had just appeared in the newspapers, and word of mouth must have rapidly elaborated the story. If there was anything that could throw the Committee into disrepute, it would be to perpetrate something resembling the mob-scene at Downieville.

That morning Sheriff Hays reported to the judge that he had been unable to find the body of James Stuart, although he had made "diligent search."

The Executive Committee met both morning and afternoon, but did not concern itself directly with Stuart. Members were dispatched to Sacramento and to Sonora in search of various men implicated in the confession. Hogan and his wife were reported under arrest and being examined. Hetherington made a further statement, in which he reported (to Payran alone, all the others withdrawing) that Stuart had murdered Charles Moore in cold blood: "Long Jim shot him — that he shot him with a shot gun." It was hearsay evidence, but it could be reported to the Committee.

Hogan's statement in general bore out the assertion in the confession that he was innocent, at least in the sense of not having committed crimes, however much he may have known about them. He admitted being a deceived husband, "the affairs between myself and wife can never be settled." He considered his wife to be involved with Whittaker, and did not mention Stuart at all.

Mrs. Hogan followed the generally safe policy of stoutly denying everything criminal or incriminating. About the only useful information which she supplied was that Stuart sometimes went by the *alias* Mason. She even denied (a blow to his *amour propre,* it would have been, if he had ever learned it) that she had Stuart's daguerreotype.

The truth seems to have been that Sam Whittaker was in possession of such heart as Mary Hogan possessed. He had lived with her openly during the absence of Hogan in the mines, and Hetherington testified that he had frequently seen them in bed together. Hogan, returning, raised a rumpus. Whittaker, who had remained in the city in spite of the activities of the Committee, did not care to brave out this personal difficulty, and left. That very day (if the testimony as to date is accurate)

Stuart arrived in town. Mary Hogan, lover absent and husband estranged, received him hospitably.

As such information became available, we may imagine that some members of the Executive Committee smiled a little, remembering Stuart's gallantry in withholding the name of the "female." Still, Mrs. Hogan made not too bad an impression. A reporter described her as "thirty-five years of age, quite genteel in appearance." And he added, "one who might safely keep a crib without ever being suspected."

The general Committee also met. It heard a report of the Executive Committee in the case of Stuart, but this did not involve the presentation of the confession. In fact, the meeting was concerned that the *Picayune* had published something about the confession, even though in a vague and general fashion. A committee was appointed to inquire of the editors how they had come by this information.

This same evening, for the first time in about a month, a Law-and-Order meeting was held. Several speakers addressed it — chief among them, Broderick. Another speaker, listed as Duane, was presumably Charles Duane, commonly known as "Dutch Charlie." The Law-and-Order people could hardly have done worse in their choice of a spokesman, since Duane was notoriously lawless and disorderly.

The meeting appointed a committee to wait upon the city authorities and to offer them help in case of an emergency. Such an action was almost the equivalent of a declaration of war against the Committee.

A crisis was at hand. Before long, probably before the next day should pass, the Committee would have to make its decision about Stuart, and take action — or attempt to take action. The Committee could now muster some hundreds, and had many sympathizers. The sheriff and the city marshal could muster about a hundred men, and could enroll deputies from the volunteers that were offered by the numerous Law-and-Order party. The two military companies could be expected to take no official action, many of their officers and members being also members of the Committee. The city was not too far removed from civil war.

Next morning, July 11, the city was still peaceful. The streets were busy with the comings and goings of many men of many kinds — prosperous merchants and lawyers, in top-hats and flowered vests; workmen, in rough clothes, with their tools; pipe-smoking Irish laborers, carrying picks and shovels; pig-tailed Chinese; cigarette-smoking Latin-Americans in colorful cloaks or serapes; booted miners, wearing the conventional red shirt, down from the Yuba or the Stanislaus.

Preparing an editorial to be published that afternoon, the editor of the *Picayune* wrote its title, "The Impending Crisis." Though the streets were quiet, he began, "Any person acquainted with the tone of the public mind of this city must be aware that a crisis is impending over us." Of the Committee he declared that their critical decision must be whether to "yield formal obedience" to the law, and "thereby defeat the ends of justice," or to "attain the ends of justice at the expense of legal forms." Chiefly, however, he urged the people not to be carried "beyond the limits of discretion and calmness." He did not attempt to veil his own anxiety: "we are in dangerous times — trembling as it were upon the brink of a volcano that yawns to engulph us." Clearly, the editor feared an armed clash.

Shortly after nine o'clock came the first stroke of the bell.

CHAPTER 18

## INTENSE EXCITEMENT

*(July 11, 9:15 A.M.–2:45 P.M.)*

THE BELL at the Plaza sounded first, and the bell on the California Engine House answered back. Each was beating out the minute-stroke which on the night of the taking of Jenkins had summoned the men of the Committee together.

The meeting could have been called privately, or even secretly. But the Committee had acted secretly and hastily with Jenkins. Now the signal sounded out clearly on a bright summer morning. If there were those who wished to make something of it, let them!

All over the city the members of the Committee looked to their revolvers, and then started for the rooms. Work stopped everywhere. Within a few minutes a crowd of three thousand people had jammed into Battery Street in front of the Committee rooms. To add to the excitement, some shipmaster began firing a cannon at five-minute intervals. Rumors flew through the crowd that Stuart was about to be hanged, and perhaps someone else too. The mayor, the marshal, and the sheriff were getting their men together.

The crowd waited. After a while the bells stopped ringing, and the cannon fired no more. The members of the Committee had been admitted into the rooms, and the doors were closed. The crowd began to drift away.

Inside, the meeting convened about ten o'clock, Selim Woodworth in the chair. At this time the total number of men who had signed the constitution was about 580. A few of these had been expelled; some others for various reasons (most commonly, absence from the city) had severed their connections; some members had been sent to other towns to arrest Stuart's accomplices; some members may have been on duty elsewhere in San Francisco. Those present numbered about four hundred.

The meeting was held in the large room, which must have been crowded. The prisoner was confined in the smaller, adjacent room, usually reserved for the Executive Committee.

Stuart, still manacled, could probably hear everything that was said in the meeting. The guards reported that he felt, or affected, indifference. Once or twice, in the course of the morning, he put his hands behind his head, and yawned, and said that it was "damned tiresome." He asked for a piece of tobacco, and then chewed on it with satisfaction.

The meeting proceeded. The assemblage must be considered, not as a jury, but as a court of review. The Executive Committee had already conducted the trial, and the duty of the general Committee was now to approve or disapprove the recommendation. No one, indeed, could have had much doubt as to how the decision would go — as Coleman wrote, "his guilt being plain, and the volume of it so vast and enormous."

The evidence in the case was first read. Such a procedure, considering the length of the confession and the number of the witnesses, must have consumed an hour and a half.

Two questions were then put to the meeting, apparently as "sense motions." The first was: "Has the prisoner performed his contract or not?" There must have been some discussion of the contract, and of the significance of the question. The answer rendered was a unanimous *No*.

Since the terms of the contract are not surely known, no decision can be made as to the justice of the action. The unanimity, however, is impressive. On several occasions in the last few months, individuals had stood out strongly against the majority. If the situation had warranted it, someone, we would think, would have entered his protest in this instance too.

Stuart probably was judged to have failed in his contract because he did not confess to some crimes of which the committee believed him to be guilty on good evidence — particularly, the murder of Moore.

The second question was then put: "Has the prisoner been guilty of crimes rendering him liable to the punishment of death?" Again there must have been explanation. The significant plural "crimes" may have called for comment. Under the law certain of the robberies which Stuart had confessed could be punishable by death. Moreover the Executive Committee must have judged him guilty of at least one murder. The answering vote was again unanimous, *Yes.*

A formal motion was then put: *"Resolved:* That Prisoner Stuart be hung."

This decisive motion was passed, unanimously, a little after noon.

A number of enabling resolutions were then passed, probably without debate.

> *Resolved:* That a Clergyman be sent for to remain with the Prisoner until he is hung.
> *Resolved:* That the Prisoner be hung at 2 o'clock.
> *Resolved:* That Ex Com make necessary arrangements.
> *Resolved:* That no person be allowed to leave the room.
> *Resolved:* That Prisoner receive his sentence.
> *Resolved:* That Col. Stevenson inform the populace that at 2 o'clock the prisoner Stuart will be hung.

The utility of most of these resolutions is obvious. The two-hour period granted to the prisoner was probably a compromise. It allowed a certain interval, so that the Committee would not be accused of great hurry, and so that the prisoner could have time with a clergyman. But it did not allow so much time that opposition could organize too strongly. The members of the Committee, in fact, were apprehensive lest they might meet with resistance. Rumor was circulating that the much respected

Sheriff Hays had mobilized a band of armed horsemen to take the prisoner.

The resolution that no one should leave the room was another safeguard. It would, for a while, prevent the public from knowing when the Committee intended to act, and would thus preserve an element of surprise. In addition, it would prevent any faint hearts from quietly going home.

To Stevenson was assigned the work which Brannan had done on the night of the hanging of Jenkins. Although not actually withdrawing from the Committee, Brannan was sulking. Colonel Stevenson was a wealthy and respected citizen, and possessed some talents as a public speaker.

After an interval the meeting passed two more resolutions.

> *Resolved:* That a Committee be appointed to draft a form of the testimony to be published in the papers of tomorrow morning.
> *Resolved:* That the Com. take a recess of half an hour.

The last resolution meant a recess only within the limits of the building, where (it is to be remembered) the builder had constructed a privy. But, aside from such an opportunity for physical relief, the recess provided no relaxation.

> In the interim [as the *Herald* reported, doubtless from one who was there] the four hundred members in the Committee Room sat like statues on their seats — not a word was uttered, not a sound was heard to break the solemn stillness. . . . Gravity sat upon every countenance, for all doubtless felt the awful extremity to which they were forced.

During this interval a crowd gathered outside, probably drawn together by the announcement that some explanation of the Committee's action would be forthcoming. As the *Herald* reported:

Col. Stevenson went out and addressed the citizens assembled, . . . and put the question to the vote whether they would approve the course the Committee had decided upon. Almost a unanimous voice of approval was the response.

In the same interim, the Executive Committee withdrew from the general meeting and busied itself with the details. Half of its members were absent, doubtless employed upon special assignments. The chief action taken was to authorize Captain Wakeman "to pass out to make the outdoor arrangements." That formidable shipmaster, who had placed the rope around Jenkins's neck, was again to act as executioner.

The Reverend Mr. Mines, already alerted, had been quick to respond to the call. He found Stuart much more approachable than the foul-mouthed Jenkins. Still Stuart did not think that his own case at the heavenly court of judgment would be a very strong one — "I have not thought of God for fifteen years, and I cannot expect that he would think of me in the few moments that are left to me." He was no longer convinced that the religion of his youth was even true, but he stated hypothetically, "If there are everlasting burnings, I expect to go to them, for I have led the life that must take me to them."

Shortly before two o'clock the meeting reconvened, and the members were divided into two approximately equal companies. One company, probably composed of men who had had military training, was assigned as the immediate escort for the prisoner.

Finally Mines withdrew, and all was ready. Though the response of the crowd to Colonel Stevenson had been encouraging, the fickleness of mobs is notorious, and the members of the Committee had still no idea of whether they would meet with organized resistance and how serious it might be. Nevertheless, the resolution was put that the sentence should now be carried out, and was passed unanimously. President Woodworth, thereupon, picking up his revolver, remarked, "The chair volunteers to head the procession."

The doors opened at last, and the members filed out solemnly. Two hundred of them formed into a column of twos, each pair with arms locked. The other two hundred massed into a phalanx, ten men abreast and twenty deep. In the front rank were Colonel Stevenson and nine other prominent citizens. At the center, in a small open space, stood Stuart, his arms pinioned behind him.

The march proceeded south on Battery Street. There was no sign of resistance.

Stuart strode along firmly, without evidence of weakening. His mouth was compressed, showing the strain. Those in charge had seen to it that he was well dressed. He wore a tight-fitting

HANGING OF JAMES STUART

black jacket, white shirt, brown trousers, and patent-leather shoes.

Across Pine Street and onward, scarcely two minutes' walking brought the steadily-moving column to the corner of Bush and Market. Here the leaders swung to the left, and then part way left again. Close ahead was Market Street wharf, which stretched out two hundred yards into the bay. Near the end of the wharf stood a derrick, for loading and unloading cargo. Captain Wakeman had chosen his place shrewdly. From the shoreline, from boats, and from California Street wharf, people could see what was happening, but the intervening water would prevent interference.

The four hundred men of the Committee, entering the wharf, jammed it solidly. Rescue had become almost a physical impossibility.

There was no delay or fumbling. Shortly before three o'clock, on a sunny afternoon, in the sight of three thousand citizens, after a careful trial and full deliberation, with the consolations of religion fully offered, formally and without haste or confusion, the Committee of Vigilance hanged its man.

# CHAPTER 19

# ARRESTS BY THE VIGILANCE COMMITTEE

*(July 11, 2:45 P.M.–July 20)*

C URIOUSLY, the only officer to attempt a rescue was Edward Gallagher, the city coroner. Stuart had been hanging for only a few minutes when Gallagher pushed forward through the crowd, and came to where the vigilantes, arms locked, were grimly holding their solid front across the wharf. He demanded the body.

"By God," came the reply, "you don't get through till that fellow's a fit subject for your administration."

Thus blocked, Gallagher took a boat, and rowed to a point near the derrick. Since a sufficient period was now judged to have elapsed, Wakeman permitted the body to be lowered into the boat, and the assiduous coroner hastily made off with it.

As might be suspected, his eagerness did not spring primarily from a desire to hold the inquest promptly. A quack doctor had recently approached the authorities with claims of great proficiency at the restoration of victims of strangulation. In a desperate effort to circumvent the Committee by sleight, Gallagher hurriedly took the body (or was it the living Stuart?) to some place where this restoration could be attempted. The "doctor" labored hard for some time, and claimed to observe certain traces of still-existing vitality. In the end, however, he was forced to admit the efficacy of Wakeman's work.

The macabre incident, coupled with memories of Jenkins being dragged across the Plaza, gave rise to the epigram, "The first man that they hanged was dead before they strung him up, and the second man was still living when they took him down."

The hanging inaugurated a period of about three weeks during which the Committee functioned effectively and accomplished much work. But the hanging, or the circumstances attending it, produced a new flare-up of opposition, differing greatly from that which the Committee had previously encountered.

During June and early July, the great adversary had been Broderick. He had combatted the Committee by attempting to organize what might have been called an Anti-committee. He had held mass-meetings and organized his followers. Though a Law-and-Order man, he had paid little attention to acting by legal process. Finally, when the hanging of Stuart seemed imminent, he had offered his armed cohort to the service of the city. When the authorities refused to meet the Committee head-on, Broderick was apparently disgusted, and he ceased his active and open opposition. He must have done so with the realization that he had been wholly unsuccessful.

Largely to counteract Broderick's cry of "midnight murderers," the Executive Committee had arranged for the highly formal execution of Stuart. Immediately, however, they discovered that, when it comes to a hanging, you have great difficulty in pleasing everyone. There had been, even among the officials, a tendency not to consider the Jenkins affair too deeply. Its impulsive and helter-skelter nature kept it from being a deliberate insult to the law, and even suggested a boys-will-be-boys defense. The circumstances of the Stuart affair prevented any such easy-going judgment. As a result, the members of the Committee found themselves immediately the targets of two official thunderbolts.

One of these, written on the very day of the hanging, bore the signature of that eminent and amiable nonentity Mayor Brenham. Obviously that highest officer of the city should have been a key figure in the situation. If a strong man, such as the

CHARLES J. BRENHAM

former mayor Geary, had been in office, the history of the summer might have been different. But Brenham, so far, had done
nothing at all, except to suppress an incendiary handbill, thus
helping to preserve the peace, but also to aid the Committee.
Now, though the wording would indicate that he was rather
reluctant, he issued a proclamation "to the citizens of San Francisco."

Once aroused, Brenham declared that the shortcomings of
the police and courts could not be safely remedied "by voluntary associations of citizens, assuming a superiority to the laws."
Without naming the Committee, he stated that recent events
showed "an insurrectionary tendency." He cited "the provisions of the 'Act to regulate Proceedings in Criminal Cases,

Chap. IV.' " And, in this connection, he declared that he would
not shrink "from a prompt discharge of the duties" ascribed
for the mayor in that chapter.

This proclamation had all the effect of a horrendous scare-
crow. Who was afraid of big bad Charlie Brenham? His having
done nothing in the past provided a good-enough guarantee
that he would do nothing in the future.

The second blast, somewhat more formidable, was from
Judge Alexander Campbell, in a charge to the Grand Jury.
He declared the hanging "by an organized association" to have
been an "outrage," and he reiterated that term. He also reiterated that it occurred in "open day." He contrasted it with "the
unlawful execution of a man named Jenkins," which he considered to be "greatly palliated by the circumstances under
which it was committed." He declared that the courts were
wholly competent and adequate to treat criminal cases, and
stated (with high optimism, under the circumstances) that "if
the deceased was guilty of any crime, he could have been
immediately indicted, and within a week, or at most ten
days, tried, convicted, and sentenced." Climactically he thundered, "Every person who in any manner acted, aided, abetted,
or assisted in taking Stuart's life, or counseled or encouraged
his death, is undoubtedly GUILTY OF MURDER."

If the upright judge was able to read this charge and keep a
straight face, we must consider that he was either a consummate
actor or a man wholly lacking in humor. Half of the Grand
Jury, no fewer than eight members, were also members of the
Committee, and were thus being advised to indict themselves
for murder. Obviously, they were unlikely to do so, and thus
the judge's charge, like the mayor's pronunciamento, produced
no specific result.

Perhaps, having made public statements, the mayor and the
judge rested better at ease with their consciences. Any other
effect was only to strengthen the Committee and harden the
resolution of its members. Men who are threatened with in-

dictment for murder can only decide to continue in their established course with the hope of coming out on the other side. If they were already accused of insurrection, why not go ahead and complete the revolution? Everyone knows that a successful revolutionary is remembered as the Father of his Country, that an unsuccessful one ends on the gibbet or in exile.

Both mayor and judge, in fact, seem to have been acting as futile idealists. Their statements merely tended to widen cleavages and exacerbate feelings. They offered no means of conciliation and cooperation.

At the same time, we may note, the issuance of these statements cleared the Committee of charges of tyranny. It was, *de facto*, the controlling power in the city, but it permitted freedom of speech, and it continued to give strong support to Judge Campbell, as an intelligent and uncorrupted judge.

That the Committee could thus allow freedom of speech is a good indication of its secure position. Only a strong government can permit open criticism. At this time the situation was such that Robert Lammot could declare "nine tenths of the order-loving inhabitants" to be "openly arrayed against the laws, or rather — against the administrators of the laws." The Committee, therefore, could afford to neglect counter-propaganda, and to continue with its work in full vigor. . . .

The situation, indeed, had changed tremendously since that time when fewer than a hundred men had gathered at the trial of Jenkins. The membership, spurting a little after the hanging of Stuart, was close to the six hundred mark. Moreover, throughout the state in every town and mining camp, the responsible citizens by this time had organized a committee, more or less on a model of that in San Francisco. Of a special significance, nowhere except in San Francisco had these movements met with resistance. As a result, the real power in the whole state of California now rested in the committees, which were in correspondence for mutual support and cooperation.

An indication of the strength of the Committee in San Francisco alone is afforded by the amusing shift in attitude of Aiken, the British consul. After the Jenkins affair, he had forwarded a sharp note to Governor McDougal. On the hanging of a second British subject, Aiken merely wrote to his home office, stating that Stuart had probably deserved it. . . .

The Committee, therefore, leaving its propaganda in the hands of the newspaper editors, settled down to work. But by this time, the conception of what was the proper work had altered greatly.

Originally the Committee had thought largely in terms of street-patrols after dark and of Water Police. But by now criminals had been so nearly eliminated that these activities had become unproductive. The street-patrols were perhaps given up entirely, with some concomitant strengthening of the so-called voluntary patrols, which had been organized before the Committee, to function in collaboration with the police. Since many individual vigilantes were also members of the patrol the situation was not greatly changed.

The Water Police, as vigourously conducted by Captain Wakeman and his boatmen, had been the most colorful of the regular activities. The Water Police gained the support of the shipmasters whose vessels were lying in the harbor. The officers of the revenue cutter *Polk* cooperated, thus furnishing an exception to the general rebuff of the Committee by the constituted authorities.

The Water Police had made special expeditions to the islands in the bay, to the Contra Costa, and even to the Farallones. These expeditions had resulted from reports that organized criminals maintained hang-outs in these places. The expeditions had proved to be generally fruitless, and at the same time the bills for boat-hire had caused consternation among the financial officers of the Committee. The Water Police, thus having outlived their usefulness, were restricted to a small fraction of their former activity.

On the contrary, supervision of the immigration of criminals, which had been one of the Committee's original objectives, was intensified. On July 15, a vessel from Sydney was reported entering the harbor. The Executive Committee immediately appointed four of its members "to proceed on board the ship *Adirondack* to examine the passengers." Among the four was Bluxome, who, in spite of his regular work as secretary, always seemed able to undertake an extra job if it should be necessary.

The vessel was a large one, and carried 256 passengers. Of these 118 were either children or had their papers in good order to show their identity. The other 138 were individually questioned; each of them was asked by what ship he or she had arrived in Australia, and the answer was checked against a prepared list of convict ships. The examiners asked other questions, and Bluxome carefully recorded the answers.

Preliminary to the examination, the passengers had all been collected in the forward part of the ship. After his examination, the passenger was taken aft, if he had satisfied the examiners that he had not been a convict. Those who were considered still to be under suspicion were put into a small boat alongside.

As in most of its investigation the Committee tended to err on the side of leniency. Of the large number of immigrants on the *Adirondack,* only ten were put into the boat, and were then taken ashore and held in the Committee rooms. Six of these soon managed to clear themselves. The whole operation, therefore, at the most, prevented the landing in California of four persons.

One reason why the Committee detained so few was undoubtedly the difficulty of knowing what to do with them, and the inevitable expense. The prisoners had to be housed in the small detention-room, and there they must be guarded, fed, and given humane treatment. Eventually they had to be shipped back to Australia. Those who had money could be forced to pay for their own return passage. The Committee paid the fares of the others out of its own funds, though in some instances the attempt was made to put the responsibility upon the captain who had brought them originally. . . .

On the day after the arrival of the *Adirondack* the Committee made final disposition of Hamilton Taft. His case is of interest as showing another phase of the Committee's work. . . . On July 10 two men from Placer County, believing Taft to have stolen $2300 in gold and coin, appealed to some vigilantes, and not to the regular police. After Taft had been accused but before the Committee arrested him, he expressed a pressing need to retire, and was allowed to do so. Later, he was taken to the Committee rooms, and searched. Some incriminating gold-specimens were found upon him. He thereupon broke down and confessed, adding the detail that he had got rid of much of the gold by dropping it down the privy at the time of his trip to that place of secrecy. One of the original complainants was assigned the unsavory task of recovering this portion of the evidence, and Taft was clapped into the detention-room.

Since the original crime had not occurred in San Francisco, the Committee eventually turned Taft over to one of its own members and to the original complainants, to deliver to the authorities in Placer County. The two complainants, however, were formally put under bond for one thousand dollars, the money to be paid to the County of San Francisco, in case their prisoner should not be properly delivered.

Like other cases, that of Taft illustrates the anomalies of the situation. The Committee made an illegal arrest, but turned the prisoner over to the legal authorities. It ignored the sheriff of San Francisco County, but arranged to have that county receive one thousand dollars if the bond should be forfeited. . . .

The most active work of the Committee during mid-July was in the pursuit of various individuals who had been involved in the confession of Stuart and the testimony of Hetherington. Again the Committee was lenient in its actions. Stuart had implicated not only Frank Pixley, but also two San Francisco policemen. Except for publishing the names, the Committee took no action against these persons. Probably the consensus of opinion was that the Committee should not come into such direct conflict with the constituted authorities.

But the Committee set up a vigorous hue-and-cry after the members of Stuart's gang, whom the newspapers sometimes mentioned as "Mrs. Hogan's boarders," since most of them, at one time or another, had lived at her house. The most wanted of the boarders were T. Belcher Kay and Samuel Whittaker.

Kay was a character equally colorful and slippery. He had even some international reputation:

> On the continent and in Paris he is known as Count Peri: in England and in the Colonies as Singing Billy, also as Billy Gibson.

He had got to California by escaping from Tasmania, or Van Dieman's Land, as it was then known. This, in itself, lent him some distinction, as in the words of a mere Sydney man:

> There is no comparison between the convicts of Sydney and Van Dieman's Land. The latter are so bad, that they would not allow them to come into Sydney.

Arriving in San Francisco, Kay was clever enough to establish himself as a man of respectability, and Governor McDougal appointed him to be Port Warden. By virtue of this office he had much inside information about the movements of vessels and their cargoes, and he made use of this information in planning robberies.

As might be expected, a man of such talent proved difficult to capture. Scenting trouble, or perhaps being tipped off, he had left San Francisco shortly after the arrest of Stuart. Members of the Committee followed him to Sacramento, and arrested him there on July 11. With characteristic effrontery, he talked his way out of it, persuading them that he would return to their custody if they only permitted him a day off to tend to some business. Released, he absconded immediately, and set out for San Francisco by a circuitous route, disguising himself as an old woman. He was doubtless intending to get himself smuggled aboard a ship and thus to leave California, but he was recognized or betrayed. With all the agility of a cat, however, he managed to light on his feet, by being arrested by the city police, not by the Committee. In fact, the Committee never was able to lay hands on him.

Samuel Whittaker was an Englishman, thirty-three years old, who at the age of eighteen had been transported to Australia for house-breaking. In 1849, he received a conditional pardon, and came to San Francisco. He earned an honest living for more than a year, but then lapsed into bad ways. He was one of the men who remained in the street at the time of the attack upon Jansen. Along with Kay and Stuart, he was a leader. Hetherington, who was in a position to know, declared, "I believe Whittaker to be the smartest thief of the whole gang." He was the especial favorite of Mrs. Hogan, and rivalry for her favors produced bad blood between him and Stuart.

Though lacking something of Kay's effrontery and gift of talk, Whittaker was highly intelligent, and during July he eluded the posses that the Committee sent after him.

The Committee, however, did not despair. California was a kind of natural prison. About the only way to escape from it was through the port of San Francisco. With Whittaker's description circulated to every committee of vigilance throughout the state, and to the sheriffs as well, there was a good likelihood that he would eventually be rounded up.

Balked in its attempt to seize the leaders, the Committee was forced, temporarily, to be content with some run-of-the-mill members of the gang, though even these were far from colorless characters.

One of them was James Burns, generally known by his bizarre nickname of Jemmy-from-Town. He was, to lend variety, an Irishman — a quick-tempered and quarrelsome little fellow, an adept both at burglary and at jail-breaking.

Also apprehended, was George Adams, *alias* Jack Dandy. Adams had been particularly useful to the gang, since he was a skilled craftsman, able to manufacture burglars' tools and to counterfeit keys.

Both Burns and Adams were already well known in San Francisco, being two of the nine who had escaped from jail on June 2. This had been Burns's fourth such escape.

A third to be added to the bag was Thomas Ainsworth, *alias* Tommy Roundhead, still another of the Sydney ducks named by Stuart.

The Committee was also, for a brief time, possessed of the body of a minor character known as Dab the Horsethief. The story is more important for the commotion that it aroused than for anything that happened to Dab, in whom the Committee evinced scant interest.

The committee at Marysville, one of the most active in the state, arrested Dab on the strength of his having been mentioned once in Stuart's confession. Two of the Marysville members escorted him on the steamer to San Francisco, and Brannan, who happened to be on the same steamer, took the prisoner over, conversationally at least, to such a degree that the newspapers later reported him to have been the captor. The Marysville men, accompanied by Brannan, delivered their prisoner at the Committee's rooms. This happened to be an evening of some temporary crisis. The Executive Committee had instructed Van Bokkelen, the chief of police, that he should permit no one to leave the rooms.

This unfortunate order, in a short time, aroused intense excitement among high-spirited and high-tempered members, who had finished their stint of work and wanted to leave. Violence was threatened. The mercurial Brannan, as might be expected, was among those most vociferously demanding exit, and for some reason he wished that the prisoner should go with him. Finally a near-riot developed. The rebellious members forced the door open, and several of them left. In the confusion, Brannan shoved Dab through the door, and he escaped.

No attempt seems to have been made to recapture Dab. The Executive Committee, however, appointed a sub-committee to investigate the affair, and the final decision supported Van Bokkelen. Brannan was temporarily denied access to the rooms.

During this period came the rise of Ryckman, who had been elected to the Executive Committee on July 9. At fifty-three, he was one of the oldest — perhaps, actually, the oldest — member of the Committee. He had come from Albany, New York, where he had been a printer, and later had owned a brewery. In San Francisco he was a man of property. During this summer he left his partner in charge of his affairs, and later stated that he did not do five days' work all summer.

He had signed the role as #57 during the first evening. Equally with Payran — certainly more than Coleman, as far as '51 is concerned — Ryckman may be considered the archetypal vigilante. The affairs of the Committee absorbed him passionately. At times he seems a kind of avenging angel. In his neverflagging energy, he surpassed boys in their twenties who were his fellow members. He was a teetotaler, and despised anyone (and there were many among the members) who let whiskey befuddle his faculties. Fearless and unflinching, pitiless if need was, a prosecuting attorney by instinct, he even kept a disguise handy in his room, so that he could slip it on readily for a little sleuthing. Along with Payran, he became an outstanding investigator and examiner. T. J. L. Smiley, #573, declared in his reminiscences that "the great strength" of the Committee lay in "the wonderful faculties" possessed by Payran and Ryckman.

With such talent at work, the two chief prisoners crumpled rapidly. On July 19 and 20, Burns and Adams were making

confessions, which both detailed their own crimes and incrimi-
nated their associates. The juncture again seemed to be approaching when the Committee must once more ask Captain
Wakeman to officiate.

By this time, the general situation, again, was altering. The
Committee, repulsed by the authorities immediately after the
hanging of Stuart, now was gaining more official support.

The Grand Jury — as might have been expected, since so
many of its members were also members of the Committee —
proved to be highly cooperative. It politely requested of the
Executive Committee what evidence it could supply to expedite
the indictment of Kay. On two occasions the jury met with the
Executive Committee in consultation about cases which were
of common interest. On one at least of these occasions the jury
came to the Committee rooms.

Sheriff Hays, also, was cooperative. The Committee undertook to raise money, to complete the jail, and Hays was enthu-
siastically ready to receive such funds, even though they might
come from men whom one of the judges (of whose court Hays
was an officer) had declared to be guilty of murder.

Even more important was the action of the governor. . . .
In that year John McDougal was thirty-four years old, a strikingly handsome man, in a heavy sort of way, looking as if he
could well be cast as the lead in a Shakespearean tragedy. He
had come from Indiana, where he had been in politics. Later
he had served, with distinction, as a captain in an Indiana regiment during the Mexican War.

Coming to California, he kept store for a while, and then was
elected a member of the Constitutional Convention in 1849.
His fellow delegates knew him, not so much as a statesman, but
as a good drinking-companion, something of a wit, and a little,
even, of a buffoon.

Then the Democrats nominated him for lieutenant-governor,
an office for which there was little competition. He was elected,

along with the rest of the ticket. In January, 1851, the governor resigned. And there was McDougal, the hard-drinking buffoon of the convention, in full gubernatorial power. They called him "His Accidency"!

He had physical courage, some sense of responsibility, and a few other good qualities, and so he was not an utter failure as governor. One of his faults was his readiness to grant pardons. Yet he was not a soft-hearted sentimentalist, and he had no objection, on principle, to capital punishment. Therefore, we come up hard against the unescapable conclusion that he granted pardons because there was something in it for him. This may not have been money. He was a cog in the vast, and vastly corrupt, political machine, and his pardons may have been tied in with the consolidation of power, or the enrichment of henchmen somewhere along the line.

In May, 1851, the Democrats met in convention and nominated John Bigler for governor. McDougal was through! With months left to serve, he was nothing better than a lame duck.

McDougal was thus in a weak position, and can hardly be blamed for looking the other way when trouble arose in San Francisco. As a Democrat, he could not go against Broderick. As a man soon to become a private citizen, he certainly should avoid offending all the powerful businessmen who composed the Committee. But McDougal had neither Broderick's strength nor Gwin's astuteness.

At this time, probably on July 15, the governor came to San Francisco. As a more prudent man would not have done, he visited the rooms and talked with the Executive Committee.

There is no detailed account of the conversation. The governor was noted as a man who was highly convivial, not to say, bibulous. Preparations to entertain him may therefore account for one of the still-surviving vouchers, which indicates that on July 14 the sergeant-at-arms officially purchased ten cheeses and five gallons of brandy. Tongue thus well lubricated, His Accidency may have said rather more than he meant. Certainly the members of the Executive Committee came to believe that there was nothing to fear from the governor, and that he was ready to cooperate with them. Four of its responsible and highly respected members later declared the governor to have stated "that he approved the act of the Committee, and that much good had taken place." They further quoted him, in effect:

> He hoped that they would go on, and endeavor to act in concert with the authorities, and in case any judge should be guilty of mal-administration, to hang him, and he would appoint others.

The governor made no denial, and there is every reason to believe that the four members were quoting him with essential accuracy. The violence of the words suggests a man talking irresponsibly, perhaps under the influence of brandy. But, even if we discount the words for alcoholic exaggeration, anyone would be justified in assuming that the governor would be more likely to act with the Committee than against it.

Toward the end of July, therefore, the well-informed members of the Executive Committee had much cause to believe that everything was progressing satisfactorily. At this time occurred the affair between Frank Ball and "Dutch Charlie" Duane.

# CHAPTER 20

## ASSAULT WITH INTENT TO KILL

*(July 21)*

I N THOSE DAYS — the fine term "nightclub entertainer" not
yet being invented — people talked more directly, and they
merely said of Frank Ball, "he sings in Clayton's saloon."

Though he signed himself Francis A. Ball, everyone called
him Frank. He was a well-known and well-liked young fellow.
Physically, he was slight, almost frail. Besides singing, he composed his own witty lyrics, commenting upon happenings in
town. Like other such entertainers, he was not squeamish. He
had even composed, and often sang, a comic song about the
hanging of Jenkins.

But Ball was more of a man than this introduction might
seem to indicate. He had served in the Mexican War, and part
of his frailty was the result of a wound. He was a good citizen.
During the spring he had conscientiously and courageously
served on the jury for a serious and notable trial. He was now
on the Grand Jury. Moreover, he was a member of the Committee, having joined it early, as #192.

San Francisco, even in '51, had a good-sized French colony,
and, as the cliché assures us, "The French are fond of dancing
and light wines." To illustrate the point, these French people
made plans to hold a fancy-dress ball, hiring the ample room
belonging to the Cairo Saloon. It was to be a private affair,
but a large one. The popular Frank Ball, though he was not
French, received an invitation, and he threw himself with enthusiasm into concocting a funny costume. The ball was set

FANCY BALL, CALIFORNIA EXCHANGE

Note that two of the ladies are wearing costumes suggestive of bloomers.

for the evening of Sunday, July 20, and the festivities would continue well into the hours of the next morning.

On that Sunday another well-known character of the city was much in evidence. This man, probably even better known than Frank Ball, was Charles P. Duane. Most people referred to him as "Dutch Charlie." The "Dutch" seems to have been merely a nickname. As far as can be determined, though no one can be proud of it, he was thoroughly American.

Physically, he was the opposite of Ball — tremendous and

powerful. He had perhaps been in the ring, since he strongly suggests the heavy-weight type.

Duane held some position in the Democratic political machine, a position which may be described as obscure, but disreputable. He was apparently the chief agent of physical violence that a corrupt organization maintains, and uses as needed. If someone was breaking ranks or otherwise causing trouble and so had to be threatened or actually beaten up, "Dutch Charlie" was the one to call on. He was thus, necessarily, very close to Broderick, to whom he was a kind of right-hand man. Duane had even spoken at one of the anti-Committee mass meetings, though he must have struck many people as a very curious champion of Law-and-Order.

In San Francisco, that summer, many men habitually carried arms and there was still a cult of honorable self-defense. But even in such a city Duane was hated and feared for threats and for acts of violence. Early in the year he had knocked a man down, kicked him, jumped on him with his feet, and finally shot him in the back. The case aroused such indignation that Duane was threatened with violence at the time of the general excitement over the Jansen case. Tried for "assault with intent to kill," he had escaped by means of a hung jury, when one juror refused to convict, though the case was an open-and-shut one. Apparently Duane's lawyers had done what was common (and was an important cause for the formation of the Committee), that is, they had planted in the jury one man who was in their pay.

That had been the jury on which Ball had served, and he was one of those voting for conviction. Duane held this against him, and at various times had been heard to utter threats. He had also taken offense at Ball's song about the hanging of Jenkins, saying that Jenkins was a friend of his — a statement which in itself tells a good deal about Duane.

A week after the organization of the Committee, ten rank-

and-file members had submitted a resolution asking for a move against Duane in connection with the shooting case, which had not again come to trial. The Executive Committee took no action, but the submission of this unparalleled resolution indicates the extraordinary antipathy and fear in (which the "shoulder-striker" was held.

Like many San Franciscans, Duane was a heavy drinker. On July 20, for some reason, he took to drinking even more heavily than usual. He made a round of saloons with his friend Ira Cole, and by nightfall he was, according to Cole, "pretty tight."

That evening the French held their party, and Frank Ball, true to his reputation as a fun-maker, arrived in a costume that raised great hilarity. Amelia Bloomer had just been popularizing her new mode of dress for women, and Ball appeared in knee-length skirt with bloomers beneath. Under the skirt he was wearing several petticoats gathered at the waist to create an impression of obesity, or perhaps of pregnancy. To make it all the more bizarre, he had blackened his face.

The dance was proceeding with Gallic gaiety, late into the night. About one o'clock the half-drunken Duane, accompanied by Cole, shouldered his way past the doorkeeper, and entered the ballroom. Though it was a private party, no one was prepared to ask him to leave. Duane and Cole went across to the bar, and ordered drinks.

As word spread about, a chill fell over the festivities. Couples began to leave the floor, until few were left. Ball, however, pluckily remained among those who continued dancing.

Soon Duane sent Cole to deliver an insulting message, again threatening Ball for having voted adversely on the jury. The little man in the bloomers passed it off as best he could, and continued to dance.

Duane himself then went across, menacingly, to Ball, who was dancing a quadrille.

Not restrained by the presence of ladies, Duane called out, "I want to see you now, you damned son-of-a-bitch!"

Ball said that he would see him at the proper time and place. Duane blurted, "You god-damned son-of-a-bitch, I want to kill you."

Everyone in San Francisco knew that such words from "Dutch Charlie" could not be taken lightly. Standing there in his ridiculous costume, Ball kept his nerve, and answered, "That is easily done, for I am unarmed."

The words were shrewdly chosen. If a man like Duane stood by any code at all, it would have been that he should not shoot a defenseless person.

Ball turned to go, and Duane swung on him with a tremendous open-handed stroke. Ball went to the floor. As he was rising on one arm, Duane kicked him heavily and viciously just below the heart.

Ball collapsed into unconsciousness. In the confusion that followed, his friends carried him to his room. A physician pronounced him to be probably dying.

The city police took Duane in charge. If he was sober enough to know anything, he accepted them as his best friends. As yet, the Committee had never taken a prisoner from the police. In their hands, Duane would be tried by the regular courts, and he could have every expectation of escaping punishment — things being as they were with California "justice," especially for one who could be called Broderick's right-hand man.

The assault had occurred after the morning newspapers had gone to press, and word of it began to spread by word of mouth only after people appeared on the streets that Monday morning. The news was not generally known when the Executive Committee assembled for a regular meeting. So little excitement was in the air that only six members of the Committee were present — among them, Payran and Ryckman. Immediately upon calling the meeting to order, Payran announced (it was apparently still news to some of those present) "that a member of this Committee had been assaulted with intent to kill by one Charles Duane." Action was then taken, "*Resolved* that an order be issued for the arrest of the said Charles Duane."

In all probability the men thus voting were ignorant that Duane was already in custody. Even though anger must have blazed out at the news, a small meeting of the Executive Committee would not have dared to order that a prisoner should be taken from the police.

The Committee then continued with the examinations, and word soon was brought that Duane was actually in the jail. Toward noon the Committee adjourned to meet again at seven that evening.

Throughout the day report and rumor circulated, and angry tempers flared up. The members of the French colony were particularly incensed. With them joined the men of the Committee, and Ball's numerous personal friends. In many ways the situation was tenser than it had ever been before. Not only was this a flagrant example of lawlessness by a notorious offender, but it was also marked by exceptional brutality. The sense of fair play was outraged because a big man had attacked a small man. The sense of chivalry was outraged that the assault had been perpetrated in the presence of ladies. Moreover, this might well be a deliberate attempt to bait and to intimidate the members of the Committee. Undoubtedly many of them were eagerly expecting the stroke of the bell, which would mean that they would march, hundreds strong, to take the prisoner from the jail and hang him.

By coincidence, the *Herald* published that morning a long letter from the much respected minister Flavel S. Mines, which he had originally addressed to the members of the Committee. Mines urged that "wisdom and moderation" might continue to guide the Committee in their "difficult and self-imposed task." But he was almost inflammatory in his characterization of the

San Francisco judiciary — "profane and profligate, obscene and drunken ministers of law."

With so much excitement in the air, the meeting of the Executive Committee that evening was one of the largest ever recorded, no fewer than sixteen being present. Even the terse record of the minutes indicates a tense and stormy meeting, with the proponents of moderation battling those who demanded quick and violent action.

The old case of Lewis was hotly argued. He had been arrested for arson on June 2, and his case had had much to do with the original formation of the Committee. Now, after much postponement, he was being tried. A motion was made, "that in Case of Lewis being found Guilty of Arson, that the Executive Committee recommend to the Genl. committee to take possession of the said Lewis & hang him." The motion, which could have meant direct conflict with the authorities, was tabled. Later it was taken from the table, and passed, and a sub-committee of three was appointed "to superintend the trial of Lewis."

With the radicals now in control, it was further resolved "that we recommend the Genl. Committee now in room proceed to the Court House, and remain there until the case of Lewis was disposed of — and if necessary to arrest and take Lewis and dispose of him as the People may direct." Probably the last resolution was never put into effect. The number of members present in the outer room may not have been sufficient to make such action practical.

But the Executive Committee could not stop with the case of Lewis. With regard to the Ball-Duane case, they were, indeed, rather moderate, perhaps influenced by the fact that Ball now showed signs of recovery. The resolution read

> Whereas our Brother — Frank Ball — has been violently assaulted by one Chas. Duane, alias Dutch Charley, who is now in Custody of the Civil Authorities, we hereby pledge ourselves that justice shall be meted out to said Chas. Duane.

Such wording suggested that the regular courts might do justice. The use of "brother" is interesting as one of the many indications that the Committee was coming to be considered in terms of a fraternal organization.

Still another radical resolution showed how the assaults upon Ball had exacerbated feelings, and brought the situation very close to a violent outbreak:

> *Resolved* that the Executive Committee recommend that if any Judge or Magistrate or other Administrator of the Laws can be detected in corruption or Mal-administration of their duties, they shall be arrested by this Committee, and hanged, as an example to those who have asked and received office at the hands of the People.

In support of this resolution the members of the Committee could cite the counsel and advice of the governor, for this action was just what he had recommended in his conversation, a week earlier, and the unusual word "mal-administration" was probably his. The spirit of the governor, indeed, may have hovered over this meeting rather closely. On this very day, he was writing a proclamation or open letter "to the people of the state of California," dating it from the Executive Department at Vallejo. The members of the Executive Committee may well have known that he was thus writing, and they may even have thought that the governor would make the same position which he had assumed with them in private, and might even use the same strong language.

Night thus fell with the Committee violently aroused, and the more militant faction in control. Dutch Charlie's drunken brutality had brought the city again to the brink of armed conflict.

# CHAPTER 21

# THE GOVERNOR AND THE VIGILANCE COMMITTEE

*(July 22–August 11)*

IN THE MORNING came the announcement that Ball's condition was improved. The tension grew less. . . .

By this time, the Committee had arrived at the situation which must be apparently reached, sooner or later, by every organization which has initiated a movement of revolutionary implications — and, indeed, perhaps by every organization initiating a movement of any kind. In short, the Committee had developed radical and conservative wings.

The radicals believed that the Committee should maintain, and even intensify its activities. Not only should it continue to hound the Sydney men, but also it should not shrink from direct conflict with the authorities. The logical end of such a movement would be revolution, in which the government of the city, and even of the state, would be taken over and then reconstituted.

The conservatives, on the contrary, considered that the work of the Committee was largely accomplished. They pointed to a city from which robbery and arson had almost vanished. They were looking for ways by which to diminish or end operations, and to allow the now chastened and re-activated authorities to take over.

Excitement and outbreaks of crime or violence, such as Duane's attack upon Ball, would tend to arouse and to strengthen the radicals. So would threats and active opposition from the Law-and-Order party.

Mere dullness would help the conservatives. So would any sign of collaboration from the legal authorities, and any indication that the administration of justice was improving.

Working strongly in favor of the conservatives, also, was the mere amount day-to-day labor which was proving to be necessary. A few members, such as Payran, Ryckman, and Bluxome, were willing to work full-time. But most men were not. Coleman had almost given up attendance at meetings of the Executive Committee since the hanging of Stuart. Many of the rank-and-file had grown slack. The members were evincing no enthusiasm about subscribing to the fund to complete the jail.

A good politician, either in the Committee or outside of it, could realize what was happening. Broderick was such a one, and his withdrawal of active opposition may have been the result of his realization that by vigorously opposing the Committee, he was inevitably strengthening it. Governor McDougal may have been another who sensed the situation, though his vacillating course during the summer gives little indication that he grasped anything very securely. In his conversation with the Executive Committee he had abetted the radicals. But his proclamation or open letter to the people of the state strengthened the hands of the conservatives.

This letter circulated in San Francisco on July 22. Anyone who had been thinking that the governor would say publicly what he had said privately was disappointed. The letter was chiefly remarkable for mildness of tone. One newspaper characterized it, "harmless as a bread-pill." The Law-and-Order party could seize upon the governor's words as supporting them and as opposing the Committee. Technically, they were right. The governor put himself and the state administration — and, by implication, the Democratic Party — on record as in favor of sustaining the laws. It was in the record, to be hauled out if needed.

At the same time, the members of the Committee, reading what the governor had to say, need not be alarmed. The mildness of the words suggested that he was merely making a statement *pro forma*. He did not (as Broderick had done) cry "midnight murderers," or (as the mayor had done) cite chapters in the criminal statutes, or (as Judge Campbell had done) suggest indictments for murder. By doing none of these things, he undercut the radicals.

But the conservatives, reading carefully, could see that the governor had strengthened them tremendously. In fact, he almost recognized the Committee, by noting the existence of extra-legal organizations in the state; then, instead of threatening them or calling upon them to disband, he advised them to act "in concert with the civil authorities, to detect, arrest, and punish criminals." As the result of the governor's admonition, the power shifted suddenly from the radicals to the conservatives.

On the evening of July 23 the Executive Committee (14 present) voted to hand over "to the constituted authorities for trial" the three chief prisoners, that is, James Burns, *alias* Jemmy-from-Town, Thomas Ainsworth, *alias* Tommy Roundhead, and George Adams. Thrown in for good measure was George Arthur, probably not a Sydney man, who had been recently picked up for burglary. The conservatives were thus showing themselves so ready to take the governor's word and cooperate with the authorities that they were cleaning out the detention-room.

Though there is no evidence of a split vote in the Executive Committee, there may have been some opposition. In any case, the decision about the prisoners was not put into effect, but was referred to a special meeting of the general Committee, held that same evening.

The larger meeting, for once failing to approve the proposals of the Executive Committee, refused to give Adams up. The decision was not an unreasonable one. By renouncing all its important prisoners, the Committee would virtually have been voting itself out of existence, and there would have been danger that the situation would have reverted to what it had been in early June. By retaining Adams, the Committee not only placated its own more radical element, but also made clear to the community in general that it still remained active, and was testing out how well the courts could now function. As the *Herald* stated it, "Now we shall see what the courts will do."

The new policy of cooperation proved to be popular, and allayed many apprehensions among the citizens generally, again in the words of the *Herald:*

> This course meets, as far as we have ascertained, with universal approbation, and many who were before lukewarm in their support of the Committee are now earnest in their commendations. Their opponents too have been completely disarmed, and are compelled to acknowledge the very great assistance that such a body so acting may render to the regularly constituted authorities.

The immediate result of the surrender of the prisoners was highly encouraging. The Grand Jury, after only a few hours' deliberation, found an indictment against Jemmy-from-Town, and set his trial for the succeeding day.

As such action would indicate, the Grand Jury remained one of the bright spots. Its final report excoriated the judges for failure to enforce the laws, and the people for failing to elect good officials. In its attitude to the Committee the report was ambiguous. It admitted that certain actions were "unlawful and in violation of the fundamental law of the land." But it characterized the vigilantes as "a large portion of our best and most worthy citizens," who had acted "at a great personal sacrifice to themselves," and stated, "To them we are indebted for much valuable information and many important witnesses."

While deploring certain incidents, the Grand Jury declared
that the vigilantes had acted with "no personal or private mal-
ice," and "for the best interests of the whole." It finally took
no action to indict any member of the Committee and dismissed the whole matter "as among those peculiar results of
circumstances that sometimes startle communities." . . .

Toward the end of July, however, the immediate interest cen-
tered upon the trial of Duane, for "assault with intent to kill."
Ball had now recovered sufficiently to be able to appear as a
witness.

The lawyers for the defense attempted the expedients which
might be expected when their client was a man so closely con-
nected with the political machine, and even (as his avowal of
friendship with Jenkins would indicate) had a certain linkage
with the criminal world. The case was being tried, however,
before Judge Campbell, and he allowed no easing of the rules in
favor of Duane. On the other hand, with his approval, no member of the Committee was allowed to sit on the jury. This ex-
clusion resulted in some adverse commentary in the press, to
the effect that the authorities were acting inconsistently. On
the one hand, they asked for cooperation from the Committee
and accepted the prisoners. On the other hand, they refused
to cooperate with the members of the Committee, by excluding
them from the jury. Nevertheless, the vigilantes in general
were glad that Judge Campbell was conducting the trial, since
they respected his integrity.

The feeling in the courtroom was intensely against Duane.
The presence of some members of the Committee among the
spectators had little effect upon the situation, since the ordinary citizen was already much angered by Duane's brutality.

Witnesses soon established the fact of the assault. Doubt remained only as to the intent to kill. On the side of the prosecution could be cited Duane's own threats to kill Ball, and the
very presence in the courtroom of his huge body could not be

without its effect. On the other hand, the defense could establish that Duane had used no specifically lethal weapon.

As the trial progressed, the perturbation throughout the city grew more intense. Almost everyone not only believed in Duane's guilt, but also hated and feared him. Yet everyone knew that in other flagrant cases juries had been bought, or had been confused by legal trickery, or else that corrupt judges had been able to interfere with the course of justice.

There was intense anxiety as to what might happen in the case of an acquittal. The Committee, it was feared, would move to seize the prisoner, and the result would be a full-fledged battle. There was also the possibility that a mob might rise, and be more successful than its predecessors had been.

At 10 P.M. on July 25, the jury withdrew. It remained out through the night, and all through the succeeding day, while tension in the city increased hourly. Finally, at 6 P.M., the jury returned, and its foreman announced a verdict of guilty with a recommendation of leniency.

The mention of leniency brought a hiss from the spectators, but order was quickly restored. The recommendation was later revealed to have resulted from a compromise. Certain jurors, very likely planted by the defense, had held out against conviction on the grounds that "intent to kill" had not been established. They agreed to vote for a conviction if the stipulation for leniency should be added.

Duane's lawyers appealed the verdict, on the grounds that the intense feeling against Duane in the courtroom had reached the jury. Judge Campbell quashed the appeal, declaring that the very nature of the crime was such as to arouse intense feeling. To reject the verdict would be to give automatic protection to every criminal whose acts had been particularly repulsive.

Because of the recommendation for leniency, Campbell imposed the minimum sentence, one year's imprisonment. The

attorneys declared their intention of appealing the case to the
state Supreme Court.

Victory, for the moment at least, rested with justice. It
rested also with the Committee, which in this case had whole-
heartedly supported the court. The verdict also seemed to
vindicate the governor's policy of cooperation. The light sentence might be regrettable, but none the less there was a real
victory. Even Broderick's shoulder-striker was no longer to be
considered above the law.

Two days after the conviction of Duane, there was still another encouragement. James Burns, the notorious Jemmy-from-
Town, was found guilty, and given a heavy prison sentence.
Such a decision still further strengthened the cause of the conservatives in the Committee.

Working in the opposite direction, however, was the discharge of Kay on August 1. That notoriously slippery character,
though his guilt was generally conceded, proved too much for
the processes of the law, and was allowed to go for want of specific evidence.

In its new role of cooperating with the law, the Committee
had renounced, in specific cases, its practice of holding trials
and inflicting punishment. But "cooperation" also seemed to
demand that the Committee should still arrest suspected criminals, and examine them, in the hope that further miscreants
might thus be revealed. On July 29 Robert McKenzie was
taken. He was a Sydney man, who had several times been
mentioned in Stuart's confession. On the same day the Executive Committee issued an order for the arrest of J. J. Arrentrue,
who resembled Kay in having combined public office with
private crime. On July 31 the same committee issued an order for the arrest of David Earl, who had been an active member of the Committee itself, until his criminal record had gradually been revealed, and he had been expelled.

The detention-room, which had almost been cleaned out on

July 23, was thus well-filled again. It housed Adams, McKenzie, Arrentrue, and Earl. Of lesser note was William Hays, who had first been held as a witness, but had gradually been revealed as being himself an actively practicing thief. Finally, there were a number of Sydney men who had been removed from one ship or another, and were being held until they could be sent back.

Even during these comparatively quiet days the Executive Committee met frequently. Payran and Ryckman continued to exercise their talents as examiners. Other members visited ships that arrived from Australia. . . .

When any organization has passed its apogee and has entered its later middle age, it is likely to display a certain self-consciousness, and an increased concern over details of procedure. The members of the Committee had signed, and had continued to sign, a constitution so hastily written that it contained blanks, and these blanks were never filled in. But, on the very day when the Committee voted to hand the three prisoners over to the authorities, it also adopted an elaborate new set of by-laws, largely superseding the stipulations of the original constitution. Because of the confusion resulting from Brannan's interference in the case of Dab, the new regulations spelled out the duties and responsibilities of the sergeant-at-arms and of the chief of police. A semi-military organization was adopted, the members being divided into companies of twenty men, each of these to elect its own officers. The same meeting resolved "that no Spirituous Liquors shall be introduced into the quarters of the Committee of Vigilance on any account whatever," with the stipulation that hot coffee should be supplied to the guard on duty, when a stimulant was judged necessary. A refreshment room was established.

As such legislation would indicate, the Committee was facing what we might call housekeeping problems. In spite of the serious nature of their undertaking, numbers of young men could not be thrown together and often placed on duty in the same room without tending to introduce the amenities of a social club or a fraternal lodge. Except for a few fanatics like Ryckman, the members of the Committee were social drinkers. Many of them would have expected to bring a bottle along, to while away the slow hours of guard duty. Some of them would have been heavy drinkers, and a few (Brannan and Payran are known examples) sometimes drank more than they could conveniently carry. Vouchers signed before July 23 show that the Committee officially purchased brandy on several occasions. If the amounts sometimes seem excessive, we must remember that the liquor may have been distributed among a large number of people, or may have been used as a ration over a considerable period of time. The members of the Executive Committee undoubtedly found uses for liquor other than drinking it themselves. It could have served to aid in loosening the tongues of prisoners being examined. "Brandy, gin, &c." to the total of $40 along with $18 worth of cigars, were noted as "furnished on board Ship *Adirondack.*" These commodities, in part at least, we may consider to have served as sweeteners to ensure the cooperation of the officers of that ship.

No reminiscence, unfortunately, presents us with any details of the life that went on within the rooms. Ryckman once made the comparison to a Masonic lodge. Though he was thinking particularly of the secrecy and the use of a pass-word, the resemblance undoubtedly went farther than that.

Various vouchers indicate that the rooms were funished with tables and benches, and also with three dozen chairs. Two office chairs with cushions (at $6 each) may have served for the greater comfort and dignity of president and secretary. Twenty-four single straw mattresses and pillows (total cost $60) and also twelve pairs of blue blankets, were presumably for the prisoners, but the members of the guard, on a shift off, might also have made use of them. Twenty-four oil lamps would

seem to have provided almost brilliant illumination. The purchase of two whisk brooms suggests a care for personal appearance, either of the prisoners or of the members. Seventy yards
of muslin, fifteen rolls of paper, and 60¢ worth of tacks were
used to make the "bare lofts" more presentable by the covering of the walls and the insertion of a false ceiling. In addition,
twenty-five dollars for the papering of a room and three dollars
for "Gilt Molding for windows &c." indicate that the members
retained some appreciation for the luxuries of life.

The members of the Executive Committee, in their inner
sanctum, always had so much business on hand that they had
little time for social relaxation. In the large outer room,
however, there must have been an opportunity for much good
conversation, and we must regret that no Boswell was there to
record it. You might have heard stories of the Mexican War,
experiences in crossing the plains and mountains and on the
Cape Horn voyage, anecdotes of Indian fights, or of rich strikes
in the mining-camps. You would have heard from the pre-
Forty-Niners their tales of what California was like "in the old
days," as you listened to Brannan and Bluxome, or "Don
Pedro" Carrillo, to Andy Grayson (who had crossed in '46, the
year of the Donner Party) and to Jake Snyder, (who had crossed
even a year earlier). Bill Howard remembered California
since '39. Or, if you were tired of such reminiscences, you
might get a good story out of any of a dozen ship-captains.

Only one non-member would ordinarily have been there, and
that was George Pfiester, the porter. George's duties were to
keep the place swept out and perform odd jobs. He was paid
the very low wages of ten dollars a week, but doubtless made it
up on tips, when he ran errands and otherwise performed services for individual members.

During this period, again as might be expected, there was a
certain autumnal atmosphere. Sentiment appeared. The partners George H. Plum, #240, and Charles M. Warner, #241,

presented a banner. The general Committee thereupon re-solved that the banner "be accepted and a vote of thanks be tendered to the gent for the same."

Much more significant, for public relations, was the presenta-tion of a banner on August 9. This one was the gift of the ladies of Trinity Parish and came inscribed "as a testimonial of their approbation." It was of blue satin, seven by five feet. Ap-propriate inscriptions were surrounded by "a gorgeous border of oak, olive and fig leaves, emblematic of strength, peace and plenty." On the behalf of the ladies, Benjamin S. Brooks (not a member) presented the banner "in a neat and pertinent speech."

Sentiment, also, attended the departure of Captain Wakeman on July 31. Having been appointed "as commander of the good ship Independence," he was leaving on a voyage to Panama. Without specifying that he had acted as hangman, the Execu-tive Committee voted him their thanks "for the many and very important services rendered." Eleven members of that committee signed the letter, which concluded by wishing the stalwart captain "a long and prosperous life and in the end a safe anchorage in the haven of eternal rest."

In this letter a specific reference to the fact that membership in the Committee was not lost "by reason of water" was of more significance than might seem at first. Fluidity of movement was a characteristic of California life of the time. Scarcely a week had passed since the organization of the Committee without a member submitting his resignation, because he was leaving the city. Others probably left without bothering to inform the Committee. These resignations or defections created a prob-lem. By resigning or withdrawing, a member might seem to slough off his responsibility. Eventually, those remaining as members might be so few that the authorities could bring in-dictments against them for murder, as Judge Campbell had sug-gested might occur. In the end, the Executive Committee adopted as a general principle, "Once a member, always a member." An individual leaving the city was granted indefinite leave of absence, with remission of dues, but still remained on the roll.

Other problems of housekeeping involved the unpopularity of the sergeant-at-arms, McDuffee, and boisterous and unseemly conduct at meetings. On the whole, however, the lack of internal troubles is noteworthy. The only serious difficulty was that which arose upon the evening when Brannan released Dab. Since the members were chiefly men in their twenties, high-spirited and often reckless, given to heavy drinking, the lack of quarrels speaks well for the leaders, who must have been able to impress the members with a sense of the extreme seriousness of the work which they were attempting. . . .

The new policy of cooperation, and the continuing domination of the conservatives, was put to a new test on August 5 and 6. On the former day the Executive Committee considered the disposal of four prisoners — Adams, Arrentrue, Hays, and Earl. General agreement was soon reached that Earl should be retained for further examination, that Hays should be "sent out of the Country never to return," and that Arrentrue should be handed over to the authorities for trial. As regards Adams, however, the members of the Executive Committee were unable to agree, and — for the first time, apparently — had a divided vote. Of the twelve present, six voted to hand Adams over, and six voted against that motion. The solution was to refer the case to the general Committee, without comment. Such an action, as the members of the Executive Committee must have realized, was unfortunate. In the larger meeting there would be much chance for demagoguery, and for the decisive action of passion rather than of reason. Significantly, indeed, Brannan turned up at this meeting, and took an active part in it, though he had paid little attention in the Committee in the past few weeks.

The general meeting was held on that same evening of August 5. Frederick Woodworth, as temporary chairman, presided with skill. First the minutes of the previous meeting were presented and approved, and then the whole testimony in the case of Adams was read aloud. Such a lengthy preamble allowed passions to subside. Next the *pro forma* votes were taken as to the three prisoners about whom there was general agreement. Finally, the motion was put, "That Adams be handed over to Civil Authorities." No record remains of the arguments then presented. At last, the vote was put, and the motion was lost. Finally, Brannan arose, and offered a resolution so simply worded that its real meaning might easily be missed. He moved, "That we now adjourn to meet tomorrow at 10 o'clock to meet at the sound of two bells." The deeper significance lay in the fact that the stroke on the bell indicated an emergency meeting, and that it had been used to call the members together on the occasions which had resulted in the hangings of Jenkins and Stuart.

Apparently the arguments in the meeting had been such as to make a vote not to surrender Adams to be a vote to hang him. The radicals had won a victory, and such men as Brannan considered that the next morning's gathering would be rather for action than for deliberation.

Rumor of what had happened spread around the city that same evening. In the morning, little knots of talkers on the street were excitedly discussing the possibility of another "excitement," making large predictions that Adams was to be hanged, and speculating on the possibility of a clash between the Committee and the police. No one was at all surprised when the bell began to toll the well-known signal. Hundreds of people hurried off to stand in front of the rooms. These sensation-hunters even beat the members of the Committee, since the latter preferred to move with some degree of deliberation, as befitted their responsibility. A good deal of commotion was also observed among the city authorities and the police. As the *Herald* noted, "A noted law and order supporter [doubtless, Broderick] was seen tearing through the city in search of the Mayor, and to the uninitiated, everything seemed to betoken a scene of fearful excitement."

In a short time, however, a spokesman for the Committee appeared at the front of the building, and announced to the assembled people that nothing of importance was to be done. Many people, taking his word for it, went about their business. Others remained on the spot, suspecting a ruse. These expectations were soon dampened, when the members of the Committee began to leave the building, as if after an adjournment.

Then McDuffee emerged with Adams in custody. Accompanying the two was a deputy sheriff. McDuffee and the deputy began to escort their prisoner through the streets, some members of the Committee and a large number of people following along. Gaining new recruits at each street corner, the crowd increased as it moved along, and again rumor blazed up that Adams was to be hanged. In the end, however, as the presence of the deputy should have made clear, the prisoner was merely delivered to the authorities at the jail.

As to the details of what had happened in the meeting, no record exists. Obviously, aided by an overnight cooling-off period, the moderates had been able to rally, and to regain control.

The delivery of Adams and Arrentrue, left the detention-room badly depleted again. Earl had been sentenced and was only awaiting an opportunity to leave the city. No one cared much about Hays. The Sydney ducks who were awaiting shipment to Australia called for no action. Only McKenzie was to be considered a prisoner of importance.

The surrender of Adams clinched the opinions of a great many people that the Committee was through. On August 8, two days later, the *Herald* even thought it necessary to publish an editorial that the Committee had not dissolved and still had much work to do. (The *Herald,* however, had generally been even more pro-Committee than the Committee itself was.)

Moreover, the editor of the *Herald* notwithstanding, several incidents in the next few days tended to confirm the popular opinion. For instance, Coleman resigned from the Executive Committee. He had not, indeed, been very active of late, but he was not a man to resign while the heat was on. His resignation carried with it a strong suggestion that the emergency had passed.

Also, in the next day or two, the Executive Committee faced the financial straitness that goes with declining interest. They proposed to reduce the salary of the sergeant-at-arms (a petty economy), and to rent new, and cheaper, headquarters. Smaller headquarters would mean that there was no detention-room, and an extraordinary resolution was passed that Hays and McKenzie should be sent aboard the naval vessel *Vincennes* for detention. That such a procedure could even be seriously proposed indicates that a remarkably friendly relationship existed between the Navy and the Committee. Apparently the federal officers, as the cooperation of the Revenue Service had shown already, were more inclined to act with the Committee than were the local authorities. Shortly after this time two officers of the *Vincennes* joined the Committee and for identification boldly signed themselves "U. S. Navy."

This suggestion of the transfer of the prisoners to a vessel pointed to the approaching inactivity or even dissolution of the Committee as the result of the chain of events inaugurated by the governor's open letter. But the decision in the case of Adams had been a close thing. Even a small accident or incident might, in such a situation of force and counter-force, be enough to shift the balance of power again.

# CHAPTER 22

# ARREST OF WHITTAKER

*(August 11–August 19, 9 P.M.)*

EARLY ON THE morning of August 11 the small coastal steamer *Ohio* tied up at Long Wharf. On board was Sheriff V. W. Hearne, of Santa Barbara; with him, a prisoner. The prisoner was the much-wanted Sam Whittaker.

More than a month previously, Stuart and Hetherington had implicated Whittaker. The Executive Committee had at once recognized his importance as a leader of the most aggressive gang of Sydney men, and had attempted to get hold of him. In fact, the pursuit was so vigorous that the Committee ran up a bill of $1500 in the process.

But Whittaker was no man's fool. While the search for him was hottest, he lay in hiding near Sacramento. He resumed contact with Mrs. Hogan, but so secretly that the Committee got no wind of it. The two of them agreed to make their ways, separately, to San Diego, five hundred miles to the south. Once at that port, they could hope to be smuggled aboard some vessel, and thus to escape from California.

Toward the end of July, Mrs. Hogan slipped quietly out of San Francisco, and eventually reached San Diego. But Whittaker had the bad luck to be recognized in Santa Barbara. Two citizens swore affidavits against him, and he was arrested.

Arrived at San Francisco, Sheriff Hearne at once set out to find Sheriff Hays, to deliver the prisoner. He left Whittaker, manacled, on board the *Ohio*. At this point enters an influence that may be called sheer accident.

Not knowing where to find Hays, Hearne blundered into the office of the bankers, Palmer, Cook, and Co. He talked to Joseph C. Palmer, and not only inquired for the sheriff's office, but gossiped about who his prisoner was. He then went on.

Palmer was not a member of the Committee, but was a sympathizer. In the same building was the office of J. C. L. Wadsworth, with whom Palmer was on friendly terms. Wadsworth was a member of the Executive Committee. Palmer immediately took him the news about Whittaker, and Wadsworth reacted at once.

He set out hurriedly toward Long Wharf, probably without any precise plan of action. On his way, he met James F. Curtis, also a member of the Executive Committee. The two decided to make an attempt at seizing the prisoner. There is no reason to think that either of the men was particularly a radical. Probably they reacted quickly, without much thought.

If they had stopped to think, they might well have done nothing. The policy of the Committee, during the last few weeks, had been to let the courts take over. Moreover, throughout its activities, the Committee had avoided direct conflict with the authorities, and had never taken a prisoner from the custody of the police or the sheriff.

Wadsworth and Curtis boarded the steamer. Though Hearne had brought a deputy along, Whittaker seems to have been left in charge of the captain. Wadsworth and Curtis demanded their man. Such was the prestige of the Committee that the captain (he may even have been a member) handed the prisoner over.

This action, which some members of the Executive Committee must have thought to be ill-advised, changed the situation. Whittaker was the great prize, and with him in custody the cause of the radicals was greatly strengthened. Besides, by this time there were signs that the policy of cooperation was not working out very well. Kay had escaped punishment. The course of justice against several other men was proceeding at a disappointingly slow pace. Even the moderates may have been thinking that the Committee should again assert itself.

The seizure of Whittaker, radical though it was in theory, created no excitement. After all, the Committee had of late been acting almost as an arm of the law. It had become an agency for the investigation of crime, much more skilled than anything the police could offer. People might think that the Committee had seized Whittaker to examine him, and then to pass him on to the authorities.

The only protest came from Sheriff Hearne himself, and this was in the form of a respectfully written letter, requesting that he be paid $150 for his expenses. The Committee (as a group of merchants, they never threw their money around recklessly) cut the bill to $135, and then paid it. That very evening, the Executive Committee met at half past six, and the first minute stands, "The examination of Sam Whittaker continued up to ten o'clock." The committee also noted the arrest of Mrs. Hogan, who had got back from her trip to San Diego.

The attention of the Executive Committee now concentrated upon McKenzie and Whittaker. The two offered a great contrast, the one with the other, and even their mutual peril probably did not engender any friendship or sense of community of interest. McKenzie, probably, and Whittaker, certainly, were *aliases*, but the real names were never publicly revealed.

McKenzie was English, or possibly Irish. He never admitted to having been in Australia, and there is no special reason to think that he had been. He gave his age as twenty-six and stated that he had left England as a child and had lived in New Orleans until 1849. In California he had associated with the Sydney men, and he had been implicated in Stuart's confession.

As a prisoner, McKenzie succeeded in irritating his captors

considerably. Even for Jenkins they had displayed a certain admiration, respecting his physique and his courage. But Ryckman could characterize McKenzie only as "a dirty little scrub . . . a monstrous, cowardly wretch." Part of this irritation arose from the fact that even Payran and Ryckman, with all their skill, could not break McKenzie down and obtain an easy confession. He merely cursed them and kept his own counsel. On one day the whole entry concerning him was, "Prisoner being obstinate in refusing to answer was remanded."

Obviously, McKenzie failed to strike a golden mean. By refusing to talk, he managed to avoid giving information which could be used against him. But by his bad manners and foul tongue he aroused such antipathy that any evidence against him which could be collected from other sources was certain to be used stringently.

Whittaker made a very different impression. He was more like Stuart than like any of the others — highly intelligent, pleasant in appearance and manner. Ryckman admired him, writing, "Whittaker was as brave as a little Caesar."

Naturally, Whittaker did not immediately break out with a full confession of his wrong-doing. There was even a motion to put him on bread and water, until he should decide to talk. This motion was not carried, and there is, indeed, no evidence that the Committee ever resorted to third-degree methods.

Ryckman, in his reminiscences of many years later, described the examination of Whittaker in language which was undoubtedly highly condensed, but which probably represents essential truth.

Whittaker was brought into the Executive Committee's rooms. . . . Payran was president of the Executive Committee at that time, and commenced the examination. He had been drinking evidently, and was a little tight. . . . At any rate, he could get nothing from the prisoner but "No," "No." "No." He could not get any confession or proof against the man. I took Payran aside, and said, "That is no way to examine that man. You cannot intimidate him; he is a strong-willed, fearless, iron man. That is not the way the Committee ought to work."

Payran, who had been inclined to brow-beat the prisoner, thereupon withdrew. Ryckman took over. With almost diabolical skill he proceeded to insinuate himself into the prisoner's confidence.

I sat down, and said, "Whittaker, what is your nationality?"
"I am an Englishman," said he.
"Have you any father?"
"Yes."
"Any mother?"
"Yes."
"Any sister?'
"Yes, two sisters."
I began to talk to him. Said I, "Whittaker, what must be the feeling of your father and mother at your course here in a foreign land, when they learn that you have been arrested here for infamous crimes, as you have? What will your sisters think and feel, when they know how you have disgraced yourself and them? Thus reflect what sorrow and misery you have brought upon the family by your base and unmanly conduct."

By some swift insight, Ryckman had sensed that the prisoner would be susceptible to a sentimental approach. Whittaker became deeply affected, and finally tears rolled down his cheeks. He declared, in Ryckman's words, "I have been very bad, and I want to make a confession."

Immediately Ryckman became the avenging angel, holding out no hope of sentiment to be returned for sentiment.

I said, "Don't make any confession to me. Listen to me. Don't make any confession to me with the expectation that it

will weigh anything in my mind in the way of relieving you
from punishment, if you prove to be guilty. I don't know anybody in the discharge of my duty. I will leave you, and I will
come back in an hour." I gave him a mug of ale, as he was an
Englishman, and left him.

The devious Ryckman, wrapping his cloak of righteousness
around him, thereupon withdrew to a vantage point, where he
could observe the prisoner through a peephole. He saw that in
spite of the mug of ale Whittaker was much disturbed and in
great agony of mind.

After a while [the reminiscence continues] the doorkeeper
came and said, "Whittaker says he must see you."
I went in and said, "What is the matter, Whittaker?"
"Mr. Ryckman," he said, "you are the first man that has ever
touched my heart. The world has hunted me as if I were a
monster, with bloodhounds, figuratively, and you are the only
man who has treated me like a human being. I must make a
confession to you. If I don't, I shall burst."

This incident occurred probably on August 12, the day after
Whittaker's seizure by the Committee. He thereupon began a
confession which seemed to assure him, as he had suggested it
would, an unburdening of his soul. He continued to confess for
several days, not only revealing his own misdeeds, but also
implicating numerous confederates, and even mentioning
names from hearsay.

During these days an amazing relationship, as of father and
son, developed between Whittaker and the much older Ryckman. Whittaker became dependent upon Ryckman's approbation. On the other side, Ryckman never for a moment relaxed
from the office of rigorous examiner, and potential executioner,
but he seems also to have been deeply moved and to have developed a strong affection for the younger man whose need

for a counseling father had become so overwhelming. . . .
During this period, as always, the Executive Committee had
to busy itself with many miscellaneous matters. Ships arrived
from Australia, and their passengers had to be winnowed. In
a flurry over lack of confidence, nine members of the Executive
Committee (including Payran, Ryckman, and Bluxome) submitted their resignations in a long letter. Probably they had no
expectation that their resignations would be accepted. Possibly,
even, the action was a ruse. At this time the old Metcalf-
Argenti case had come up for trial, and some of these nine
members were being summoned as witnesses. Since they had
just resigned, they were able, without perjury, to express great
ignorance on many points. Payran testified that the Committee had no secretary — true enough, since Bluxome had just
resigned.

At this time, also, as the quick result of Whittaker's confession, the Committee was able to vary its monotonous succession
of English criminals by picking up a Polish Jew whose name
was probably Aaron Ginsberg, though it stands in the record
as anything from Gainesborough to Gaenisborg. True to the
tradition, he was (like Fagan in *Oliver Twist*) acting as a re-
ceiver of stolen goods, and not as a burglar or highwayman.

There was also, this week, a possibly sinister entry in the
petty cash records, when $13.50 was expended for ammuni-
tion.

The case of the now-notorious Mrs. Hogan also demanded
some consideration. Like Stuart, Whittaker had done his best
to shield her. His statement had been, only, "Mrs. Hogan, to
do her justice, I might say that she done all in her power to
break up my associations, and to lead a different life."

"The said Mary" as the records sometimes record her, was
certainly in a dubious position. She had associated with many
of the most notorious convicts, and her boarding house had
been their principal rendezvous. If she had not actively partic-

ipated in crime, she had certainly been an accomplice both
before and after the fact. She had, also, slept with both Whittaker and Stuart, and perhaps others. But that was beside the
point, as far as the Committee was concerned.

On the whole, she made not too bad an impression both
upon the gentlemen of the Committee and the gentlemen of
the press. Some of the ladies of San Francisco became interes-
ested in her case, and declared romantically that she was
guilty only of loving a bad man. (The use of the singular in
this instance may be questioned.)

How the Committee managed to keep her under arrest without scandal is nowhere stated in the record. Doubtless they
confined her in some private room, enlisting the aid of some
member's wife or "woman." Finally, the Executive Committee
"allowed the said Mary to go at large, subject to our order
whenever she may be called for."

About noon on August 14, McKenzie broke down, and acknowledged his participation in two robberies. By the evening
of the same day, Whittaker had confessed voluminously, involv-
ing himself in a number of crimes.

The next day, the Executive Committee considered the evidence, and prepared two brief reports, to be submitted to the
general meeting. As to Whittaker, they declared that he stood
"implicated by Stuart and others, as being guilty of divers
offenses, whereby the safety of lives and property have been
endangered." The committee reported itself to be "of the
opinion that this is a case which can only be reached by this
committee," that is, a case which could not be submitted to the
courts with a reasonable chance of justice being done. The
report then recommended "the penalty of death."

The report upon McKenzie commented upon the prisoner's
troublesome character:

> Your Committee respectfully represent that they have had
> much difficulty with the Prisoner by reason of his obstinacy, in

his first examinations being guilty of lies and prevarication, whereby the patience of your Committee has been severely put to the test.

In its essence, however, the report was the same as that upon Whittaker, and it ended with the same recommendation. The day was Friday. As in the case of Stuart, the Executive Committee wished to conduct the execution with solemnity. Moreover, the week-end was intervening, and various members were being called as witnesses in the Metcalf-Argenti case. A general meeting on Saturday, therefore, took no final action. Instead, it resolved that another general meeting should be formally called by a notice in the newspapers. Since such a notice could not appear until Monday, the meeting was set for Tuesday evening, August 19. The Committee was thus taking its time, with full confidence in its own power, in order to create the maximum effect upon public opinion. . . .

If the members of the Committee had known what was occurring in the state capital at this very time, their confidence would have been shaken, and their deepest anger aroused. They would almost certainly have reacted violently.

With all the new interest in Whittaker, McKenzie, and Mrs. Hogan, the case of "Dutch Charlie" had receded into the background. The court had been commendably strict with him, and had finally refused him further bail. His lawyers' appeal to the state Supreme Court might well be refused.

But there was another possibility, which the lawyers regularly employed, and which was a useful and often successful last resort for the influential criminal. He could appeal to the governor for a pardon. McDougal was a noted pardoner.

He cannot have been happy when Duane's case was presented to him. McDougal himself must have found Duane's action somewhat repulsive. In addition, he knew the state of opinion in San Francisco, and elsewhere, about the case. By pardoning Duane, McDougal would make himself highly unpopular. Once out of office, McDougal would have to establish himself in a business. Most of the businessmen in California were in some committee of vigilance, or were highly sympathetic. To insult or outrage them all would not be an act of prudence.

Most important of all, from the point of view of any responsible governor, the pardon of Duane at this critical juncture might bring civil war and sudden revolution. Throughout the state the committees held the power. The pardon might be a final act which would push them to the final break.

On the other hand, not to pardon Duane was merely unthinkable. McDougal was only a creature of the Democratic political machine, and Duane was a useful wheel in the same machine. One of the tenets of any strong political organization has always been, "You must take care of the boys." Duane was very much one of the boys. Besides — and perhaps most important of all — Duane was a close associate of Broderick.

On Sunday, August 17, McDougal pardoned Duane. Though such a pardon was a public document, it was kept secret — good evidence that once known, it would outrage public opinion.

Because of the coincidence of timing, some may consider the pardoning of Duane to be a retort and a rebuff to the Committee for its abandonment of the policy of cooperation by its arrest and condemnation of Whittaker and McKenzie. But such an argument cannot be sustained. Duane had been tried and convicted in a regular court — we may say, one of McDougal's own courts. Duane's case was such a flagrant one that McDougal's act became a bare-faced insult to every judge and juryman in California.

From the point of view of the Committee, the governor's act represented the worst kind of a double-cross. In his conversation with the Executive Committee, McDougal had expressed sympathy and even offered cooperation. In his letter he had again proposed cooperation. The Committee, on this basis, had surrendered several prisoners, and was obviously preparing to cease its activities. Once the fact of the pardon became known, the Committee could have no feeling for the governor but enmity, hatred, and disgust.

Having signed the pardon, McDougal may have had some sense of relief. To this point, he had gone uncomfortably, carrying water on both shoulders. Now, at last, he was irretrievably committed to Law-and-Order. Moreover, he retained a certain advantage as long as the pardon remained secret. The Committee did not know that he was irrevocably their enemy.

The next day one of the papers reported that Duane had been seen on the streets of San Francisco. The Committee paid no attention, probably considering the report to be a mere rumor. Besides, the Committee was very busy with other matters. . . .

On August 18, the newspapers published the statements of Whittaker, McKenzie, and Mrs. Hogan. The last two expressed themselves briefly, and revealed little. But Whittaker's confession ran to more than ten thousand words, and bristled with names and incriminating facts.

The same papers carried the modest but significant notice:

Vigilance Committee — A punctual attendance of all members of the Vigilance Committee of San Francisco is requested on Tuesday evening, August 19th, at 7½ o'clock, as business of the utmost importance is to come before them. By order No. 67, Secretary.

The Committee met as thus scheduled, President Selim Woodworth in the chair. The total membership had now passed 650, and probably several hundred attended.

Some preliminary business was transacted. Then there was a blanket motion, "Reports of Ex Com all excepted [sic]." Only the writing of the wrong word suggests the tension of the moment, when the lives of two men hung on this single vote.

Another motion set the next meeting for eight o'clock the next morning. The approximate time of execution was thus determined.

There followed the usual motion, "That the final arrangements be left to the Ex Com."

Two somewhat unusual motions then passed, both of them made by Van Bokkelen, the chief of police. The first was, "That the Roll be called at the meeting on tomorrow morning." Apparently this was an attempt to establish responsibility, and to spot the shirkers.

Van Bokkelen's second motion was, "That all those persons who have not paid their dues be compelled to remain in the room as a guard tonight." Obviously the chief of police expected no trouble, or he would not have moved that the slackest members, probably against their own wishes, should stand the death-watch with him.

The brevity of the minutes suggest that the meeting itself was brief. Adjournment may have been as early as half past eight. Then the members scattered among their favorite saloons, and word soon began to spread through the city that something of importance would happen shortly after eight o'clock in the morning. . . .

That evening Governor McDougal was in the hotel at Benicia, a few miles from Vallejo. The town had connection with San Francisco by steamboat, and the run took about three hours.

The governor must have been suffering from acute anxiety, and not of the kind that either whiskey or brandy would easily alleviate. Because of his pardon of Duane he was now, in secret, the committed enemy of the vigilantes, but they were preparing what might well be considered their greatest triumph. Things seemed to be coming to the situation where if he did not get them, they would get him. His move should be to circumvent the Committee and render it harmless. Just how he could do so was not easy to determine. The Committee seemed to have things completely under control.

Biographical information on McDougal is scanty, but one would venture to think that the catalogue of his virtues would not be a long one. In this list, however, one would have to include physical courage. He had, we should remember, a good war-record. On this evening, also, he showed courage.

A boat was leaving for San Francisco. McDougal stepped aboard.

Probably he had little idea of what he was going to do. But, to do anything at all, he would have to be in San Francisco. He was acting according to a military adage of the day, "When uncertain, move toward the sound of the heaviest firing."

# CHAPTER 23

# THE RESCUE OF WHITTAKER
## AND McKENZIE

*(August 19, 9 P.M.–August 20, 4 A.M.)*

B Y THE TIME the steamboat bearing the governor was leaving the strait and meeting the heavier waves of the bay,
the death-watch at the Committee rooms was settling in for
the night. Van Bokkelen was in command, and he had made
his dispositions carefully. His guard comprised about thirty
men. It was divided into two watches, the men who had gone
on duty at nine o'clock to be relieved at midnight, and then to
take over again at three. During that three-hour interval, however, they would merely take what rest they might, not leave
the room or undress.

In addition to the guard, half-a-dozen members of the Executive Committee were there, including its president, Payran,
and its secretary, Bluxome. That committee thus had a *quo-
rum* present at all times for emergency action.

Arrangements were being made to have the two men hanged
from the yardarm of a ship in the harbor. A vessel had been
selected which was in full view from Telegraph Hill, in the
hope that the Sydney ducks who inhabited that disreputable
neighborhood would observe and take heed. At eight in the
morning, the alarm bell would sound, and the members would
assemble. As soon as possible thereafter, the execution would
take place.

During the earlier hours of the evening there was some coming and going of members concerned with the business in hand.
As midnight neared, however, a quiet — as of death — began
to settle over the rooms. . . .

The steamboat got to San Francisco after eleven o'clock. Mc-Dougal went ashore.

He apparently had no precise plan, but he needed, first of all, to get some information. He headed for the Union Saloon, on the Plaza, a few minutes' walk from Long Wharf. The Un-

INTERIOR OF THE EL DORADO

The combined saloon and gambling-house was an important factor in the life of 1851. Note the high-hatted gentlemen, democratically mingling with long-haired Mexicans (?) in serapes and dubious-looking characters in slouch hats. There are also several ladies. Note the roulette table, seven-piece orchestra, and show-off bartender.

ion was the particular rendezvous of politicians, and the governor could not help but find acquaintances there, even at a late
hour.

In fact, McDougal may have had a more definite motive. He
may have been expecting to make contact, at the Union, with
Broderick's agents who had infiltrated the Committee.

In any case, he did so. About midnight — probably at the
bar, over appropriate drinks — McDougal was talking with two
members of the Committee. Whether they can have told him
anything of much importance is questionable. The approximate time of the hanging was already known throughout the
city. They could have told him something about the number
and arrangements of the guard. Having learned that he would
have to act within eight hours and in the face of thirty armed
men, the governor might well have been discouraged. That he
continued with his project at all speaks well for both his courage and his resolution.

The two informers may also have told the governor that
Mayor Brenham was planning to do something. The governor
decided to go to the mayor.

McDougal stepped outside the door, and then took an action
which might well have been disastrous. In the saloon he had
noticed an acquaintance, Colonel George Washington White.
From the doorway, McDougal called to White, and then asked
him to go along to find the mayor.

McDougal did not know that White had recently joined the
Committee. Such membership could no longer be called really
secret, but members did not wear badges, or proclaim themselves from street corners.

McDougal hired a carriage, and he and White drove off to
find the mayor. McDougal said that he had come to San Francisco to prevent the hanging. They came to the mayor's house,
and there was further conversation. Brenham explained the
plans which already had been set afoot — information which

must have been especially interesting to White, as a member of the Committee. Brenham intended to appear at eight o'clock, leading his fully mobilized force of marshals and policemen. He thus intended to take the prisoners, or at least prevent their execution. The governor apparently accepted this course of action. The governor and the mayor then decided to go off in the carriage and hunt up Sheriff Hays. White found this an excellent opportunity to part company from them. . . .

White, true to his duty as #668, went off to the Committee rooms, knowing that the mayor planned to attempt a rescue when the Committee brought the prisoners out. He passed this word on to Van Bokkelen, and the latter addressed a note to the Executive Committee, that "from information received" he requested permission to remove the condemned prisoners "to some proper place outside this building, where they will be at the proper time executed." Probably he intended to take them aboard the ship, thus wholly frustrating the mayor's attempt. The Executive Committee approved the request, in an endorsement carefully marked 12:50 and initialed by Payran.

Van Bokkelen began to make arrangements for the transfer, but he was in no hurry. The mayor was not planning the rescue until after eight o'clock, and that was seven hours off. . . .

And now the governor had a bit of good luck. Talking things over, after White had left, he came to the conclusion that the mayor's plan was not a good one. (It was, in fact, about the worst plan possible. It was an invitation to civil war. It would probably not even be successful in rescuing the prisoners. The mobilized police and marshals, even with some reinforcement from Broderick's men, would scarcely equal the Committee in numbers. Finally, at the first sign of an imminent rescue, the guards who had been especially assigned to that purpose would shoot the prisoners to prevent their rescue.)

The governor — for all his faults, a much better man than the mayor — evolved another plan. It might not have much chance of success, but its failure would not result in any major disaster.

The carriage, rattling along the unpaved streets, came to where Sheriff Hays lived.

He was doubtless surprised to be routed out of bed at one o'clock by two no less distinguished visitors than the governor of the state and the mayor of the city. Still, the redoubtable sheriff was probably no more pleased than any other man would be at being rudely awakened from his first sleep. Besides, the rash proposal that the governor now presented was one at which even a former Texas ranger could not be happy. The sheriff was asked to serve a writ of *habeas corpus* and to take the two prisoners into his own custody. Hays's first reaction was to refuse the duty — probably considering it to be that of the city police; in his own words he "rather roughly declined." (Just what words constituted rather rough language for Jack Hays intrigue the imagination.)

But the governor would not take no. He apparently presented a good argument that this was really the duty of the sheriff, and Hays was never a man to refuse duty. He got up, dressed (including revolver), and summoned his chief deputy, John Caperton.

The next problem was to obtain a writ, and they all went off in the carriage to find a judge. They first went to the house of Nathaniel Bennett of the Supreme Court. But, though the hour was now past one o'clock, the judge was not in — evidently a gay nighthawk. Eventually they found Judge Myron Norton of the Superior Court. The governor himself swore out an affidavit. Since there was no time for the procedure of issuing a *habeas corpus,* the judge issued a warrant for the sheriff to arrest Whittaker and McKenzie.

Hunting for a judge, explaining the situation, making out the documents — all this had taken two hours. When the warrant was placed in Hays's hands, he noted the time as 3 A.M. . . .

At that same hour, in the Committee rooms, the watch shifted. The night had been passing quietly.

Preparations were under way to move Whittaker and Mc-Kenzie, according to the orders issued two hours earlier. Since the removal was imminent, the two prisoners had not been shackled with leg-irons, as was customary, but they were handcuffed.

In the weariness that comes with early morning, everyone not directly concerned with guard-duty was trying to get a little sleep. McDuffee was asleep, having completed his duties by sending for Mines, the minister. Bluxome had gone to sleep on a table. Payran was sleeping in the Executive Committee room. The fifteen members of the guard who had just gone off duty were resting, but they were clothed and armed, and could be roused at any moment.

The members of the guard who were actively on duty were properly placed. A few of them were in the detention-room, keeping direct watch upon the prisoners. A hefty blacksmith (almost too appropriately named Steele) was the doorkeeper. The others kept their positions in the large room.

In spite of the hour a few curiosity-seekers had gathered. Some of these had come up the stairway, and were hanging about, just outside the door to the main room. John B. Evans, #330, was ordered to go outside and get these people to leave, since it was feared that they might cause confusion when the prisoners were being removed. While Evans was outside, a man whom he knew as Yorker asked him to give a message to Vi Turner, #313, to the effect that he, Yorker, had been looking for the governor all over town, and could not find him. . . .

Sheriff Hays, having received the warrant, laid his plans. He knew the situation that he was facing, and it was a most unhappy one. Through information received from spies, Hays knew the number of the guard, and he could only assume that they were well-armed, courageous, determined, and alert. The

situation might well be considered hopeless. In fifteen minutes, Jack Hays might be dead, and there is always something
repugnant in the idea of being killed by your own friends.

The mayor offered him a posse of police. Hays refused. He
wanted no trigger-happy blunderers.

Of course, Hays was not irrevocably faced with victory-or-
death. If he entered the room, and found himself facing cocked
revolvers, he could back out, and then tell the governor and the
mayor that he had done his best, and that they would need
troops with artillery.

Hays could count a few advantages on his own side. Most of
all, he had the offensive, and could hope for surprise. He
could act quickly, before the others had time to know what
was happening. Through the spies, moreover, Hays knew exactly the situation he was facing — that the prisoners were not
chained to the benches, and that they had been told to expect a rescue. Still, counting all the advantages, anyone could
see that the odds against success were heavy.

Nevertheless, the four of them would attempt it. Hays settled his plan. They would drive in the carriage to a place near
the street-door which opened on the stairway leading up to the
Committee rooms. The mayor would then sit in the carriage,
and be sure that the horses were ready. The other three
would enter the door, which was not guarded, and climb the
stairs. At the landing, in front of the guarded door to the
rooms, McDougal would stop. He would stay there, and be of
what help he might be to keep the exit clear. Hays and
Caperton would boldly push in.

Once inside, Hays planned to halt and remain there, attempting to keep the door open for Caperton's return. He
would shout loudly, "I am the sheriff of the county," thus calling attention to himself and making anyone hesitate to offer
violence to the sheriff.

Under cover of the shout, Caperton would move quickly

across the room, and enter the detention-room. Once there, he would call out, "I am the officer; I come to save you!" Presumably the spies had given these words to the prisoners as a kind of code.

The prisoners were then expected to spring up and accompany Caperton, out into the main room, and then to the door which Hays would (hopefully) be keeping open. Hays would step out with them, and they would all go down the stairs, picking up McDougal on the way. Once in the street, they would pile into the carriage, and drive rapidly to the jail. A good plan, if it would work!

The four men drove to a spot near the Committee rooms. In front of the doorway another carriage was standing; it belonged to the minister. Farther along the street, a number of policemen were standing. They were there in an unofficial capacity, having heard what was being planned, and having come to see how it would work out.

Hays, Caperton, and McDougal got out of the carriage. Doubtless they checked that their revolvers were ready.

The mayor, ignominiously, remained with the carriage. We can pity him the tension of his waiting.

He saw the three men enter the door. He listened for sounds of outcry and shooting. There was nothing.

Suddenly, after about two minutes, someone threw a rope over one of the beams projecting from below the upper windows. Then a man sprang out, and slid down the rope to the street.

Immediately Hays, Caperton, and McDougal came out of the door with the two prisoners. The man who had slid down the rope saw them, and drew a revolver, but did not fire. Hays and the others bundled the prisoners into the carriage. It had been as simple as that.

# CHAPTER 24

# GOVERNOR McDOUGAL'S PROCLAMATION

*(August 20, 4 A.M.–August 20, evening)*

T HE MAN WHO had slid down the rope was William Hogg, #220, and what he did was the result of quick and clear thinking. Having seen the prisoners taken, he supposed that any force capable of so doing would be strong enough to post guards at the door. He therefore made a hasty exit through the window. Though his nerve failed him when it came to shooting at the sheriff, he ran off to the Monumental Firehouse, to ring the alarm bell. He there met with another frustration — not being able to find the rope, he could not ring the bell.

Eventually someone found the rope, and in a few minutes the members began hurrying in from all directions. At the same time, the citizens generally, thus awakened just before daybreak, also turned out, and came pouring through the streets.

In the rooms, for once, all order seemed to have broken down, and the Committee became little more than a mob. Hearing that the prisoners had been rescued, some members merely left in disgust.

Eventually the meeting came to some kind of order, but no minutes were kept. The *Herald* reported:

Amid intense excitement the meeting organized and the circumstances were detailed. The person who had charge of the room [Van Bokkelen] was bitterly denounced; various propositions were made, each more violent than the other.

But what action could be taken? No one even knew what had happened to the prisoners. In addition, charges of treachery were flying about, and no member knew whether he could trust the man who stood beside him.

But force of habit was strong. The members of the Committee had been well schooled against mob-action and hasty movements. Habit, along with the mere difficulty of knowing what action could be taken, got control. The crowd became enough of a parliamentary body to adjourn itself, with the stipulation that another meeting would be held at eight o'clock.

At the same time, excitement and confusion seized the victors. "The authorities," declared the *Herald*, "were seized with the most absurd and ludicrous panic — absolutely as it would appear frightened at their own boldness." One mad proposal was that the captain of the *Vincennes* should train his guns upon the city, aiming them in the direction of the Committee rooms — as if an American captain could assume the responsibility of bombarding an American city, or as if the mayor of that city could request such action! As the *Herald* continued:

> Others were for a parley. Orders were issued to repair to the Presidio, and bring in some of the honey-combed pieces of ordnance which graced that interesting ruin. Brigadier General Addison received hurried commands to get his epaulettes in readiness, and that distinguished officer, with a humorous smile, gave orders to Capt. Howard to have the Guards prepared to do duty at a moment's notice.

The mention of the general's epaulettes was a reminder to the reader that Addison was a mere figurehead of militia, with no troops at all. The smile at giving orders to Captain Howard would have been the result of his knowing the captain to be a member of the Committee.

Probably there was not so much panic as the pro-

Committee *Herald* liked to imagine. In any case, the jail soon was strongly garrisoned.

The ringing of the alarm bell at 7:30, having been pre-arranged, created less excitement. The members, slightly diminished by those who had quit in disgust, assembled and came to order. In the few intervening hours some progress had been made. The intense excitement had somewhat abated. But in its place had succeeded an equally intense feeling of bitterness and resentment. The situation was critical. Civil war was close, and beyond civil war could lie only revolution.

Colonel Stevenson was in the chair. No member of the Executive Committee presided, doubtless because they were all under suspicion of treachery.

A member reported that the two prisoners were in the county jail. Now, at least, there could be an objective for action.

Then came the inevitable push for an immediate counter-stroke. Payran, usually far from being a hothead, submitted a resolution written under such pressure of excitement that it was largely incoherent. But its last words were clear enough, "to at once rouse our City to Action, and show who has the supremacy." Another resolution was coldly brief and dangerously clear. No name is attached to it in the minutes, but it could have been written by Coleman or Ryckman:

> *Resolved* that this Com proceed en masse to the prison and take from the Authorities the prisoners taken from us last night.

Who rose to oppose these resolutions and with what argument was not recorded. The best argument against them, perhaps, was mere uncertainty. Who wishes to march into the battle, behind a captain who may be a traitor, and not trusting the man at his shoulder? Both resolutions were laid on the table.

The decision was wise from the military point of view as well. The storming of a strong and strongly garrisoned building is likely to be a bloody business, and might well have been beyond the capacities of the Committee.

While the Committee was thus meeting, a large and excited crowd had, as usual, gathered outside. Presently someone took it upon himself to announce that an immediate attack was to be made upon the jail. The crowd took the announcement seriously. There was a tremendous rush to the vicinity of the jail, each man wishing to get a good location from which to see the battle.

Unaware of what was happening outside, the members continued their meeting. They took positive action by suspending Van Bokkelen from duty, an inevitable procedure under the circumstances.

The meeting took another positive action by the appointment of a committee to inquire into the whole affair. No member of the Executive Committee was appointed for this investigation, another indication that all of its members had fallen under suspicion. Colonel Stevenson was a member of the investigating committee, and so was Brannan. The appointment of Brannan indicated that the radicals, as would be certain under the circumstances, had come back into power. The situation demanded that the investigation should be placed in the hands of those who could most be trusted to remain true to the original objective. Brannan, who came as close as anyone to being the founder, was in a good position.

The meeting adjourned, and the committee prepared to begin its investigation. At the same time, the opponents were equally busy. By this time anyone could see the armed sentries, posted conspicuously on the flat roof of the jail.

In addition, the governor had been plying his pen, and the typesetters had been furiously busy. At half past ten, a handbill was being distributed on the streets, with the title in huge capitals:

## PROCLAMATION!
### BY THE GOVERNOR.

This full-fledged proclamation was a great contrast to the earlier open letter. The governor now wrapped himself in the full dignity of his office, loosed a full blast against "an armed and organized body of the citizens," and threatened all such with specific paragraphs of the criminal code. He declared that further activities might well result in "all the horrors of Civil War."

Considered by itself, the proclamation was a vigorous and sometimes eloquent plea for the support of lawful modes of government. Coming from the man who had just secretly pardoned Duane, the proclamation was a masterpiece of hypocrisy.

It probably had no effect, except to add to the already intense excitement, and to irritate the members of the Committee and still further stiffen their resistance. The friends of the Committee rallied around, and the newspapers, though printing the governor's proclamation, cast ridicule upon it. The same newspapers that published the proclamation published also the statement by four members of the Executive Committee, declaring that the governor in his interview with them had supported the Committee's acts and had even urged them to hang any guilty judges.

The opening sentence of the second paragraph began, "Now therefore, I, JOHN McDOUGAL, Governor of the state of California." Seizing upon this bombastic use of capitals, the local wits saw the possibility of another nickname. In the future the governor was known not only as "His Accidency," but also as "I, John."

Yet, in some ways, the governor was riding high that morning. The side to which he had committed himself had achieved, at his insistence, a brilliant exploit. He himself had even contributed physically. At the very crisis some of the guard had forced the door shut while Hays, Caperton, and the prisoners were still inside. McDougal had then shoved it vigorously from the outside, opening it and allowing the others to pass through.

But the governor must have been, that morning, a very worried man. He had brought the city and the state to the verge of civil war and revolution. Perhaps for that reason, as well as with the magnanimity of a victor, he was willing to be conciliatory. He agreed to appear before the Committee's investigating committee.

All this summer is full of paradox. This is, perhaps, a characteristic of civil disturbances. Two men who at one moment seem to be opposed in deadly enmity, at another moment have a friendly drink together. But of all the paradoxes, none is more striking than the appearance of McDougal before the investigating committee within twelve hours of the seizure of the prisoners. He told, apparently with great affability, of his actions throughout the preceding night. He admitted that at the Union he had received information from "two gentlemen, who represented that they were, or had been, members of V. C.," but he declined giving the names.

Next appeared (in this incredible investigation) his Honor the Mayor himself! After confirming the governor's testimony, he stated that he himself had had no collusion with any member of the Committee.

The third man to testify was Sheriff Hays. He declared that there was no resistance to his entrance, "and but slight resistance to their departing with the prisoners."

Since the deputy sheriff appeared later in the day, the testimony of all four principals was preserved. Caperton stated that "the persons in the room were so taken by surprise that they could not resist." When the doorway was blocked he had told Van Bokkelen that resistance was useless, that they were too strong, and he then called out "Police!" as if to summon reinforcements from outside.

In addition the committee took statements from McDuffee,

Van Bokkelen, Payran, ten members of the guard, and James Nelligan (*alias* Yorker) who was not a member of the Committee but had apparently been a go-between carrying news from the spies to the governor.

This mass of testimony made clear some of the details of Hays's almost inexplicable success. He had gained one bit of good luck in that Van Bokkelen, at the moment of the attack, had gone to the refreshment room. He returned, but had lost irreplaceable seconds. He reacted, quickly enough under the circumstances, and tried to argue with Hays. At the critical moment, some unidentified guardsman had the presence of mind merely to put his back against the door and shove it shut. It looked, for an instant, as if Hays and Caperton would be overwhelmed by the rapidly rallying guards. This was the moment, however, when McDougal burst the door open from the outside, and the escape was effected.

The investigating committee, which had thus done so well at fact-finding, prepared a somewhat disappointing report. It gave a blanket exoneration against charges of bribery and connivance, but condemned "those members of the Vigilance Com, who were so derelict in duty as to inform the Governor." The report, also, in a measure, exonerated the governor, declaring that the receipt of this information "rendered it imperative upon him to adopt the course he did." The report declared Van Bokkelen to have been "guilty of gross neglect." Actually his conduct had not been too bad, but a scapegoat was necessary, and the direct responsibility for the disaster was obviously his.

At four o'clock, the general meeting reconvened. By this time the members were beginning to rally from the demoralization which had at first overwhelmed them. This was, in most respects, the most momentous meeting yet to be held. If the radicals took over, there might be an immediate march on the jail. Another possibility was even more likely. The Committee, plagued by sudden disaster and the accompanying sus-

272 Committee of Vigilance

picion of treachery, might merely fizzle out in impotence, and disintegrate.

The meeting came to order under good auspices. Selim Woodworth, the proper president, was in the chair.

First, the investigating committee presented its report, which was reassuring in its conclusions that there had been no serious treachery. Most important, because of this report, the members could have a restored confidence in Payran and the other members of the Executive Committee. The report was accepted and placed on file.

A letter was then presented from Messrs. Flint, and Peabody, and Co. The partners in this firm were not members, but they wrote, "We have sympathized with you since your first organization." The letter continued:

> We trust that in the present crisis your action will be characterized by your usual prudence and firmness, and that you will not entertain a thought of discontinuing your effort in so noble a cause.

As an evidence of sincerity, the partners enclosed a check for $100 "as a small token of our appreciation of your efforts to punish and suppress crime in our midst." It was ordered that a letter of thanks be sent.

The third item of business involved more difficulty. In the meeting that morning Van Bokkelen had been suspended from duty as chief of police. In addition the examining committee had charged him with "gross neglect." Still, the case against him was not strong, and there was the possibility that he was merely being made to take the blame. His reinstatement was now moved. Although there must have been opposition, the motion carried.

The fourth motion came from W. L. Higgins, #410, who had been one of the guard. He was not a man of importance, but democracy ruled in the meetings of the Committee. Much of its strength came from men of little note, who thought for themselves and acted on their own convictions. Now, as Higgins was granted the floor, the affairs of the Committee moved forward again, for the first time since the seizure of the prisoners. He moved, "That the Chief of Police keep a constant guard of 20 men over the 2 prisoners arrested by the sheriff of the county." This would mean that the Committee threw a cordon around the jail, to prevent the removal of the prisoners to some other place. The motion passed, and we can only think that it passed with a low growl which carried a touch of threat in it.

The joint resignation of H. D. Evans, #33, and J. W. Salmon, #34, was then presented. The two friends, as their low numbers indicated, had signed on the first night. Salmon had been for a time the treasurer. Their resignation bore the date of the present day, and they left the Committee, presumably, in disgust at the fiasco.

The resignations were accepted. Perhaps even in this we may read a sign of returning confidence. Usually members were not allowed to resign, but were granted indefinite leave of absence. The actual acceptance of the resignations was a sign that the Committee was not forced to maintain its hold on recalcitrants, but could let them go.

Then Charles A. Poor, #591, gained the floor. Like Higgins, he was a man of little importance, but he presented the motion that could be decisive. He made it, we would think, to an assemblage hushed in dead silence, and as he finished, there would have come the letting out of breath.

*Resolved* that the sentence of Death pronounced on the two men, Whittaker & McKenzie, still remains in full force, and that all necessary means shall be resorted to, to obtain possession of these men & when taken that they shall meet the punishment due their crimes as the voice of the people demands it.

The motion passed. It was decided. The Committee had defied the governor, and resolved to continue upon its course.

The final motion was anticlimatic. It was made by one member of the investigating committee, and was to the effect that anyone found guilty of revealing the business of the Committee should be expelled, and his name published in the papers.

In spite of the last resolution, we can only suppose that some news of the action of this meeting soon came to the governor's ears. He may have realized, then, that he had been unsuccessful. His only hope had been by a *coup de main* to make the Committee ridiculous, to set the members fighting among themselves, or to incapacitate them by suspicion of treachery among their leaders. He had failed.

Under cover of darkness, that evening, the city authorities conveyed two hundred muskets from the Presidio to the jail, and many of them were then loaded. This cooperation of the Army with the local authorities was the first suggestion of federal opposition to the Committee.

The situation was perilous, and throughout the state it was just as perilous as it was in San Francisco. Feeling in Sacramento ran so high that McDougal was hanged in effigy. And, as yet, his pardoning of Duane was kept secret.

# CHAPTER 25

# A DAY OF TERROR!

*(August 21–24)*

GREAT EXCITEMENT had served as a headline for the account of the midnight hanging of Jenkins, as if this were a diversion by which the citizens might while away an empty hour. INTENSE EXCITEMENT had announced the hanging of Stuart, with an implication of greater seriousness. But, for an occasion in August, the editor of the *Alta* used the headline A DAY OF TERROR! . . .

Hays had seized the prisoners early on Wednesday morning. By that evening the Committee had pulled itself together, held its investigation, resolved to inflict its sentence of death, and thus — in effect — accepted the governor's challenge to open warfare. But to pass such a resolution and to implement it were two different things. In spite of resolutions, the Committee was still shaken. Many members had lost confidence in Van Bokkelen. Payran and the other leaders who had been present at the time of the rescue were inevitably under suspicion. The prestige of the Executive Committee was weakened for the first time.

Before there could be a counterstroke, someone must plan it with care, and in the interests of security the Executive Committee itself must be scrutinized.

When men face such times of uncertainty and suspicion, in a nation or in a Committee of Vigilance, the moderates go under. Necessarily, those assume leadership who have always committed themselves to extreme measures, since only they can be above suspicion.

Thursday, August 21, must have been a day when much was happening in secret. But nothing got into the record, even into that private record which the Committee kept of its own transactions. The fact in itself speaks eloquently, if ambiguously. Since the Committee first was well organized in June, no day had passed without documents being added to the file. Every Sunday, and even the Fourth of July, had seen business transacted. On August 21 — nothing!

It must have been a day when the Committee was reconstituting itself — a day of quiet conversations, of men gathering into little groups, of friend drawing close to friend. Who can be trusted, in such a situation? But someone must be trusted, or nothing can be done. Some group must exist, of men having confidence in one another, bound by that subtle and sometimes dubious tie known as loyalty.

Though there is no record for this day, the records of the succeeding days would indicate that by that evening the once-seemingly-united Committee might be considered as having divided into three parts. At one extreme, were the hard-core men. In the middle remained the great mass of the members, probably to be considered loyal, but doubtless with a few who were either disloyal or so lukewarm that they might yield to subornation. The third group was composed of a few men who were definitely under suspicion. Chief among them were James L. Malony, #250, and Vicesimus (Vi) Turner, #218, both of whom had connections with Broderick and were known to have been talking with McDougal at the Union.

In the first excitement suspicion had fallen upon some half-dozen members of the Executive Committee. The serious investigation cleared them, and without any change of membership that committee continued to direct affairs. There was however, a reorganization. The new president was James B. Huie.

Huie was a prominent commission-merchant. He was a man in middle age, having a son old enough to be a member of the

Committee. His title "Colonel" may have been a courtesy one, but such titles usually indicated some military experience. Far back, at the time of the Jansen trial, Huie had been one of the three who supported Brannan in his push to hang the prisoners. Such an alliance marked him as a radical. After the Jansen case he had served notably as foreman of the Grand Jury. He had joined the Committee on the first night as #16, and had served throughout as a member of the Executive Committee. Now, in the crisis, that committee made him its head, as a man of undoubted loyalty and of iron determination. . . .

Throughout this time of hesitation and defeat there was at least one member who never faltered. This, as one might guess, was Ryckman — "the old man," as he was in the thoughts of most of his colleagues. As he told it a quarter-century later, he may have built himself up a little — being, as are many strong and able men, something of an egotist.

Ryckman had been working hard for several days, and on the critical evening he had gone home to pick up some sleep. So exhausted was he that he slept right through the sounding of the alarm bell. Only later did he learn that "the prisoners had been rescued, and the whole city was in commotion." He then went to the rooms, and found everything in excitement. While suggestions were being made, as Ryckman put it, to "tear down the jail," he himself lashed out at those who had been the guards, and "told them they were a nice set of men, who had been put there for the protection of the prisoners, and had let them go."

On the next day, he went to the jail. Lambert, the jailer, faced him at the door, saying, "Mr. Ryckman, I don't want any trouble with you." Ryckman took the words as only a deserved compliment, and replied that he came merely to see that the prisoners "were properly cared for, and that he did not allow them to escape." Lambert then allowed him to enter.

Once in the jail, he had a chance to talk with Whittaker. The younger man again spoke as a son might to a father, "I hope you are not sorry, Mr. Ryckman, that we made our escape."

But if Ryckman was a father, he was of the Roman breed. He replied sternly, "You have not made your escape. You have been convicted, and you will be executed beyond a shadow of doubt. There is no power on earth that can save you."

Ryckman also made use of his time in jail to observe its armament. He saw the stacks of muskets which had been brought from the Presidio. But he noted that many of them were ancient flintlocks, even lacking flints. He decided that the armament was not very formidable.

On this day the ever-loyal *Herald* ran an editorial:

> We are gratified to announce that the occurrence of Wednesday morning, so far from paralyzing the energies or usefulness of the Vigilance Committee, have [sic] stimulated them to renewed exertion, and drawn into the association a large number of our most respectable citizens who had not before joined.

A consideration of the records of the Qualifications Committee makes one think that "large number" represents propaganda rather than reality. Still, as always, the excitement brought in some new members, and the total began to approach seven hundred.

The editorial included a sentence which was not, indeed, without a suggestion of threat — that the people might "confidently expect" the members of the Committee to "extend the sphere of their usefulness throughout the entire State, in conjunction with the Vigilance Committees of the sister cities." The suggestion was one, not of a surrender, but of an offensive against the governor.

The slightly sinister implication of this editorial was reinforced by some resolutions passed on this same day by the Santa Clara Vigilance Association, and forwarded to the Committee in San Francisco.

Santa Clara was a small town, fifty miles south of San Francisco. The membership in its association probably did not exceed twenty-five. These members labored under no illusions of their own greatness, but still they proffered their "feeble but hearty cooperation." The Santa Clarans expressed themselves as having learned "with unfeigned astonishment" of the rescue of the two "notorious villains." They went on to "denounce in the most bitter and unqualified terms the recent shameful conduct of Gov. McDougal." They expressed themselves as offering their "unqualified services to be commanded by the shortest notice."

Though the language was a little tortuous, the meaning was clear enough. The Santa Clarans were saying, "If you need us, call on us." If it came to a show of strength, or to shooting, San Francisco could count on the backing of Santa Clara.

There is no reason to doubt that San Jose, Sacramento, Marysville, and a score of other towns, also stood ready to rise at the signal. We must remember that only in San Francisco had the Committee met with appreciable opposition. Revolution awaited only a leader and a word of command.

On this day, also, Huie addressed a letter, by order of the Executive Committee, to John W. Cartwright, #234. Known as "Captain," Cartwright probably had, like Huie, some military experience. He had served the Committee as deputy marshal. He was now selected for the supreme test. The letter read:

> You are hereby authorized to detail a guard such as you think proper, and arrest two Prisoners, to wit — Sam Whittaker & R. McKenzie and bring them into custody of the Committee of Vigilance.

This simple note represented the implementation of the declaration of war against the governor, already passed at the general meeting.

Cartwright set about organizing. The situation facing him

might seem even more desperate than its counterpart which Hays had faced on Wednesday morning. The jail was heavily garrisoned with armed men. Under the circumstances, they could be expected to be much more alert than the guards at the Committee rooms. The jail was a strongly-constructed building. Finally, with the Committee infiltrated by no one knew how many spies, secrecy would be difficult.

Under such circumstances, the fewer men the better. Cartwright, compromising between need of strength and fear of betrayal, decided that thirty would be the proper number. He divided his men into three squads, each with a leader.

The men must have been selected with the utmost care, probably with the collaboration of some members of the Executive Committee. One of the squad leaders was Colonel White, who had proved his loyalty by reporting the governor's conversation on Wednesday night. Another squad leader was Captain Reuben Calhoun, #620, who had commanded one of the posses sent to hunt for Whittaker. The third squad leader was Oscar Smith, #267. The names of about half the thirty are preserved, but so little is known about the men themselves that the mere listing of the names is futile. At least two members of the Executive Committee, Huie and Bluxome, served in the ranks, waiving any prerogative. Huie's son was also in the group. Payran and Schenck may have been of the number, though the evidence is not clear. Ryckman was not; he had most of the qualifications, but would have been ruled out because of age, in a desperate venture which might call for physical activity.

On Saturday, Cartwright matured his plans. There was need of haste. The authorities might decide to move the prisoners. Besides, any delay greatly increased the chance of the opposite side getting wind of something.

To preserve secrecy, Cartwright kept away from the Committee rooms, and gathered his thirty together in an old iron building at the corner of California and Leidesdorff streets. As Bluxome stated, at that meeting "we agreed to take that jail or sacrifice our lives."

The attempt was set for the next day. The time was advantageous. Every Sunday afternoon services were held in the jail. The prisoners were then brought from their cells to a central court. On this Sunday the Reverend Albert Williams was to officiate.

At this time an accident may have helped focus attention upon the possibility offered by the services. Williams, like some other ministers, was apparently not without a touch of vanity. Meeting Payran on the street, he asked him to come and hear the sermon. Payran saw the possibilities, and several of Cartwright's men were smitten with religious fervour, and made arrangements to attend the services.

There were other preliminaries. If possible, Hays must be eliminated. No one wished to tangle with such a quick-thinking, fearless, and dangerous fighter. George Schenck was a good friend of Hays, and undertook the job. He told Hays about an interesting bull-fight which was to take place at the Mission that very Sunday afternoon. Jack Hays could see through a millstone with a hole in it, and he may have got the idea that his absence from the city was desirable. Or he may merely have been interested in the bull-fight. At least, he said that he would go.

Another preliminary was a second check on the muskets. Ryckman had decided that they were not formidable, but they might have been repaired and loaded since he had seen them. Lots were drawn, and Bluxome was chosen.

He went at once to the jail. Outside, he came upon Hays, saddling a mule, about to set out somewhere on a mount which scarcely befitted a dashing Texas ranger. Bluxome spoke to him, and said that he would like to see Berdue, who had recently been brought down from Marysville, and was still held, pending a final hearing. Bluxome said that he wanted to observe whether Berdue really resembled Stuart as closely as had been reported. Hays ordered Bluxome's admittance.

Once inside, Bluxome let his eye be caught by a rack of muskets. As if on impulse, he said to the jailer, "Lambert, you are an old infantry fellow, so am I."

> He had a stock of muskets there. I took one out of the rack. "Now put me through the drill," said I.
> "What drill?" said he.
> "Loading and firing," said I.
> "All right, sir," said he.
> We went on, and presently I said, "This musket is not well balanced," and threw it down and picked up another. I found that they were empty. I took up about a dozen, on one pretense or another, and they were every one empty.

On Sunday afternoon Cartwright completed his dispositions. The jail was as yet unfinished, and the central court was open to the sky. From the slope of near-by Telegraph Hill a man could see into the court. William Higgins, who had made the critical motion on August 20, took his post on the hill; at the end of the services he was to give the signal by opening his arms wide.

The jail was on Broadway between Kearny and Dupont streets. At the proper time, one of Cartwright's men drove up in a carriage, drawn by two fine white horses. To avoid suspicion, he stationed himself a little way off from the jail, facing away from the jail and also away from the Committee rooms.

As the time approached, a half-dozen of the thirty asked permission, and were allowed to enter the jail, to hear the services. A squad, properly concealed, was stationed near the front door of the jail. Another squad, this one commanded by Smith, was stationed so that it could attack the rear door. Either squad might be stopped, and the other carry out the mission. Both of the parties were furnished with sledges and crowbars.

A few other members who were in on the secret lingered in the vicinity, but remained inconspicuous. Some members of the Executive Committee, including Ryckman, were at the Committee rooms, awaiting the alarm signal, which would indicate success.

Williams, the minister, had arrived with his two young children, a sufficient evidence that he was not expecting trouble and therefore was not in collusion with the Committee. The prisoners were brought from their cells, and stood in the court. The half-dozen members of the Committee who were present, we may assume, appeared to be attentive, but no one afterwards reported as to the text, and as to whether the sermon was as moving as Williams had apparently thought it might be.

As the services ended, Higgins observed from the hill, and spread his arms wide. From front and rear the squads rushed at the jail. The guards on the roof fired a few wild shots.

At the front door the squad pounded for admission. An unwary jailer opened the door a little. With a rush, the squad knocked him backward, and poured in.

At the rear door Smith swung with his sledge, and smashed the lock. That squad burst through.

In an instant, both squads rushed together in the central courtyard. The innocent clergyman stood amazed. The prisoners scattered, each to his own cell, as if to a place of refuge. Huie, with a big revolver leveled, kept the guards quiet.

The two prisoners were rushed from the jail, and bundled into the carriage. Several of the thirty, revolvers ready, leaped into the carriage as guards, or hung to the outside. The driver lashed with his whip, and the horses sprang forward.

The carriage dashed up Broadway, and swung left into Stockton Street, careening at the turn, as the whip slashed and the white horses galloped.

In the Committee rooms, Ryckman laid his watch on the table, saying, "If that bell doesn't strike in two minutes, it is a failure." Almost as he spoke, the alert guard at the bellrope saw the signal from the hill, and struck the alarm.

At the gallop the horses dashed on. To confuse pursuers, the driver followed a zig-zag course across the city, the carriage swaying wildly at the turn of every corner. The men on the outside hung on grimly.

Those of the thirty who had been left at the jail were running hard across the city toward the Committee rooms. Other members were hurrying at the alarm.

With sounding bell and running men and galloping horses, the city was suddenly alarmed. Some dashed toward the jail, where trouble had been expected. Most people, realizing what the bell meant, hurried toward the Committee rooms.

As if reacting to human mood, the wind blew fiercely, sweeping the dust through the air.

In seven or eight minutes, before the crowd had grown very dense, the driver pulled his galloping horses to a halt in front of the Committee rooms, and the prisoners were hurried inside.

Already, it was judged, a sufficient number of members had assembled to prevent any attempt at rescue. The doors were thrown shut and locked, and late-comers beat in vain for admittance. A few climbed up ropes which their friends let down from the windows.

Outside, the whole city seemed to be assembling in Battery Street, and on the vacant ground across from the building. One reporter estimated the crowd at six or seven thousand, and another gave it as ten thousand.

Inside, everything had been prepared, even to the making ready of the ropes. The two projecting beams were at last to serve as gallows.

The ropes were quickly rigged to the beams. Inside, a noose was placed around each prisoner's neck.

At the last moment, Whittaker asked to speak with Ryckman. Ryckman went up behind him, and pressed the hand that was tied there.

HANGING OF WHITTAKER AND MCKENZIE

A contemporary letter mentions this drawing as being wholly accurate, except that the artist could not represent the crowd as being so large as it actually was. This is the best picture of the Committee's quarters. Note bare-legged Chinese with pigtail, and several ladies.

"Whittaker," he said, "what do you want of me?" With his own death at hand, Whittaker gave warning, a story doubtless heard in the jail, that the Sydney ducks were planning to take Ryckman's life.

A moment later, a little before three o'clock, the two bodies were hanging, each from its beam.

About twenty minutes had elapsed since the first rush on the jail. As the bodies swung, the great crowd grew quiet, until few spoke except in a whisper. Soon people began to drift away, but others arrived. The *Alta* estimated that as many as fifteen thousand people, half the population of the city, viewed the bodies.

# CHAPTER 26

# QUIET

*(August 25–September 16)*

L IKE AN aging fighter, the Committee had pulled itself to- gether and scored another knockout. But its days of vigor had passed.

The bold and spectacular recapture of the prisoners might be considered a sign of strength — and so, in some respects, it was. But also there was about the whole affair a suggestion of weakness. The Committee had not mustered its hundreds, and marched serenely to work its will, confident in its own strength. Instead, it had been forced to work by stealth, by sleight, and by surprise. Even worse, it had been forced into precipitate hurry, so that the hanging of Whittaker and Mc- Kenzie resembled that of Jenkins, not that of Stuart.

Moreover, the intense concern about the whole incident was a symptom of weakness. If the Committee had been developing its work, investigating and trying more prisoners, it might have been able to be little concerned about what happened to any two of them.

Finally, the whole affair left a bad taste in the mouth. In- stead of being primarily a part of the effort to suppress crime, the capture and recapture of the two prisoners had turned into a power-struggle between the Committee and the authorities. Two miserable lives had been, somehow, at stake, and the swinging bodies had demonstrated, in people's minds, not so much the triumph of justice over crime, as the triumph of the Committee over the governor.

Following that day of terror came a quick reaction. To describe Monday, August 25, the editor of the *Alta* used the simple headline QUIET, writing:

> After a storm comes a calm. The great waves of our city's life which surged and dashed so on Sunday, yesterday had calmed down into a quiet sea, peaceful as a summer lake.

He then commented upon the situation with complacency and civic pride:

> In other countries among other people such terrible excitement as that of Sunday would have lasted for many days, and great excesses would have been committed, but our people, impulsive but not rash, allow their excited feelings to die out with the occasion which has created them.

Undoubtedly the editor was right that an emotional exhaustion had settled upon the citizens, and among the citizens must be included the members of the Committee.

To record events on that quiet Monday, no single scrap of paper is preserved in the Committee's records. Apparently, no business was done even by the usually busy members of the Executive Committee.

Yet they must have been taking thought, and talking among themselves. Except for a revolt of the general membership — and such an event seemed unlikely — the members of the Executive Committee would determine the course of events. And these men, now more than ever, must have seen that things could not continue to be uncertain and half-hearted.

But to go forward could only be interpreted as meaning to move toward revolution. There is, however, no record that such a move was considered.

If not to go forward, then, it must be to go back! These were terms in which a merchant could think. The business must be liquidated. It had been a thriving enterprise for a while, but there seemed little likelihood that it would pay dividends in the future. Therefore — cut your losses, get out, close the shop!

This would not mean that you merely, one day, declared the Committee no longer to exist. The Committee, we might say, had accumulated assets, and had a duty to its stockholders. Its assets, not counting a few chairs and lamps, were a more orderly city and an enhanced public conscience. Its stockholders were not only its own members, but also the law-abiding citizens generally. Therefore, the chief objective of the Committee became how to liquidate itself most efficiently, with least loss of prestige.

In the meantime, in a kind of valedictory atmosphere, there was a general closing-up of cases.

One of these was the most ancient of all. . . . The assault upon Jansen had occurred on February 19; the extra-legal trial of Berdue and Windred, on February 23. Since that time, Windred had escaped from jail, and had finally been smuggled aboard a ship and off to Australia. Berdue had suffered many hardships, but the Committee's lucky discovery of the true Stuart at the proper time had resulted in Berdue's being freed from the charge of murder. He was thereupon returned to San Francisco, where his conviction for assault still stood. Finally, on August 25, again by help of members of the Committee, he was set at liberty.

The *Herald* concluded its account of the case:

Mr. Jansen, who was present, came forward and declared his readiness to return to Berdue the money taken from him at the time of his conviction, and the court, upon information that the unfortunate man was now without means, suggested the propriety of a subscription for his benefit, which was immediately set on foot by those assembled in the court room.

The Committee took special action to forward this subscription. With respect to Berdue, however, it need have no sense of guilt. It had taken no action against him, and had contributed essentially to his release.

The celebrated resemblance between Berdue and Stuart proved to be much less startling than was at first assumed. Members of the Committee who had a good opportunity to observe both of the men declared that there was really no very striking resemblance. As so often, we must attribute much to the hysteria of the moment. People were convinced that Berdue looked like Stuart because someone said so in the first place, and everyone desperately wanted a conviction.

Other famous cases were gradually being cleared. On August 29, Adams was convicted of grand larceny, and sentenced to ten years in the state prison. Some members of the jury, it was reported, had been in favor of inflicting the death penalty. In any case, the Committee could congratulate itself. This was that Adams, known commonly as "the burglar," whom the Committee had come close to hanging on August 6, but had finally handed over to the authorities.

The case of Duane also proceeded in its somewhat mysterious way. He had received his pardon on August 17, and had been reported in San Francisco the next day. During the few days of excitement over Whittaker and McKenzie neither the newspapers nor the records of the Committee made mention of Duane. Probably he realized that for him to appear openly at such a time would add to the tension. Only on August 26, at a general meeting, did two members submit a resolution:

> That said Charley Duane have notice to leave this City of San Francisco and not to return under penalty of *Death* and that this act of the Governor meets with our unqualified disapprobation.

The resolution was passed, but it was ordered that no action should be taken "until it is ascertained positively that pardon has been granted." Even at this time, the Committee did not have sure information, and its members could hardly believe that even McDougal could have committed such an act.

The case remained the most ticklish one still on the Committee's docket, the one which would be most likely to arouse the members to violent action. . . .

As day followed day, the Executive Committee continued to examine suspects and to question witnesses, but little of interest came to light.

During this last week of August, the prisoners' room was still populated. Incarcerated there were seven Sydney ducks, who had either been implicated in some of the testimony taken, or had been identified as criminals during one of the inspections of a ship. An eighth prisoner was David Earl, who had once been #264, and was now being held on charges of burglary. In addition, the Committee was holding three married couples from Sydney, who could not have been kept in the common detention room.

The leaders of the Committee were also considering plans for reorganization or dissolution. An election for state and county officials was to be held on September 1. If good men could be put into office, the responsibilities of the Committee would be lightened.

The original organization had been on a strictly non-partisan basis, and many of the members objected strongly to any attempt to put the Committee into politics. There was no reason, however, why an individual member should not take any stand that he wished to take.

The result was the organization of an independent ticket. On August 27 the papers published a non-partisan address to the voters of San Francisco. It urged:

> Sweep clean the Augean stables of legislation; purify the ermine; show by your votes that honesty and virtue are at a premium in public estimation.

A slate of candidates was presented — some Whig and some Democratic. The address made no mention of the Committee, and was merely signed by fourteen men, calling themselves a nominating committee. It can have been little secret to anyone, however, that every one of these was a vigilante.

The movement grew rapidly. On August 28 the papers published an endorsement of the ticket, and a call for a meeting. This announcement bore the signatures of 203 citizens, more than a third of this number being members of the Committee.

The final result, as the election approached, was somewhat complicated, and must have been confusing to the average voter. If he wished to support the independent ticket, he would have to vote for certain Whigs and for certain Democrats, and there were also seven candidates who were running with merely independent endorsement, lacking the support of either political party. Among these latter were three prominent members — Payran, Ryckman, and Huie — who were presenting themselves to the electorate for various offices having to do with law-enforcement. In addition, the voter might have been confused by the fact that Judge Campbell and Sheriff Hays had the independent endorsement, though Campbell had excoriated the Committee, and Hays had taken its two prisoners.

The election was a triumph for the independents — and thus, indirectly, for the Committee. The independents held the balance of power, so that whether they supported a Whig or a Democrat that candidate's election was assured. On the other hand, the independents running without party affiliation were badly defeated. It was apparently another exemplification of the well-known political rule that the amateurs are not likely to defeat the professionals. Three members of the Committee (two Democrats and one Whig) were elected to the state legislature.

With the better candidates elected, with the city quiet, with the crime rate low, plans for the deactivization of the Commit-

tee could proceed. There was, however, the beginning of a
flare-up on September 4. On that day, a member of the Committee communicated with Payran about a certified copy of
McDougal's pardon of Duane. The member wrote:

> I believe that this community will hold us responsible if we
> allow so great a rascal as Duane to go at large. I have already
> had it said to me that if the Committee are consistent they will
> either have to confine Duane or send him out of the country.

Even here, however, we should notice that the proposition
was to confine or exile. Even in the case of "Dutch Charlie" the
Committee was no longer thinking in terms of hanging.

Next day, the Executive Committee ordered that Duane
should be arrested, and kept "in a good and secure place." At
this point, however, Duane solved the situation himself, by quietly going aboard the steamer *Pacific,* and leaving for Panama.

Perhaps he was tipped off by some spy. Perhaps, indeed, the
members of the Executive Committee itself let the news leak.
They could not, in conscience and honor, refuse to take action
against Duane, but they undoubtedly were very happy to have
him leave of his own accord. Thus, by good luck, the case of
Duane never created as much excitement as it might have done.
It was, in many ways, the most flagrant case occurring during
the period of the Committee's activity. To its original brutality was added the governor's shameless interference with the
course of justice.

On the day when the Executive Committee ordered Duane's
arrest, it also disposed of David Earl, by ordering him to leave
the state within ten days. An ex-convict, named David Turner,
was also directed to leave, and to pay for his own passage.

As the second week of September opened, the Executive
Committee was still working on plans for reorganization.
Financial difficulties were arising. The Committee was looking

for cheaper rooms. It was beginning, like all human beings and all human institutions, to feel the effects of old age.

On September 9 there was a belated flare-up of the Duane case. The Grand Jury of the Court of Sessions unanimously asked to be discharged, the jurors declaring that they were not willing to jeopardize their lives under such an abuse of pardoning. Though the judge did not discharge them, the incident shows the depth of feeling which the case had aroused, particularly because Ball had suffered for his conscientious jury-service.

On September 10, George Schenck offered his resignation from the Executive Committee. In a sense, this event may be considered cataclysmic. Without Schenck the Committee of Vigilance would never have been what it had been.

In any episode of history there are men like Schenck. Without them, indeed, we may doubt whether the events of history would ever get themselves consummated. These men are not the great leaders, but they make the great leaders possible. They are men who are able, conscientious, and courageous, but lack the flare of leadership.

Schenck came of an old Dutch family of New Amsterdam. Reaching San Francisco in October, 1849, he became a commission-merchant. He served on the jury of the Berdue trial, and was one of the three jurors who courageously, and correctly, voted for acquittal. On the night of June 9 he signed as #68. Elected to the Executive Committee, he served on that body continuously, but without being an officer. He was responsible for the arrest of Jenkins, and was present at the hanging. He was involved with the identification of Stuart. He got rid of Sheriff Hays before the rescue of Whittaker and McKenzie.

He now resigned because he was forced to make a trip to New York. We may consider, however, that if the Committee had not been on the point of dissolution, Schenck would not have left San Francisco.

The lines of his letter were emotionally charged, as they well might be. He had experienced deeply in the company of his colleagues of the Executive Committee. He expressed his regret "at parting with Gentlemen who by their many Virtues have so endeared themselves to me that their names shall ever hold a place in my memory." He urged their continuance "in this good cause of reform." Showing even broader interest, he advised:

> Use your influence, Gentlemen, for the establishment of Schools, Academies, and Seminaries, of learning and virtue. This accomplished, you can say with pride that this — our state of California — has become one of the brightest stars in the great galaxy of our glorious Union.

The letter of acceptance, written for the Executive Committee and signed by Payran, was equally charged with feeling, for "our Brother G. E. Schenck." Payran, in his somewhat florid style, recalled the dangerous and desperate days of arson and assault during which the Committee had first been organized:

> Although the day was dark, and danger stared us in the face, we assayed to meet the storm and test the consequence; the spirits of our revolutionary Sires prompted us; virtue guided our acts; corrupt representatives yielded; Felons and Incendiaries fled. Light has taken the place of darkness, and a calm has succeeded the storm; peace and security are restored.

Such words, written to a friend and colleague, and not for publication, may be accepted as sincere. The members of the Executive Committee thought that their work had been brought to a successful conclusion.

On September 15 the prisoners' room had at last been emptied. On the next evening a general meeting was held, and a reorganization was effected. The Committee renounced its power. Its period of activity had totaled exactly one hundred days.

# POSTSCRIPT

THE COMMITTEE did not disband on September 16, and technically it never disbanded. Members were relieved of active duties, but they remained members.

From this time on, the Committee met infrequently. The reduced activities were entrusted to an Executive Committee which was doubled in size. This committee was to be primarily a watchdog, observing the conduct of public courts and officers, and holding itself in readiness for action, if needed, against ill-doers. Most of the members of the old Executive Committee continued to serve upon the new one. Brannan and Coleman became members once more. Payran and Bluxome again served as president and secretary.

Two incidents of the next month were of significance. . . . On October 8 Andrew Goodwin presented a petition. His ten-year-old niece, Mary Lye, had been taken from him by a certain Ernest Kohle and his wife, and was being held in a house of prostitution at Marysville.

Payran was deputed to attend to the business. He went to Marysville, and consulted with the committee there; then, accompanied by several of its members, he went to the house and made his demand. The owners of the house responded at first with bluster and threats, but soon quieted down, and handed the girl over. . . .

On October 31, the mob rose again. The sloop *Challenge* had arrived in the harbor, and its men, on going ashore, were loud in their complaints at the brutality that they had suffered from their officers. Angry sailors and stevedores soon collected. The excitement grew, and the mob began to cry for a lynching.

At this point a curious reversal occurred. The mayor himself ordered that the bell should be tapped, thus sounding what had been known as the signal for the assembling of the Committee. (He later explained that he had ordered the bell to be tapped as a signal to law-abiding citizens to assemble for the suppression of the mob.) Naturally, at the well-known signal, the members of the Committee rapidly rallied. The mayor was reported to have accepted their services, not as a Committee, but "as a body of citizens, merely" — a fine distinction.

In any case, the show of force was sufficient to quiet the mob, and the sailors were placated by promises of a legal investigation. The captain was eventually tried and fined.

This incident marked what we may call the domestication of the Committee. Since its reorganization, indeed, it could scarcely have been called an illegal organization. It was, rather, a group functioning in support of the laws, and in cooperation with the authorities.

On December 10 the Executive Committee authorized the issuance of certificates of membership. These were printed on vellum and sold for five dollars. Although prepared so late as to be only *ex post facto* evidence, the language of the certificates shows something of how the vigilantes thought of themselves. The highest-placed motto was in Latin, "Fiat justitia ruat coelum," which may be translated "Let justice be done, even though heaven fall." Below this was the symbol of the watchful eye. There were also the mottoes in English, "Self preservation, the first law of nature," and "Be just and fear not." The Committee was stated to have been organized "For the mutual protection of life & property, rendered insecure by the general inefficiency of the laws and their maladministration."

On into 1852, the Executive Committee continued to meet and to record its minutes. There were no spectacular developments, and probably this was just as the leaders wished. By continuing to remain "in being," by the very power of its dread name, the Committee of Vigilance could exercise a salutary effect upon the life of the city.

A few items of old business continued to crop up. On February 13, Sheriff Hays reported that he had received $4694.29 from the funds raised by the Committee, and that he had expended this amount for the completion of the county jail.

The old Metcalf-Argenti case dragged on for some months. Originally there had been much excitement about the threat to private liberties represented by the assumption of the right of search by the Committee. But the Committee had not made excessive use of search, and after its reorganization the question ceased to be current. Metcalf's lawyers, scenting high profits, pushed the case persistently. They twice won hollow victories, receiving once a judgment for $201, and finally the nominal verdict of six cents.

Late in 1852, the city was alarmed by an increase of crime and by several fires, some of them thought to be the work of incendiaries. In this emergency a general meeting of the Committee was called, by notice in the newspapers, for the evening of November 19. No record exists of this meeting, good evidence that nothing of much importance happened. On November 25, a certain Charles Talbot was arrested on a charge of arson, "by Number 1." (This should have been Selim Woodworth.) A deposition was taken from Talbot and also from a man called as a witness.

The Executive Committee, meeting on the next day, took no action on Talbot. Presumably, he had either been discharged or turned over to the authorities. The meeting concerned itself with elections. Ryckman was chosen as president, and Bluxome was continued as secretary. These actions would indicate that the Committee was to continue indefinitely. There are, however, no later records in the official papers.

Nevertheless, in January, 1853, the newspapers were publish-

ing notices under the heading "Committee of Vigilance."
These notices requested the cooperation of the citizens in the
suppression of arson, burglary, and highway robbery, and offered $2000 for "the arrest, with sufficient testimony for con-
viction, of any person setting fire to any building." Thus the
Committee retained a special interest in incendiarism.

The Committee never followed Schenck's admonition to become a general agent of good by founding "Schools, Acade-
mies, and Seminaries, of learning and virtue." One might note,
however, that Dr. Samuel Merritt, #507, became a regent of
the University of California, and left his fortune to found Merritt Hospital in Oakland. Moreover, according to Bluxome's
reminiscences, the Committee took action to establish a library.
Bluxome himself contributed some five hundred volumes,
and these books eventually went to the Mercantile Library,
which merged with the still-existing Mechanics Library.

There is a newspaper mention of a meeting of the Executive
Committee in March, 1853. The authors of *The Annals of
San Francisco,* written in 1854, were probably well informed in
declaring:

> The Vigilance Committee has long ceased to act, but the
> association has never been formally dissolved. The original
> members are doubtless ready, if ever sad occasion should re-
> quire, again to assert the right of self-preservation, and the su-
> premacy of natural law.

In 1856 the city suffered new troubles, different in nature
from those of 1851. A new committee was then organized.
Many members of 1851 joined that of 1856, and the connection by tradition was close. But the new committee was
not formed by reactivating the earlier one. Some members of
the original Committee, notably Ryckman, refused to join
that of 1856. We may therefore consider that the later com-

mittee was a new organization, and that its story is therefore a different one. In any case, its formation may be said finally to have put an end to the story.

In a sense, then, the Committee faded out, and ended ingloriously. Perhaps, however, this was the best way. A disbanding ceremony, with bugles blowing and cannon saluting, might have seemed to be a signal for criminals to resume activities, or could have been interpreted as a final defiance of the authorities.

# RETROSPECT

T HE COMMITTEE did not vanish without trace. It continued to exist in the records, in the lives of its members,
and in a tradition.

It can scarcely, however, be said to exist still as a place.
Although downtown San Francisco is a modern American reality, neither stick nor brick nor tree survives from 1851. Only
the pattern of the streets, their names, and the general shapes
of the hills remain. The Plaza is still an open space, but it is
terraced in concrete and a parking facility underlies it. On
the site of the Committee rooms stands an office-building. You
can still walk down Battery Street, as the four hundred marched
with Stuart — but, where they turned into the wharf, now
stretches out the broad reach of lower Market Street.

On the other hand, the Committee's original papers have
lasted intact through fire, earthquake, and ravaging time.
Their careful preservation was urged by the Executive Committee at the time of the reorganization. These papers should
be kept, that committee declared, as an evidence of the good
faith of the members, and "that in the future their actions may
be shown to any representative body, should it be required."

This attitude is remarkable. These men had been accused of
capital crimes. Yet they chose to preserve the records which
might be thought to incriminate each of them as individuals.
Such action is evidence of good conscience.

The Committee took no official action about the papers, and

they merely remained in the possession of Bluxome as secretary. After about twenty-five years he presented them to the historian H. H. BANCROFT, who used them for his *Popular Tribunals* and *History of California.* In 1906 his great collection became the property of the University of California, and the papers now rest in the Bancroft Library at Berkeley.

The Academy of Pacific Coast History undertook publication, and Porter Garnett made a beginning in 1910-1911. The bulk of the papers appeared in 1919, as the result of the herculean labors of Mary Floyd Williams, in a massive volume of 906 pages.

The existence of the papers allows the historian to treat the Committee with some degree of confidence. The newspaper accounts, though vivid, lie on the surface. The reminiscences, most of them collected by Bancroft a generation after the events, deal chiefly with a few dramatic episodes, and are inaccurate even about these. But the minutes and miscellaneous papers permit a penetration into what was actually happening, and why.

Even the financial accounts and the vouchers have their interest, and sometimes their importance. Nor, even after publication, can a scholar wholly neglect the yellowing papers themselves. I have several times consulted the original documents, and, on the evidence of changes of pen and ink and other such details, have been able to wring significant information from them. . . .

The Committee also continued to exist in the lives of its 710 members. Some of them, indeed, did not last long. Oakes, who might be called the founder, died before the year was out. A hundred members, with the banner of the Committee, marched in his procession. The rooms were draped in black for thirty days, and the members wore mourning.

Though the Committee had directed its activity against violence, John J. McKaraher, #115, was murdered a few days after the reorganization. He had had the bad judgment to visit a low drinking-house across the bay, with $150 on his person. An investigating posse reported "his body disposed of in some manner to conceal it."

Others lived on. The two oldsters, Ryckman and Stevenson, survived into their eighties, remaining prominent citizens. Others also passed many years in San Francisco, and among these we may note Schenck and Bluxome, who remained prosperous merchants. Others went elsewhere. Watson, who as "Justice" had done much to start matters, lived in Massachusetts. There he wrote his memoirs, and eventually, through the agency of Chief Justice Earl Warren, a copy was deposited in the California State Library. Payran went to live at Petaluma, fifty miles to the north, where Payran Street commemorates him.

Captain Ned Wakeman, Chief of the Water Police and principal handler of nooses, continued to live colorfully, and eventually published his memoirs, *The Log of an Ancient Mariner*. In 1866 he had as a passenger on his ship a young journalist named Sam Clemens. As a result, Wakeman is generally considered to have achieved immortality as Captain Stormfield, whom Mark Twain sent upon a voyage that might well be the envy of even the most ancient of mariners.

As might be expected from their temperaments, the members reacted quickly to war. H. M. Naglee, #132, and James F. Curtis, #35, were Union generals; Selim Woodworth served as a commodore in the Union navy. A. Van Horne Ellis, #682, as colonel, took the 124th New York into the second day's fighting at Gettysburg, and died there.

Brannan, who even more perhaps than Oakes might be claimed as the founder, generally went downhill from this time onward. His was the old story of the California millionaire. He lost his money and took to drink (or perhaps it was the other way around), and eventually died in poverty.

Coleman, the prudent young man who had gone home to

change his coat that Sunday morning, was destined to live so eventfully that his lively experiences in 1851 shrank to the dimensions of a passing incident. Even though his name does not appear in the records often, he had managed to impress his colleagues with his courage, wisdom, initiative, and integrity. Soon afterwards, Coleman went to New York, and there he devoted himself successfully to making money. Returning to San Francisco, he found himself selected — or drafted — to be the head of the Vigilance Committee of 1856. He was undisputed leader of this great organization, which mustered its thousands to the hundreds of '51. Having taken care of his city's business, Coleman — in the tradition of Cincinnatus — retired to private life. He rapidly became one of the wealthiest men of the state. At the same time, in spite of his gaudy participation in two illegal committees, he remained a pillar of society, of almost oppressive respectability.

During the disturbances of 1877, Coleman was again forced to act as a kind of temporaray dictator to the city. This time, however, as head of the Committee of Safety, he was acting in collaboration with the authorities. His reputation became such that he received some support for the presidential nomination of 1884.

Coleman's firm failed in 1886, and the creditors could be paid only 46¢ on the dollar. In the heroic tradition of personal responsibility, he refused to accept the solution of bankruptcy, and managed to pay his creditors in full before his death in 1893.

But Coleman, though the greatest, was not the longest-lived. That title, it would seem, must go to James R. Duff, #169, who died in San Francisco on August 9, 1917, at the age of ninety-two. He had been young enough on that August day when he had been one of Cartwright's thirty. Then he had clung to the box of the perilously careening carriage, as it had gone dashing through the streets behind the white horses.

Since the principle had been established "Once a member, always a member," we must therefore consider that the Committee, in a certain sense, remained in existence until 1917. . . .

The Committee lived on, also, in a tradition. The events of that summer established in general American speech the terms *Vigilance Committee* and *vigilante*. *Vigilantism* has also become a recognized word.

Inevitably, the tradition has created new conceptions which are sometimes misconceptions. Gradually, the term *committee* has gone out of use, and *vigilante* has remained. In 1851, the Committee was organized largely to forestall mob-action, but in present usage, there has ceased to be any distinction between vigilantes and a mob. The fact is, however, that not only in San Francisco, but also in Sonora and Downieville, the organization of a committee followed upon an outbreak of mob-violence with the purpose of preventing another such incident.

Throughout many years the tradition remained pro-vigilante. People remembered, more and more vaguely as time progressed, that the Committee had rescued the city from criminals and dishonest officials. Almost all the historians, though sometimes offering adverse criticisms, supported the Committee on the whole.

Only in the last few years has there been some tendency toward a reversal of opinion. The reasons for such a reversal are fairly clear. The semantic shift of the word *vigilante* has emphasized the mob-action. The frontier, with its associated violence, has vanished, and people have forgotten its stresses. A more effectively functioning democracy has increased confidence in the ballot. Finally, a strongly developed objection to capital punishment has made the actions of the Committee the more repellent. . . .

The members of the Committee, on their own part, never flinched in their conviction that they were acting from the highest motives. When challenged in court with being a member, James Wilber, #260, snapped back, "I am proud to say that I am able to present a character that entitles me to a membership in the Vigilance Committee." Payran, writing to the newly-organized committee in Nevada City, declared:

> Our great aim, gentlemen, is to remove corruption from high places, to advance the safety and the interest of our adopted state, to establish justice and virtue. . . . That your course may be marked with prudence and justice, may God grant. Do not permit vindictiveness to enter into your deliberations. Be calm and determined; swerve not to the right nor to the left, but go onward in your pursuit of right.

To some, such words may smack of hypocrisy, and there is no doubt but that the worst deeds may be committed by men with high ideals, or self-deceived. Yet, at least, these men should be allowed to present their case.

The Committee, in so far as it acted to enforce the laws, was in itself acting illegally. From the strictly legal point of view it was no different from any lynching mob or band of murderers. Some people, interpreting the situation wholly by logic, have thus concluded.

But the situation is not so black-and-white. It involves the problem of the relationship of the individual and the state, and this problem is perpetual, complicated, difficult, and not wholly soluble.

When the individual acts against the state in certain ways, we classify the action as crime. When he behaves somewhat differently, we call it conscientious objection, though it is still illegal. When the action against the state is of still another kind, we employ the terms insurrection, rebellion, and revolution, and such action also is illegal.

"Dutch Charlie" kicking Frank Ball, Thoreau refusing to pay his poll-tax, the embattled farmers shooting down the redcoats at Concord bridge — all performed illegal acts. But only a pedant, one would think, could maintain that no distinction may be made among the actions, and that they are all, being illegal, the same. Most people would attempt to make some distinction on the basis of such standards as those of motivation and individual conscience. The San Franciscans themselves did so, even in 1851, and the theories of justification are still of interest.

The men who organized the Committee acted hastily. They seem to have been intelligent, but few of them were highly educated or well read. They were not lawyers, and they had little sense of the tradition of the law.

At the time they were not much concerned with a theoretical legality. Crime was rampant, and the administration of justice seemed to have broken down. The mob had risen, more than once, and had been with difficulty restrained from violent action. Into such a situation Jenkins had the misfortune to be precipitated, and the members of the Committee were swept into their first illegal action with little time for reflection.

If any member had been called upon at that time to justify himself, he would probably have raised the plea of self-defense. "To be sure," he might have said, "no Sydney duck is at this moment pointing a revolver at me or pressing a knife against my throat. But potentially it is so! Look at what happened to Jansen! Why should we wait until they attack us at their chosen time and place? Law-enforcement is a farce. The police, the judges, the lawyers — many of them are allied with the criminals. Therefore I plead, 'Self-defense.' "

Under the circumstances, in a disturbed frontier city, the plea was a strong and convincing one. The chances are that many members never needed to go beyond it, to satisfy their consciences. On this basis, we may also believe, most of the citizens of San Francisco supported the Committee. Among these supporters were all but one of the newspaper editors, and many of the ministers. Even some of the public officials, such as Sheriff

Hays, were sympathetic, and probably on the basis of self-defense.

As time went on, other doctrines were developed. There were the conceptions of the "higher law," or "natural law," and of the individual conscience. Hunt presented such ideas strikingly in his sermon. Usually, in this connection, we think primarily in negative terms. We are familiar with the conscientious objector, whose conscience forbids him to perform certain actions, though the law enjoins him to perform them. But cannot conscience be positive? Cannot it force a man to defend his city personally, when he believes that the emergency so demands? Just as a man may refuse to bear arms because his conscience so forbids him, similarly a man, we might think, may go out and hang someone because his conscience so commands him.

Another argument was raised that the Committee represented the will of the people, and therefore had democratic justification. Though the Committee certainly did not represent the people as the result of an election or through the process of any legal machinery, still the argument had some basis of reality. Before the hanging of Jenkins and before the hanging of Stuart a crowd gathered. On each occasion a spokesman for the Committee went out, explained the situation, and then put the question whether the citizens thus assembled would approve the proposed act. Each time, a shout went up in the affirmative.

These expressions of popular approval were highly comforting to the members of the Committee. If such a crowd was not wholly representative of the citizenry, its shout at least came as close to expressing the real will of the people as did one of the notoriously dishonest elections.

Eventually, however, still another argument was put forward — one which seems both to come closest to reality, and to give to the Committee its deepest significance. The argument was that the action constituted a revolution.

This idea of revolution had cropped up at the very beginning. In one of the riots about the Jansen case in February, some excited Frenchmen were heard crying, "Une révolution! Une révolution!" These Frenchmen may well have fought at the barricades in '48. Perhaps they sensed a deep reality.

Soon after the organization of the Committee, its very size suggested a revolutionary movement. Although there was never an appeal for mass-membership, the numbers soon passed five hundred, and in a city of not more than thirty thousand, such a group was far from negligible.

Now, in connection with numbers, the law is far from being divinely consistent. When John Brown with a few followers begins shooting, the law condemns and hangs him as an individual criminal. When the people of eleven states begin shooting, those captured are treated as prisoners of war. For, behind all its high pronouncements of equal justice for all, the law must be practical. If we hang our prisoners, you hang your prisoners. So neither side hangs prisoners, and never mind about having hanged old John Brown.

But this affair of 1851 was not an ordinary revolution. That kind we know. It strikes at the sovereign or at the national power. It gains control at the top, and therefore dominates all branches of government. It takes over permanently, that is, until it is overthrown in its turn. Such revolutions loom large in history.

But the Committee did not strike at the national power, or even at the state power. It took over at the bottom — with the city and county. Moreover, it renounced its own power, thus becoming temporary. Also, it affected the different branches of government differently.

One can scarcely say that the Committee concerned itself at all with the legislative branch. It passed no laws. In general it seems to have accepted the criminal code of California, somewhat liberally interpreted on a commonsense basis, without the aid of lawyers. The Committee affected the executive branch chiefly by assuming certain police powers. It had nothing to do with such executive functions as collecting taxes. Even the judicial branch was not wholly superseded. The Committee tried no civil cases, rejected many criminal cases, and turned many prisoners over to the authorities. The Committee allowed the courts to function against its own members, even in cases which concerned the work of the Committee itself.

The idea that the movement was a revolution appeared in print as early as June 14 in an editorial in the *Alta*. Hunt did not hesitate to use the term in his sermon.

One of the most interesting discussions appeared in the *Herald* of August 11 in a communication signed "Cuidado." The writer presented a theory of revolution — or of "insurrection," as he termed it. In maintaining "the indisputable right of insurrection," he made an interesting analogy with war. When two nations sign a treaty, he declared, they lay down certain stipulations. They insert, however, no stipulation as to the penalty for violation. Both sides know that the penalty is war. So, he continued, it is with individuals and the state. It is nowhere written into a constitution that, if the government governs badly, the people will revolt against it. But everyone knows that this has always happened, and inevitably must happen, and so is really a part of the constitution, even though it is not included in any article. He summed up by declaring the present one to be "an imperfect insurrection," because it had not assumed all the governmental functions.

Inevitably comparisons were made with the American Revolution. "Pacific," writing to the *Herald* on July 16, shortly after Judge Campbell's blast against the Committee, stated that George Washington would have been hanged by the same reasoning. "Justice," in the *Herald* of September 28, pointed out that the Founding Fathers were "rebels" and "committee men," since the Committee of Safety was then much in fashion. The Executive Committee, in accepting Schenck's resignation, declared, "the spirits of our revolutionary Sires prompted us."

In 1851 Americans thought rather commonly in terms of revolution. The revolt against King George was only three-quarters of a century in the past, and the older members of the Committee may literally have had "Revolutionary sires." More recently, American sentiment had supported revolutions in Latin America, and in many European countries. Writing in *Civil Disobedience*, published in 1849, Thoreau could state:

> All men recognize the right of revolution; that is, the right to refuse allegiance to, and to resist, the government, when its tyranny or its inefficiency are great and unendurable.

There was, indeed, a certain feeling that the Committee might actually have made a mistake by not going farther than it did. To have seized the city government completely and then to have administered it on an emergency basis might have produced less disturbance than what actually occurred.

There is always difficulty in stopping halfway. But the Committee, not yielding to the intoxication of power, so stopped, and finally withdrew, of its own accord. It has thus supplied an almost unique episode in history.

Nevertheless the situation was critical on August 20. Had the Committee acted favorably on the proposition laid before it, its members would have marched on the jail, and after that there might have been no turning back.

If the Committee had moved forward, its course toward revolution could have led to two possible consummations. The more radical of these, by following a conventional course, would have been somewhat commonplace, and therefore, historically speaking, of less interest.

This more conventional revolution would have been against the federal government. Since the Committee could not have hoped to overthrow the government in Washington, their revolution would have set its goal as independence, after the pattern of the thirteen colonies, and of Texas against Mexico. The examples were well known, and just ten years later there was to be a large-scale experiment in secession.

Such a contingency would have been possible. Some rash and foolish federal official might have allied himself with the foolish governor, and begun to breathe fire and sword. With visions of trials before hostile juries, imprisonments and firing squads, the men of the Committee might have preferred to try ordeal by battle, and thus to become fully revolutionary.

In such a situation the odds would have been on the side of the Committee. The federal troops in California were possibly two thousand strong, were not remarkable for armament or leadership, and were in a strategically impossible position, being garrisoned in posts of company strength all over the state. The Navy had the *Vincennes,* and a revenue cutter or two. On the other side, the Committee could muster its own hundreds, plus contingents of allied committees from every town and mining-camp in the state. We should remember that the Santa Clarans had volunteered their services.

The Committee could hardly have failed to win. Most of the little Army garrisons, isolated from their high command, would probably have made terms after token resistance or none at all. He would have been a rash captain or lieutenant who would have ordered his men to fire upon the local citizens.

Then we should have had the Pacific Republic. Mere distance would probably have prevented an attempt at re-conquest, though we can hardly doubt that a peace would have been patched up and a reunion effected.

The more interesting situation would have been to have the Committee stage its revolution against the state. No such overthrow of a state government by revolution has occurred in our history. Somewhat similar revolutions, however, are known in Mexico.

At the beginning, Governor McDougal ignored the whole affair. When he visited the rooms, he was actually, if the testimony of the four members is to be trusted, in a friendly state of mind to the Committee. Then, having taken decisive action by his secret pardon of Duane, he declared war by taking the prisoners and launching his violent proclamation.

If the Committee had accepted his challenge, as it was very close to doing, the whole state would probably have gone off like a powder barrel. All the advantage would have been on the side of the Committee, reinforced by the committees from all over the state.

The governor had no troops; there was no organized militia. The only non-federal military companies functioned as private clubs; the governor could merely request their cooperation. Since many of the officers and men were also members of some committees, the governor could not have raised any troops from them. The federal troops would probably have stood neutral.

In actuality, everything would have been a *fait accompli* before the federal officers could have intervened, if they had attempted to do so. In a few hours from the opening of hostilities a steamboat would have docked at Vallejo with a strong-enough contingent aboard to have sent McDougal hustling and capture the state capital. Within twenty-four hours, in all likelihood, the government would have been firmly in the hands of the amalgamated committees. They would then have set up a provisional *de facto* administration. Soon this latter would have held an election, either returning itself to office or being replaced by a friendly governor.

Such was the isolation of California that word of all this would not even have reached the East for a month. Washington could scarcely have done anything but accept the situation. Practical politicians like Broderick would have made their peace with the new regime, and Gwin would probably have continued to represent California in the Senate.

Thus, paradoxically, we may even consider the Committee to

be remarkable, not so much for what it did as for what it did not do. Against the background of all the executions and killings of history, the hanging of four rascals is insignificant. We should rather remember that the Committee did *not* yield to the temptations of power, and did *not* carry its revolution to a logical conclusion.

This remarkable ending may be explained as the result of several influences. . . . In spite of 1776 there was no active tradition of revolution in the United States, so that the members of the Committee had neither the drive nor the technique toward that end. No individual in the Committee, it would appear, possessed at once the urge toward power and the personal strength to become a leader of revolution. The merchants, who controlled the Committee, looked upon the whole affair as a time-consuming and generally tedious interference with business — the sooner to be safely liquidated, the better. The Committee had no practising lawyers among its members, and lawyers were the most politically conscious group, and were likely to be individually ambitious and able.

Not only was it a partial revolution, but it was also, we must remember, a successful partial revolution. Those who participated in it were honored in their city, throughout the years, as the leaders of a successful revolution may expect to be honored. They were heroes not only to the citizens generally, but also to the historians. Even Josiah Royce, a philosopher-turned-historian, concluded his account of the Committee with the words, "a good beginning had been made in righteousness."

One of the most interesting judgments came from Richard Henry Dana, Jr., at the time of his visit to San Francisco only eight years after 1851. He wrote then, referring to the Committee of 1856 as well as to the earlier one, that the city had been

handed back to soberness, morality, and good government, by that peculiar invention of Anglo-Saxon Republican America, the solemn awe-inspiring Vigilance Committee of the most grave and responsible citizens.

Dana was a lawyer, a Harvard graduate, a member of an old Boston family, and a man particularly interested in human rights. He was a contemporary of the Committees, but far enough removed to have some objectivity. His endorsement cannot be lightly rejected. Of especial interest is his comment that the Committee of Vigilance was a "peculiar invention" of the United States. Now, certainly, mobs have raged and killed in most parts of the world, and the United States can claim no priority in such actions. What Dana meant was that only in the United States has there existed that curious halfway institution which was fully manifested in the San Francisco of 1851. This cannot be justly called a mob, for it does not act like a mob. Yet its actions are just as illegal as those of a mob. It is a Committee of Vigilance.

More strictly speaking, it *was* a Committee of Vigilance, for no example has occurred in many years. In fact, the only two full-fledged examples were those of San Francisco in '51 and '56.

The historians have not usually approved the Committee wholly, and in the general judgment of good citizens its record leaves much to be desired. A common criticism has been that it effected little permanent change, and that the criminals and corrupt officials again became rampant in the city. Yet this in itself cannot be considered a very serious charge. What reform-movement was ever wholly successful?

Attack has also been made upon the Committee on the grounds that the situation was not really so bad as to warrant interference, and that the legal authorities would have got things under control. But this is merely one of the "ifs" of history. No one knows, or ever can know. The very fact that the Committee took action makes it impossible for us to know what would have happened if it had not taken action.

The most serious charge against the Committee is that it weakened the respect for law, and in the long run tended to make the situation worse instead of better. The charge cannot be lightly dismissed, but some defense is possible. The men of 1851 did not even invent the term Committee of Vigilance, much less the practice of vigilantism. That practice was the heritage of the turbulent frontier. Historically considered, the Committee, organized to forestall mob-action, may even be said to represent a step in the direction of ordered justice. The later semantic evolution of the words *vigilante* and *vigilantism* should not be held against the Committee.

If the Committee is to be judged on the basis of its results as shown by conditions at the present day, we may indeed maintain no high opinion of it. One of the chief reasons for its organization was the law's delay. But, reading the record of 1851, a modern citizen is impressed by the rapidity of the courts' actions. The interval between arrest and trial is now much greater than it was then. Nor has crime declined. San Francisco is about the same as other American cities, and its streets are now more dangerous, probably, than in 1851. Bank robbery is of weekly, or even of daily, occurrence. Rape and purse-snatching with violence are too common to get much space in the newspapers. An old man, inoffensively taking a walk after dark, is viciously beaten for no reason at all. As a result, people are warned not to go walking after dark, and we move a little closer to the time when each man must again carry his own weapon.

Such a crime as the attack upon Jansen would not raise a mob now. It would scarcely make the newspapers.

The present apathetic acceptance of a high crime-rate is disturbing. The men of 1851 may have got too much excited over a few crimes. But the citizen of today, though he may object to the illegal actions of 1851, has no reason to be smug about how he is keeping his own house in order. . . .

The record may be summarized. The Committee made ninety-one recorded arrests. Four men were hanged and one was whipped. Fourteen persons were deported to Australia, and fourteen were more informally ordered to leave California. Fifteen were handed over to the authorities. Forty-one were discharged. Two others, of whom no disposition is noted, were probably discharged. There is, of course, no summation of those who fled to escape arrest, or of those who may have been dissuaded from ways of crime by fear of punishment.

The record is eloquent in itself. It speaks of moderation and of the attempt to render justice. There were no mass hangings, no men shot down in the street. There was none of that grim nonsense, "Give him a fair trial and then hang him!" To be arrested did not mean that a man was already condemned, but only that he stood trial, with a half-and-half chance of being cleanly acquitted.

The record indicates that the police-methods were humane. If the whipping of a man is to be considered cruel punishment, let it also be remembered that knots were removed from the cords before the cat was applied. There are several notes in the records indicating concern for the prisoners' well-being. Nothing, even in accusations by enemies, suggests that the prisoners were treated roughly to break them down into confessions. The small proportion of convictions in itself supplies evidence that the accused was allowed to make the best defense possible. Even the most violent opponents of the Committee, though they attacked it vigorously for illegality, did not attack it on the grounds of inhumanity or the punishment of innocent men.

The saying "Desperate ills demand desperate remedies" is one that may mask much evil. It is akin to that other, "The end justifies the means." Some believe that certain remedies are too desperate ever to be used, and therefore they wholly eschew war, revolution, and capital punishment. But in the rough-and-tumble that is human history men have often turned to such expedients, in hope of escaping from conditions which they find intolerable. If such desperate remedies are ever to be tried, at least the Committee of Vigilance of 1851, throughout its hundred days, applied them with courage and moderation, and with a sense of responsibility to humanity and justice.

SOURCES AND ACKNOWLEDGMENTS

NOTES

INDEX

# SOURCES AND ACKNOWLEDGMENTS

M Y INTEREST in the Committee began in 1920, when I first read the newspaper accounts and prepared a report in a class at the University of California under Professor C. W. Wells. In the early thirties I attempted to tell the story by means of newspaper clippings. The present book thus represents a return to unfinished business.

The major sources are (1) the contemporary San Francisco newspapers, and (2) the papers of the Committee itself.

Of the newspapers the most valuable are the *Daily Alta California* and the *Herald.* I have also used the *Courier,* the *Pacific News,* and the *Evening Picayune.*

The papers of the Committee have been edited by Porter Garnett (*Acad. of Pac. Coast Hist., Publications,* i and ii) and Mary Floyd Williams (*idem,* iv). Certain of the papers remain unpublished in the Bancroft Library, and I have also used these. (See also, *Retrospect*).

Reminiscences constitute a third but much less important source. These were mostly collected in the 1870s at the instance of H. H. Bancroft, and are preserved in manuscript in the Bancroft Library. Here are the statements of the members Isaac Bluxome, W. T. Coleman, James Dows, J. D. Farwell, C. V. Gillespie, J. P. Manrow, James Neall, G. W. Ryckman, G. E. Schenck, T. L. Smiley, J. C. L. Wadsworth. Also of interest, in the Bancroft Library, is the anti-Committee statement of Harvey S. Brown. The reminiscences of R. S. Watson (photographic copy) are in the California State Library. Edgar Wakeman included a brief account of his services in his *Log of an Ancient Mariner* (1878). W. W. Carpenter (*Oakland*

*Transcript,* March 29, 1878) records some of Stephen Payran's memories. The reminiscences of Charles P. Kimball, *San Francisco Vigilence [sic] Committee of 1851* are in the Bancroft Library.

As would be expected of writings based upon recollections of events many years in the past, the reminiscences are generally inaccurate, as checked against the newspapers and the Committee's own records. They are valuable as recording vivid impressions of particular incidents.

Of all the participants Coleman wrote most voluminously on the subject. Besides the statement already mentioned, he prepared a manuscript about his life for Bancroft's *Chronicles of the Builders.* In addition to what was published in that volume, the original statement is in the Bancroft Library. He also wrote *San Francisco Vigilance Committees* (*Century Illustrated Monthly Magazine,* xliii). These statements are repetitive, and are chiefly valuable as showing what Coleman thought in later years, not what actually happened in 1851 or what he thought about it then.

The only contemporary journals that I have found are those of Martha H. Hitchcock (Mills College Library) and J. Goldsborough Bruff (*Gold Rush,* New York, 1944.) Neither of these is of much value, but we may note that both of them seem at least to accept, and even to favor, the Committee.

A few contemporary letters are of interest as preserving the immediate impressions of events upon individuals. I have used the published correspondence of Alonzo Delano (*California Correspondence,* 1952), and the manuscript letters of Martha H. Hitchcock (Mills College Library) and R. S. La Motte, or Lammot (Bancroft Library). A letter from an anonymous correspondent appeared in the *Illustrated London News* (Aug. 9, 1851).

A contemporary publication of importance is: T. Dwight Hunt, *Sermon suggested by the Execution of Jenkins* (1851). Of similar significance is Frank Soulé, John H. Gihon, and James Nisbet, *The Annals of San Francisco* (1855); compiled in 1854, it gives a contemporary impression of the events. Some interesting details are preserved in the correspondence of the British consul (photocopies in Bancroft Library, and C. S. Forester, *S. F. Chronicle,* May 20, 1951.)

The first important historical treatment of the Committee was by Josiah Royce, *California from the Conquest in 1846 to the Second Vigilance Committee in San Francisco* (1886). Royce based his account chiefly on the newspapers and *The Annals of San Francisco,* but he also had some direct contact with R. S. Watson.

H. H. Bancroft, in *Popular Tribunals* (i, 1887), treated the Committee at length, making use of the Committee's papers and of the reminiscences which he had himself collected. The text is further built up by the use of constructed conversations and by the insertion of remarkable details for which no source is given and for which I can find no contemporary authority. I have therefore made little use of the volume as an original source. Bancroft's treatment of the Committee in his *History of California* is brief and unimportant.

A basic work is Mary Floyd Williams, *History of the San Francisco Committee of Vigilance of 1851* (1921). Although I differ from Dr. Williams in some matters of interpretation and presentation, I remain greatly impressed by the accuracy of her work and by the comprehensiveness of her research, and I happily remember a conversation with her some years ago.

Later treatments have been Stanton A. Coblentz, *Villains and Vigilantes* (1936); J. A. B. Scherer, *The Lion of the Vigilantes* (1939); Alan Valentine, *Vigilante Justice* (1956). Since each of these volumes covers a much larger field than the history of the Committee of 1851, the affairs of that committee are presented in summary only.

The bibliography in Dr. Williams's history may be consulted for the numerous scattered (and generally valueless) references to the Committee. Since the date of her compilation, little of importance on the subject has come to light. One might, however, mention the Watson reminiscences and the La Motte letters.

Many individuals have kindly offered cooperation. I wish especially to thank Walton E. Bean, C. S. Forester, Helen S. Giffen, G. W. R. Gilbert (H. M. Vice-Consul, San Francisco), James D. Hart, G. Brett Melendy, Bill Woods, and my wife, Theodosia B. Stewart.

The Bancroft Library holds the original sources, with some minor exceptions. I used its facilities to the full, and wish to thank, as so often before, all of its staff. I also used the University of California

Library; the Library of the California Historical Society (with special thanks to James de T. Abajian) and the California State Library (with special thanks to Allan R. Ottley).

G. R. S.

Berkeley, California

October 15, 1963

# NOTES

THE ORIGINAL sources are often spelled and punctuated care-
lessly. I have generally normalized these details in the quota-
tions.

Chap. 1. In the reconstruction of the crime I have largely ignored
Jansen's testimony, which conflicts with the confessions of Stuart
and Whittaker. Jansen was, I believe, too badly injured to remember clearly.

Chap. 2. There has been a tendency among historians to exagger-
ate the amount of crime before the attack on Jansen, and to consider
that this attack was merely the last straw. Study of the newspapers,
however, leads me to the conclusions stated in the text. As modern
citizens we must feel some humiliation to think that our ancestors
could get so excited about what we would consider a very mild
crime.

Chap. 3. In considering the story one should remember that
mob-action was prevalent in cities of the eighteenth and early nine-
teenth centuries. The American Revolution was notable for a great
amount of such activity.

Just what the captain meant by saying that the Washington
Guards had merely done their duty is hard to tell. Since the Guards
were a private club, they had no duty in the military sense. The
Recorder was not an officer empowered to enroll military forces for
the city or the state. The position of these private organizations was
somewhat anomalous.

Chap. 9. This standard account of the origin of the Committee is derived from Neall's reminiscences. It was adopted by Bancroft and by Williams. Possibly, however, the importance of the Brannan-Oakes group has been exaggerated. Neither Watson nor Bluxome in his reminiscence, when discussing the origin of the Committee, mentions Brannan or Oakes. Moreover, Neall did not join until some time later, since he was #178. Of course, his high number does not necessarily mean that he was not at the meeting of the four on Sunday, since some accident may have prevented his being at the meeting when the constitution was originally signed.

The position and importance of Brannan in the Committee (not only at the beginning, but also later) is difficult to appraise. But then everything about Brannan is difficult to appraise. I have tried to let the incidents speak for themselves.

Various statements indicate that the number of original signers was about one hundred. I have examined the original constitution, and I note a change of ink, after 103 signatures. This change suggests strongly that the original signing ended at this point.

The assignment of a number to each member was an obvious device to aid the maintenance of secrecy. Since the Committee worked away from the idea of secrecy, the numbers became of little importance. Names and not numbers are generally used in the *Papers*. Public notices were sometimes signed, "No. 67, Secretary."

Each new member signed the constitution, and thus automatically received a number from the already-numbered line on which he signed. But the numbers 172-175 were accidentally repeated. Moreover, the names and numbers were copied into the *Book of Names*, which was used as a record-book by the sergeant-at-arms. Some mistakes were made in the copying, and as a result each member numbered from 17 to 178 in the original list (with a few exceptions) bears a different number in the *Book of Names*. Thus Bluxome signed originally as 71, but as secretary used 67. I have used the original numbers.

Chap. 11. In the rough treatment of Clark there is no reason to see any action, direct or indirect, of the members of the Committee. The whole philosophy of the Committee was opposed to such mob-action.

A compilation indicates that the number of members at the time of the issuance of the public statement was 186, though the highest numbered member was 187. Three members, therefore, did not sign. One of these, Henry S. Brown, #82, had probably gone on a sea-voyage. What had happened to the other two (Thomas W. Walker, #80, and Charles B. Marvin, #183) I do not know. In any case, the attaining of such a large proportion of signatures is remarkable, and shows the tension of the time.

Chapter 13. Though Schenck quotes Sullivan as saying that Stuart "murdered the sheriff of Auburn," we may doubt whether Sullivan said so. There were two murders — of Echols, the so-called sheriff of Auburn, on June 2, 1850, and of Charles Moore, on October 7, 1850. Echols was killed by the brothers Samuel H. and William Stewart (Williams, p. 253, note). Moore was killed by James Stuart. Partly because of the duplication of the name the two murders became confused. Sullivan would have been more likely to know about the murder of Moore than about the murder of Echols, though even in Marysville, at the time of the attempted lynching, Stuart may have been accused of both murders. Sullivan worked for Stuart only during a few weeks, not for six months. We must remember that the conversation is being reported by Schenck twenty-five years later.

Chap. 14. Berdue's letter is in *Papers,* pp. 222-223, and in *Popular Tribunals,* i, pp. 197-198. The details of his trial are given in *Popular Tribunals,* i, 194ff.

Though there is much controversy about the details of the hanging at Downieville, the main facts are well enough established. I have chiefly used Royce, Chap. iv, #9; *Illustrated Hist. of Plumas, Lassen and Sierra Counties,* pp. 445-447; D. P. Barstow, "Statement" (MS in Bancroft Library). Royce is important since his account is based upon that in the *Daily Pacific Star,* and I have not been able to find a copy of that issue still extant. The other San Francisco papers presented summaries (e.g., *Alta* and *Herald,* both on July 9) based upon a brief account in the Marysville *Herald.* The *Picayune* on July 14 gave a longer account under the heading *Murder at Downieville,* but this was largely editorializing. The Downieville

*Mountain Messenger* in 1961 ran a series of articles and correspondence on the subject.

Chap. 22. H. Brett Melendy has published "Who was John McDougal?" (*Pacific Hist. Rev.,* v. 29, pp. 231-243). A photograph of McDougal, with biographical notes by his son, is in the Bancroft Library.

Chaps. 25, 26. Judge Harvey S. Brown, of the Court of Sessions, (See also Chap. 6) resigned on August 24, following the double hanging, in protest against the lack of respect which the city was showing for the constituted courts. He had been, and remained, a violent opponent of the Committee, and his "Early Days of California" (MS, Bancroft Library) is the most notable anti-Committee document that remains extant. In it, Brown stated, "The first Vigilance Committee was absolutely without any cause," maintaining that the courts were working hard to correct matters. He credits to himself the garrisoning of the jail on August 24. He also states, that "the Vigilance Committee men" assured Hays "on their honor" that they would make no attempt to recapture the prisoners and that Hays thereupon discharged the guard at the jail. (But not all of the guard was discharged.) Brown's reminiscences, like the other reminiscences, cannot be wholly trusted, but they are interesting for their presentation of a strongly anti-Committee attitude.

Chap. 26. The exaggerated idea of the resemblance between Berdue and Stuart has even got into the historical tradition. Bancroft (*Popular Tribunals,* i. 181f) tells the story that Berdue had three times been arrested for crimes committed by Stuart. I have found no contemporary evidence to this effect.

Postscript. Though the Committee of 1856 is best considered a new organization, the medal of that Committee bore the legend, "Organized 9th June, 1851; reorganized, 14th May, 1856."

Retrospect. Since the kind of man constituting the Committee is a matter of first importance, I add some details. I differ to some extent from Dr. Williams. She gives the total as 707, but I make it out to be 710. The record, however, is sufficiently confused to allow us both to be wrong by a count or two. Ten of these members joined after the reorganization. Dr. Williams suggests (p. 178) that she identified about one in ten; I have been able to identify more than half. I am therefore in a position to differ from her when she states (p. 188), "The majority . . . were clerks or small tradesmen."

Enough data are available to plot the growth of membership:

|  | Approximate Number | Gain |
|---|---|---|
| End of first week | 250 | — |
| " " second " | 390 | 140 |
| " " third " | 490 | 100 |
| " " fourth " | 560 | 70 |
| " " fifth " | 600 | 40 |
| " " sixth " | 625 | 25 |
| " " seventh " | 650 | 25 |

After the end of the seventh week (July 28) growth almost stopped, except for a slight flurry of new memberships just after Hays's rescue of Whittaker and McKenzie. One must remember that the Committee was not interested in large numbers, and never made a general appeal for membership.

About a half-dozen members were from towns other than San Francisco, and probably joined on a kind of honorary basis. About a half-dozen members were expelled. About fifteen members are noted as having left San Francisco, and probably a number of others did so without formally withdrawing. No death is noted before the time of the reorganization.

It was the era of the independent businessman, before the growth of large corporations. The typical San Francisco enterprise was a partnership of two or three individuals. Men of this sort formed the strength of the Committee, and almost wholly directed its affairs by composing the Executive Commitee. I have identified about 50 commission merchants, and about 170 other members in the business of buying and selling — everything from liquors and tea to paints and crockery. I have identified, though somewhat uncertainly, 22 shipmasters, 13 physicians, and 2 dentists. In my list are 10 bankers, 10 clerks, 5 journalists, 2 customs officers, 2 blacksmiths, 2 naval officers, a pilot, an undertaker, a saloonkeeper, an insurance-agent.

The "trades" are represented chiefly through men who were apparently small employers or kept their own shops. One "drayman" apparently had a small livery stable. Two watchmakers may have kept their own shops, as may the carriage-maker. One of the two carpenters, was what we should now call a builder.

Of course, the lower a man in the social scale the harder he is to identify. Still, I have spotted 5 watermen.

Completely missing are practising lawyers, though a few members were lawyers involved in business-management. Gamblers were apparently excluded. Since the Committee had to do with violence, it included no ministers. There were no teachers, since there were scarcely any of them in the city at that time. Completely missing, also, are laborers. Such obscure persons would be hard to identify, but I think that they were kept out by design. The Committee was the organization of those who by owning property or a business had a stake in the community.

The Committee was politically non-partisan. Probably a majority of its members were without religious affiliation, but it included both Christians and Jews. As would be expected of the time, it included neither Negroes nor Chinese. Actually very few of these would have fulfilled the qualification of having a stake in the community. George Pfiester, the porter, may have been a Negro, but I have found no definite evidence. Though some were foreign-born, the members were predominantly American.

Of the sixteen directors of the Pacific Marine Insurance Company, five were members of the Committee. These inadequate figures would suggest that the Committee did not enlist more than about half of those who might have been considered eligible, but the other directors may have been lawyers. Still, many men who might have joined (e.g., Jansen and Payne) did not do so. There may have been many reasons — mere timidity, conscientious scruples, old age, physical disability. Some who did not join salved their consciences by gifts of money, and other forms of aid.

# INDEX

Academy of Pacific Coast History, 304

Adair, James, 143f

Adams, George, 78, 213f, 229f, 234, 238-240, 290

Addison, J. E., 266

Adelaide, 177

*Adirondack* (ship), 209f, 235

Afoy-whang, 65

Aiken, C. D., 159

Aiken, George, 128f, 208

Ainsworth, Thomas, 213, 229

Albany, 214

*Alta California*, editorial attitudes of, 18, 42, 126, 129, 312; quoted, 7f, 9, 27, 59, 60, 67, 69, 73, 75, 76, 77, 78, 84, 89, 122, 131, 275, 288; see also, 87, 285

*Annals of San Francisco*, vii, 300

Argenti, Felix, 128, 136f, 147, 167, 170, 249, 251, 299

Arrentrue, J. J., 170, 233f, 238, 240

Arrowsmith, D. B., 104f

Arthur, George, 229

Auburn, 36, 148, 179

Austin, E. G., 187f

Australia, 2, 53

Ball, F. A., 217, 219-227, 231, 294, 308

Bancroft, H. H., 304

Bancroft Library, 304

Barbary Coast, 50

Battelle, T. K., 125

Benicia, 74, 254

Bennett, Nathaniel, 166, 173f, 261

Berdue, Thomas, 10, 34f, 46, 58, 60f, 67, 75, 85, 149, 151-154, 156, 163, 165, 173, 186, 281f, 289f, 294

Bloomer, Amelia, 222

Bluxome, Isaac, 100f, 131, 165f, 175, 177f, 182, 189, 209, 228, 249, 257, 262, 280f, 297, 299f, 304f

Boston, 66

Brannan, Samuel, in Jansen affair, 23-25, 27, 29, 32; early life of, 44f; in Lewis affair, 80-82; helps organize Com. of Vig., 87-89, 91, 93, 95; Pres. of Com. of Vig., 101; in Jenkins affair, 106, 108-110, 123-125; quits presidency, 146f, 189; quarrels with Van Bokkelen, 213f, 234, 238; in Adams case, 239; serves on investigating committee, 268; later life of, 305; portrait of, 88; see also, 100, 121, 131f, 144, 163, 167, 198, 235, 277, 297

Brenham, C. J., 71, 80, 204-206, 240, 259-261, 263f, 270, 298; portrait of, 205

Qualifications, Com. on, see Com.
   on Qualifications

Ray, Ben, 107, 113
Revolution, American, 312
Reyes, Justo, 136
Rincon Hill, 50
Roach, William, 181
Robinson, Ben, 139
Robinson, Margaret, 139
Rose, John, 158
Roundhead, Tommy, see Ainsworth,
   Thomas
Royce, Josiah, 315
Russian Hill, 49, 72
Ryckman, G. W., 99, 105, 108-110,
   189, 214, 223, 228, 234f, 246-249,
   267, 277f, 280f, 283-285, 292, 299f,
   305

Sacramento, 36, 74, 141, 153, 169,
   178-180, 191, 274, 279
Salmon, J. W., 273
San Diego, 243, 245
San Francisco, crime in, 7-9, 53f, 67;
   description of in 1851, 49-52;
   elections in, 71, 292; fires in, 72-
   75, 89, 135, 299f; jail, 64, 69, 78,
   147; law-enforcement in, 14-16,
   53, 83; police of, 7f, 10; politics
   in, 64f; see also, *passim*
San Francisco County, 210
San Jose, 279
Santa Barbara, 243
Santa Clara, 278f, 314
Schenck, G. E., 43, 100, 105f, 110f,
   131, 144-146, 148f, 151, 175, 280f,
   294f, 300, 305, 312
Shattuck, J. J., 33, 35-39, 43
Shepheard, P. W., 34, 46

Shinn, C. H., 14
Simpson, ——, 59
Simpton, ——, see Jenkins, John
Slater, ——, 68
Smiley, T. J. L., 214
Smith, J. T., 133
Smith, Napoleon, 127
Smith, Oscar, 280, 283
Smith, ——, 183
Snyder, J. R., 236
Sonora, 144, 146, 191, 307
Spear, William, 158
Spence, J. F., 33, 43, 133, 169, 175,
   182f
Spring Valley, 49
"steam paddy," 65
Steele, J. A., 262
Stephens, John, 164
Stephens, William, see Stuart, James
Stevenson, J. D., 80, 82, 97, 100f,
   106, 197-200, 267f, 305; portrait of,
   81
Stuart, James ("English Jim," James
   Stephens, etc.), in Jansen affair,
   3, 7, 10; apprehension of, 143-
   146, 148; resemblance of to Ber-
   due, 151-153, 290; examination,
   164-175; confession of, 177-184;
   events succeeding confession of,
   185-193; trial of, 194-198; hanging
   of, 199-201; attempted resuscita-
   tion of, 203; see also, 58, 60f, 71,
   206, 208, 210, 212f, 215, 243, 246,
   250, 282, 287, 290, 294, 310
Sullivan, John, 104f, 133f, 148, 164,
   178
Supreme Court (California), 166,
   187, 233
*Surprise* (ship), 59
Sussex, 144, 177